The Original Hot Five Recordings of Louis Armstrong

CMS SOURCEBOOKS IN AMERICAN MUSIC
No. 3

Series Editor
Michael J. Budds, University of Missouri-Columbia

CMS Sourcebooks in American Music

No. 1 — Larry Starr: The Dickinson Songs of Aaron Copland
No. 2 — Neil Minturn: The Last Waltz of The Band

Pendragon Press Journals and Series

Aesthetics in Music
Annotated Reference Tools in Music
Bucina: The Historic Brass Society Series
CMS Sourcebooks in American Music
The Complete Organ
The Complete Works of G. B. Pergolesi
The Croatian Musicological Society Series
Dance & Music
Dimension & Diversity: Studies in 20th-Century Music
Distinguished Reprints
The Festschrift Series
The Franz Liszt Studies Series
The Free-Reed Journal
French Opera in the 17th and 18th Centuries
Harmonologia: Studies in Music Theory
Historical Harpsichord
Interplay: Music in Interdisciplinary Dialogue
The Juilliard Performance Guides
Lives in Music Series
Monographs & Bibliographies in American Music
Monographs in Musicology
Musical Life in 19th-Century France
The Opera Series
Pergolesi Studies Series / Studi Pergolesiani
The Pendragon Review: A Journal of Musical Romanticism
The Polish Music History Series
The Sociology of Music
Studies in Central and Eastern European Music
Studies in Czech Music
Thematic Catalogues
Vox Musicae: The Voice, Vocal Pedagogy, and Song
The Wendy Hilton Dance & Music Series

CMS Sourcebooks
in American Music

The Original Hot Five Recordings of Louis Armstrong

by GENE H. ANDERSON

Edited by Michael J. Budds

Pendragon Press
Hillsdale, New York

Publicity photographs of the Hot Five are reproduced courtesy of the Hogan Jazz Archive, Tulane University.

Permission to reprint "The Hot Five Session," by Edward "Kid" Ory and Lester Koenig, published in *The Record Changer* (July-August 1950), 17, 45, was granted by Richard Hadlock, editor / publisher of *The Record Changer*.

Permission to reprint "The Original Hot Five" by Johnny St. Cyr, published in *Second Line* V/9-10 (September-October 1954), 1-2, was requested from the New Orleans Jazz Club.

Permission to provide the twenty recorded performances of the Hot Five found on the compact disc accompanying this text was granted by Sony Music Entertainment.

Portions of the text were previously published in *College Music Symposium: Journal of The College Music Society* 43 (2003).

Cover design for *CMS Sourcebooks in American Music* series by Michael Graves. Mechanical production by Roger Parchen, Ad-Art.

Library of Congress Cataloging-in-Publication Data

Anderson, Gene Henry.
The original Hot Five recordings of Louis Armstrong / by Gene H. Anderson ; edited by Michael J. Budds.
p. cm. — (CMS sourcebooks in American music ; no. 3)
Includes bibliographical references (p.) and index.
ISBN 978-1-57647-120-3 (alk. paper)
1. Armstrong, Louis, 1901-1971—Analysis, appreciation. 2. Jazz—1921-1930—History and criticism. 3. Hot Five—Discography. I. Budds, Michael J., 1947- II. Title.
ML419.A75A83 2007
781.65092—dc22

2006032572

From the Series Editor

The College Music Society can boast of a proud tradition of contributions to the study of American music with its series *Monographs and Bibliographies in American Music*. For many years, volumes disseminated under this banner were rather lavishly produced and fell into the category of reference works, the majority of which were devoted to individual—and sometimes neglected—musical figures. In more recent times, the Society has determined to intensify its efforts by considering a greater range of topics and formats and by making available publications in paperback editions at reasonable prices.

In this spirit and in cooperation with Pendragon Press of Hillsdale, New York, The College Music Society has initiated a correlative series titled *CMS Sourcebooks in American Music*. The new venture was conceived to underscore the remarkable diversity in our nation's musical expression and to call special attention to both landmark and representative achievements in its evolution. Whether the subject is a concert or stage work communicated through a notated score, a virtual performance frozen in time by modern technology (such as a film score or a recording), or some other mode of preservation not yet invented or standardized, the goal is the same: to gather materials for study, to reconsider and synthesize existing commentary and criticism, and to offer a fresh assessment or appreciation. Although a canonizing tendency is implicit in any selection process, every attempt has been made to address as many strands in the fabric of American music as possible.

These texts should not be perceived as ends in themselves, moreover, but as educational resources directed to teachers of music, students of music, and other lovers of music. Each author has been advised to take the benefit of primary sources of various kinds as well as the generous body of relevant scholarship and to place his or her subject in contexts most meaningful to contemporary readers. Although there is no intent to provide scholastic tracts of the most exacting rigor, these studies have been carefully and engagingly written and fully documented. Whenever possible, a compact disc featuring performances of historical importance has been attached to the volume as both an added value and as a convenience.

It is always prudent to question the feasibility of yet another series of music publications. This is so especially now—when the fruits of the "Information Age" overwhelm the most curious, voracious, or dedicated reader and when the capacity and immediacy of the Internet challenge traditional practice. And yet it is never foolhardy to respond to the needs of an honorable profession in the service of a glorious art.

Michael J. Budds
Columbia, Missouri

I wish to acknowledge with genuine gratitude the contributions of Gail Yaffe, Elizabeth Baird, and Megan Ruyle to the production of this volume.

From the Author

Most of the research for this study was conducted at the Hogan Jazz Archive of Tulane University in New Orleans, the Rutgers Institute of Jazz Studies in Newark, the Louis Armstrong Archive at Queens College in New York City, and the Music Division of the Library of Congress, Washington, D.C. Without the invaluable resources held at these institutions and their helpful managers and staff members, such an undertaking would have been impossible.

For providing reproductions of Armstrong copyright deposits, I am indebted to Jan Lauridsen of the Library of Congress, Lawrence Gushee of the University of Illinois, and David Chevan of Southern Connecticut State University. Tina McCarthy from the Sony Archives facilitated my access to OKeh record label copy, and Lewis Porter of Rutgers University-Newark, Maurizio Franco from *Musica Oggi* in Milan, and Stefano Zenni from Prado, Italy, helped me obtain obscure Armstrong materials. The utility of this volume has been immeasurably enhanced through the efforts of Robby Gunstream, the Executive Director of The College Music Society, who obtained from Sony Music Entertainment copyright permissions for the Hot Five performances found on the companion compact disc.

I am obliged to Michael Davison, jazz trumpeter and my University of Richmond colleague, for his insights into the technical aspects of Louis Armstrong's playing; to librarians Bonlyn Hall, Linda Fairtile, and Lynn Smith from the University of Richmond's Parsons Music Library for fulfilling endless interlibrary loan requests; and to music tech lab assistant Jacob Monaco for file conversion of the musical examples. Most importantly, without the encouragement of research grants and release-time from the University of Richmond, my institutional home for the past twenty-four years, this project would have been severely delayed or denied fruition.

I was fortunate to receive careful readings of the final draft by Quentin Kuyper of Augusta State University and Lawrence Gushee of the University of Illinois. Gushee's work, in particular, has long been a model for my own. His and Kuyper's thoughtful commentary on issues large and small have made this a much better book. Any lingering misrepresentations, misjudgments, and mistakes must, of course, remain my own.

Finally, I thank Michael J. Budds, editor of the *CMS Sourcebooks in American Music* series, for his acceptance of my original proposal, his support of its several transformations, his unerring suggestions for its improvement, and his patience with its desultory progress toward completion.

With love and gratitude I dedicate this book to my wife Barbara, whose Christmas gift of Gunther Schuller's *Early Jazz* over thirty years ago precipitated my enduring passion for, admiration of, and commitment to the music of Johnny Dodds, "King" Oliver, "Jelly Roll" Morton, and Louis Armstrong.

Gene Anderson
Richmond, Virginia

Contents

Musical Examples

Illustrations

The advertisements interspersed throughout the text originally appeared in the pages of the *Chicago Defender*. The reproductions of copyright deposits are based on the originals submitted to the Library of Congress.

Structural Outlines of Recorded Performances and Other Tabular Explanations

| TABLE

Introduction

"... just glad to play."
Louis Armstrong, quoted in Max Jones and John Chilton, *Louis* (1971), 112.

Contemporary musicians—black and white—recognized the genius of Louis Armstrong immediately on the release of his Original Hot Five recordings. By the time of the New Orleans revival in the late 1930s and early 1940s, he and these performances were already well on their way to achieving the iconic status famously articulated by French critic André Hodeir a decade or so later:

> On November 12, 1925, in its Chicago studios, the OKeh Company recorded a little five-piece Negro ensemble for the first time. This apparently insignificant event was to have quite a repercussion on the history of jazz. . . .[1]
>
> Just as they are, the Hot Five recordings . . . constitute the most impressive, if not the most authentic, evidence of what the New Orleans style was like in its Golden Age. Beneath an apparent equilibrium, there are already signs of the powerful creative urge which, through Louis Armstrong's perfect rhythm and settled individual style, was going to lead to classicism. More than a quarter of a century later, these records . . . show clearly that Johnny Dodds and Kid Ory may have been precursors but Louis Armstrong was the first great classical figure of jazz.[2]

Although one might argue how authentically the Hot Five embodied the New Orleans style, Hodeir's assessment of the quintet's importance has become commonplace since his 1956 pronouncement. Today, the ensemble's position in jazz hagiography long secure, its music has been extolled as probably contributing "more than any other single group of

[1]André Hodeir, *Jazz, Its Evolution and Essence*, trans. David Noakes (New York: Grove Press, 1956; reprinted New York: Da Capo Press, 1975), 49. For early recognition of Armstrong's importance to jazz history, see Frederic Ramsey, Jr., and Charles Edward Smith, *Jazzmen* (New York: Harcourt Brace Jovanovich, 1939; reprinted New York: Limelight Editions, 1985), 130-34; and Charles Edward Smith, Frederic Ramsey, Jr., Charles Payne Rogers, and William Russell, *The Jazz Record Book* (New York: Smith & Durrell, 1942; reprinted Westport, CT: Greenwood Press, 1978), 130-36.

[2]Ibid., 62.

recordings to making jazz famous and a music to be taken seriously."[3] With time the Hot Five performances established beyond any dispute Armstrong's titanic profile as the "first great soloist,"[4] an "American genius,"[5] and the "single most creative and innovative force in jazz history."[6] The impact of his example, of course, extended powerfully beyond the nebulous boundaries of the jazz tradition in the years to follow.

The Nature of This Study

When determining the scope of a Hot Five-related project, perhaps surprisingly, one encounters the problem of what to include. In addition to the fifty-three titles released as Hot Fives or Hot Sevens between 1925 and 1928, Armstrong recorded almost two dozen more with the same or similar personnel under an assortment of names: Lil's Hot Shots, Johnny Dodds's Black Bottom Stompers, Jimmy Bertrand's Washboard Wizards, Carroll Dickerson's Savoyagers, Armstrong's Stompers, Armstrong's Orchestra,[7] and Armstrong's Savoy Ballroom Five. Some or all have been considered by various compilers to fall under the Hot Five / Seven rubric.[8] Complicating matters further, the style and personnel of the first Hot Five changed radically with the formation in 1928 of a second or "Chicago" Hot Five, which, by the addition of drums, was actually a "Hot Six."

In this study I avoid questions of inclusion or omission by limiting my consideration to the recorded performances of the "Original" or "New Orleans" Hot Five, under the assumption that examination of thirty-three

[3]Gunther Schuller, *Early Jazz: Its Roots and Musical Development* (New York: Oxford University Press, 1968), 98.

[4]*Ibid.*, 89.

[5]James Lincoln Collier, *Louis Armstrong: An American Genius* (New York: Oxford University Press, 1983). Collier's title makes his assessment explicit.

[6]Gary Giddins, *Satchmo* (New York: Doubleday, 1988), 86.

[7]Editor's Note: The indiscriminate application of the term "orchestra" to groupings of instrumentalists became commonplace in the realm of popular entertainment during the early twentieth century. Up to that time the word had been primarily used to designate string-dominated ensembles, often with additional instruments, dedicated to the performance of fine art music, theatrical music, or music for social dancing. Careful usage would prevent a connection to any combo of jazz soloists. Presumably, in the spirit of Madison Avenue, by borrowing it, prestige and a desired cachet of "class" accrued to musicians and their audiences.

[8]For the most inclusive compilation yet, see *Louis Armstrong: The Complete Hot Five and Hot Seven Recordings* (Sony Music Entertainment, 2000). On page 20 of the accompanying booklet, Phil Schaap argues for a total of eighty-nine cuts (including alternate takes) to be regarded as Hot Fives or Hot Sevens.

recordings by the same group, leader, and record company over a two-year period allows the most meaningful comparisons to be drawn and conclusions to be made.[9] Unfortunately, this approach filters out such acknowledged masterpieces as "Potato Head Blues," "West End Blues," and "Weather Bird." These titles, nevertheless, are among the most thoroughly discussed in the literature and, in my opinion, deserve separate attention in the context of their own Hot Seven or Chicago Hot Five milieu.

The purpose of this investigation is to determine the extent to which the Original Hot Five and its leader deserve their hallowed position in jazz history. Despite the plethora of Armstrong-related materials, few writers scrutinize his music beyond his most celebrated solos; fewer still attempt to contextualize his achievements, to develop a reliable chronology of his activities during his music-making, and to relate individual pieces to available copyright deposits; and none provide a satisfactory explanation for the origin of his pioneering recordings. I hope that applying these heretofore neglected strategies to a comprehensive study of the Original Hot Fives will help clarify and verify Armstrong's and the group's already formidable stature in jazz history.

Because the analytical portions of this study are best confirmed by ear as well as by eye, those Hot Five performances discussed in the greatest detail are supplied on the compact disc that accompanies this volume. Its playlist is provided on page 258. An asterisk (*) following a title in both the Table of Contents and chapter subheadings identifies the twenty pieces under special scrutiny.

The Transcriptions

The unique quality of Armstrong's solos was recognized from the beginning. His slightly younger contemporary, "Bix" Beiderbecke, noted their coherent structure,[10] Tiny Parham transcribed one for his 1927 arrangement of "Wild Man Blues,"[11] and a collection of them was

[9]Allowance must be made for the inclusion of Hy Clark as Ory's substitute on two of the Original Hot Fives and of guitarist Lonnie Johnson as an invited guest on three of the Original Hot Fives. Hereafter for the sake of simplicity, "Hot Five" is synonymous with Original Hot Five.

[10]Leon "Bix" Beiderbecke, quoted in Richard M. Sudhalter and Philip R. Evans, *Bix: Man & Legend* (New Rochelle, NY: Arlington House, 1974), 100-01.

[11] Recorded with Johnny Dodds's Black Bottom Stompers on 22 April 1927.

published the same year.[12] Later players memorized his solos, and a discussion of Armstrong's style appeared in his own 1936 autobiography, *Swing That Music*.[13] Transcriptions of Armstrong's most memorable Hot Five and Hot Seven solos can presently be found in numerous studies of his music as well as in several collections; entire pieces have also been fully or partially transcribed (see my bibliography). In 1989 the Hot Five repertory was written out for *The Louis Armstrong Connection*, a fifteen-CD re-creation of Armstrong's pioneering works.[14] Efforts to locate relevant transcriptions for this project, produced in Germany and featuring British trumpet player Kenny Baker, have so far proved unsuccessful.

Jazz is notoriously difficult to write down in European notation. Communicating pitches, rhythms, harmonies, and their inflections is challenging enough, but changes in tone quality, varieties of articulation, and the elusive ingredient called swing can at best be only approximated in notation, if at all.[15] Armstrong's performances often embody all these features in the extreme. His rhythm, in particular, frequently seems to float above or hover around the beat rather than being exactly on top of it.[16]

Transcriptions for this inquiry attempt to balance accuracy with utility. Swing eighths are understood unless otherwise indicated. Excessive playing before or behind the beat and timbral variety are designated. Unless important to the analysis, articulation signs have been kept to a minimum. Ascending or descending straight lines identify rips and fall-offs; a wavy line specifies a shake; an ascending wavy line represents a long glissando; and u-shaped lines mark bends or lipped pitches. Ghost notes or fluffs are shown by x note-heads. All transcriptions and tempo markings are based on Sony's *Complete Hot Five and Hot Seven Recordings* (see note 8) and, unless otherwise indicated, are my own.

[12]Louis Armstrong, *50 Hot Choruses for Cornet* (Chicago: Melrose Bros., 1927).

[13]Louis Armstrong, *Swing That Music* (New York: Longmans, Green, 1936; reprinted New York: Da Capo Press, 1993), 125-34.

[14]Werner Burkhardt, liner notes to *The Louis Armstrong Connection, Vol. I: The Hot Five* (Germany: Pastels, 20.1801-PA, 1989).

[15]On defining "swing," see James Lincoln Collier, *Jazz: The American Theme Song* (New York: Oxford University Press, 1993), 71-88.

[16]My assessment of Armstrong's rhythm is based on the numerous transcriptions made for this book and shared by many other writers. A recent study by James Lincoln Collier and Geoffrey L. Collier found, however, that in "Cornet Chop Suey" and "Potato Head Blues," both with substantial sections in stop-time, Armstrong tended to play off-beat notes behind the beat but downbeat notes on the beat; see "A Study of Timing in Two Louis Armstrong Solos," *Music Perception* 19/3 (Spring 2002), 463-83.

The Early New Orleans Jazz Band

The instrumentation of the Original Hot Five combo—cornet, clarinet, trombone, banjo, and piano—emerged from the pragmatic spirit of early New Orleans practice, which embraced various ensemble combinations. Rooted in the tradition as well was a distribution of labor within such entertainment units, that is, the assignment of specific duties to specific instruments. In this case, the cornet, clarinet, and trombone carried out the tasks of the "melody group," and the banjo and piano functioned as the "rhythm group." It is equally important to appreciate this system's general fluidity, which allowed the banjo or the piano to participate as a "melody" instrument in addition to providing a bass line, supplying harmony, and keeping time.

The make-up of Armstrong's Hot Seven—cornet, clarinet, trombone, piano, banjo, tuba, and drums—is more reflective of early New Orleans jazz or ragtime bands than that of the Original Hot Five. Even so, there are major differences. New Orleans dance bands used a string bass instead of a tuba or a sousaphone (considered marching band instruments) and a guitar instead of a banjo. They seldom had the benefit of a pianist but frequently included a violinist, whose responsibility as the only music reader was to play parts from stock arrangements for his comrades to learn by rote. "Kid" Ory's band in New Orleans was a seven-man outfit with a violin but no piano,[17] as was the Creole Band (all New Orleanians) that toured the country on various vaudeville circuits between 1914 and 1918.[18] The possible model for these was Buddy Bolden's 1905 band of cornet, two clarinets, trombone, guitar, string bass, and drums.[19]

When New Orleans bands left the Crescent City, they dropped the violin; retained the standard front line of cornet, clarinet, and trombone; and varied the rhythm section. In 1915 Tom Brown's Ragtime Band (cornet, clarinet, trombone, piano, drums), which may have lacked a regular violinist, initially left its bassist behind for an engagement at Chicago's Lamb's Café.[20] The following year Stein's Band from Dixie,

[17]Gene Anderson, "Johnny Dodds in New Orleans," *American Music* 8/4 (Winter 1990), 423.

[18]Lawrence Gushee, "How the Creole Band Came to Be," *Black Music Research Journal* 8/1 (1988), 83-100.

[19]Don M. Marquis, *In Search of Buddy Bolden: First Man of Jazz* (Baton Rouge: Louisiana State University Press, 1978), 78-79.

[20]Richard M. Sudhalter, *Lost Chords: White Musicians and Their Contributions to Jazz, 1915-1945* (New York: Oxford University Press, 1999), 4-5.

the progenitor of the Original Dixieland Jazz Band (ODJB), assembled in the New Schiller Café on Chicago's South Side with instrumentation identical to Brown's.[21] Pianist Lil Hardin's replacement of guitarist Louis Keppard and the subsequent departure of violinist Herb Lindsay produced an ODJB instrumentation plus string bass in Lawrence Duhé's band at Chicago's DeLuxe Gardens in 1917.[22] The 1921 Friars Society Orchestra, the first incarnation of the New Orleans Rhythm Kings (NORK), added a tenor saxophone and banjo for a total of eight pieces on the bandstand at Chicago's Friar's Inn,[23] and in Los Angeles "Kid" Ory's 1922 Sunshine Orchestra (Spikes' Seven Pods of Pepper) recorded with the same instrumentation as Duhé.[24]

Adopted by NORK, "King" Oliver's Creole Jazz Band, and numerous others groups, the banjo became the string instrument of choice in the Windy City. Hot Five member Johnny St. Cyr bought his unique guitar-banjo hybrid in 1919, when on the riverboats with Armstrong in Fate Marable's band, and played it on all of his Chicago recordings.[25] But to my ears, St. Cyr never takes full advantage of the instrument's guitar capabilities during Hot Five or Hot Seven sessions with the possible exception of "Savoy Blues" (see Table 9.7). It would seem, then, that without either a drum or bass instrument, the makeup of Armstrong's Original Hot Five was anomalous. In anticipation of the discussion to follow, it is my contention that the instrumentation of the Hot Five was driven more by commercial than artistic reasons.

[21] *Ibid.*, 11.

[22] Gene Anderson, "The Genesis of King Oliver's Creole Jazz Band," *American Music* 12/3 (Fall 1994), 286.

[23] Richard M. Sudhalter, *Lost Chords*, 28-32.

[24] Brian Rust, *Jazz and Ragtime Records, 1897-1942*, 2 vols. (Denver: Mainspring Press, 2002), II, 1610. Saxophonist Earl Whaley, reported in the *Chicago Defender* (28 August 1920), 5, as a member of Ory's band at Oakland's Creole Café and identified in the *Chicago Defender* (22 July 1922), 8, as a member of the Sunshine Orchestra, did not participate in the recordings. He may have rejoined Ory in Los Angeles for ensuing radio broadcasts and dance gigs.

[25] Johnny St. Cyr, "Jazz as I Remember It, Part Three: The Riverboats," *Jazz Journal* 19/11 (November 1966), 9. For a consideration of the guitar-banjo, see John Bright, "Idle Musings on a Banjo Theme: Johnny St. Cyr," *New Orleans Music* 8/4 (December 1999), 6-9.

The Origin of the Original Hot Five

CHAPTER 2

The OKeh Connection

The seeds of the idea that germinated into the Hot Five recordings were sown in the early morning of 8 June 1923 at the Convention of Applied Music Trades in Chicago's Drake Hotel. On that date "King" Oliver's Creole Jazz Band, one of several groups hired to entertain the conventioneers at a "midnight frolic," was scheduled at 3 a.m. for a twenty-minute set. Because of repeated calls for encores from the band's "mob of admirers," its performance lasted almost two hours. But typical of the racist attitudes of the time, twenty-one-year-old Louis Armstrong—in his first notice by the white press—found himself an attraction more for his appearance than for his playing: "The 'dark horse' orchestra of the whole bunch was sure dark. Especially the little frog-mouthed boy who played the cornet."[1]

Two weeks later Oliver recorded for OKeh Records, and, in Chicago's annual Elks Parade the following month, his band rolled through town on a flatbed truck advertising the special release of "Where Did You Stay Last Night?" and "Dippermouth Blues." Posters of OKeh race artists were prominently displayed along the line of march, with the placarding of the black district personally supervised by E. A. Fearn, "who spared no expense in this work."[2] Thus are introduced into Hot Five lore two names indissolubly linked: OKeh and Elmer [E. A.] Fearn. Without either the celebrated recordings would never have been made.

OKeh was formed in 1918 by Otto Heineman, president of the prosperous Heineman Phonograph Supply Company (later reorganized as the General Phonograph Corporation), to complement and expand his business of manufacturing high-quality phonograph motors, needles, and parts. Fancifully derived from the "original Indian spelling of the term colloquially known as O. K.," the label's name in its earliest version fortuitously happened to highlight (in the manner of bookends) the founder's initials—OkeH.[3] Retailing the first good records playable on

[1] *Talking Machine World* [hereafter *TMW*] 19/6 (15 June 1923), 73; *TMW* 19/8 (15 August 1923), 103. The Creole Band, representing the Gennett label for which it recorded in April, was the only black band on the program that included, among others, Benson's Orchestra (Victor), Guyon's Paradise Orchestra (OKeh), Albert E. Short's Tivoli Syncopators (Vocalion), Yerkes's S.S. Flotilla Orchestra (Vocalion), and Isham Jones's Orchestra (Brunswick).

[2] *TMW* 19/9 (15 September 1923), 102.

[3] *TMW* 14/5 (15 May 1918), 95. For a comprehensive history of OKeh, see Ross Laird and Brian Rust, *Discography of OKeh Records, 1918-1934* (Westport, CT: Praeger, 2004), 1-18.

any machine, the new company prospered.[4] OKeh's creation of the race record market—*i.e.*, black music for black audiences—with the serendipitous success of Mamie Smith's "Crazy Blues" in 1920 need not be recounted here, but when the Hot Five began recording in late 1925, the firm was the race market leader with dozens of black artists signed to exclusive contracts.[5]

A technological leader of the industry as well, OKeh raised standards for quality under the supervision of C. L. Hibbard, recognized as "one of the foremost recording engineers in the country" and the inventor of the first portable recording studio, along with a number of new methods and devices.[6] In 1925 Hibbard perfected the "Truetone" process that enhanced the tone quality of acoustic and electric recordings.[7] The novel process and Hibbard's technical ingenuity, however, could not compete with electric recording (*i.e.*, using microphones), a recently-patented procedure by Western Electric offered to Columbia and Victor but not made available to the independent General Phonograph Corporation. Lack of access to the electric process finally prompted Heineman to sell his OKeh-Odeon record division to Columbia in October 1926.[8]

[4]William Howland Kenney, *Recorded Music in American Life: The Phonograph and Popular Memory, 1890-1945* (New York: Oxford University Press, 1999), 115-16.

[5]For the "Crazy Blues" story, see Samuel B. Charters and Leonard Kunstadt, *Jazz: A History of the New York Scene* (Garden City, NY: Doubleday, 1962), 82-94; Perry Bradford, *Born with the Blues: Perry Bradford's Own Story* (New York: Oak Publications, 1965), 114-29; Brian Rust, *The American Record Label Book* (New Rochelle, NY: Arlington House, 1978; reprinted New York: Da Capo Press, 1984), 212-17; Daphne Duval Harrison, *Black Pearls: Blues Queens of the 1920s* (New Brunswick, NJ: Rutgers University Press, 1988), 42-61; David A. Jasen and Gene Jones, *Spreadin' Rhythm Around: Black Songwriters, 1880-1930* (New York: Schirmer, 1998), 263-69; and William Howland Kenney, *Recorded Music in American Life*, 116-18.

[6]*TMW* 20/2 (15 February 1924), 120.

[7]*TMW* 21/5 (15 May 1925), 1, and 22/1 (15 January 1926), 1. Brian Rust, in *The American Record Label Book* (New Rochelle, NY: Arlington House, 1978; reprinted New York: Da Capo Press, 1984), 6, speculates that Truetone was an early form of electric recording, but a statement in the *TMW* article (15 January 1926) refutes that possibility: "[the Truetone process] can be applied to either acoustic or electric recording and has been of particular value in eliminating the uncertainties from electric recording."

[8]*TMW* 22/11 (15 November 1926), 1; and Ronald Foreman, *Jazz and Race Records, 1920-32: Their Origins and Their Significance for the Record Industry and Society* (Ph.D. dissertation, University of Illinois, 1968), 201, 210. "Truetone," emblazoned on 1926 OKeh labels, was replaced by "Electric" after the company announced its adoption of the process in the March 1927 issue of *TMW* 23/3, 6. The first OKeh ad in the *Chicago Defender* (12 March 1927), 6, touting the technique, promoted a release by New York-based Clarence Williams recorded in late January; the first "electric" ad for a Chicago-based performer did not appear until 17 September. The delay suggests that Fearn's Chicago studio was not equipped to make electric recordings until several months after the company's New York studio. Thus, the Hot Sevens of May 1927 were probably not Armstrong's first electric recordings, leaving that distinction to the Hot Fives of 2 September 1927; see Phil Schaap, liner notes to Sony's *Complete Hot Five and Hot Seven Recordings* (Sony Music Entertainment, 2000), 28. Once purchased by Columbia, the reorganized OKeh Phonograph Corporation apparently pressed copies of earlier acoustic recordings bearing "Electric" labels, *e.g.*, "Heebie Jeebies"; the label is reproduced in Jim

E. A. Fearn, a native of Chicago, formed the Consolidated Talking Machine Company from five smaller firms with himself as president in 1918 and undertook the businesses of phonograph sale and repair and of record distribution from his downtown store at 227 West Lake Street. Displaying early a flair for promotion that was to mark his career, Fearn sponsored an "OKeh Record Football Team" with a mammoth OKeh disk as its team mascot. Five years after its founding, Fearn's enterprise moved from West Lake to a four-story building at 227-229 West Washington, boasted a local sales force of fourteen plus several "road men," and added branches in Detroit and Minneapolis. Consolidated Talking Machine had by now grown to be "one of the most successful OKeh jobbers in the country," whose president's observations about the industry were sought frequently by the head of OKeh's parent firm, Otto Heineman himself.[9]

The "King" Oliver recordings of 22-23 June 1923 were the first to be made by OKeh in Chicago. Although the notice in *Talking Machine World* failed to specify the location of the temporary recording laboratory for the first Oliver dates, it was almost certainly situated in the fourth floor stockroom of Consolidated Talking Machine where Oliver recorded his second OKeh session the following October. Because fire had damaged the top two floors of its headquarters the previous December, Consolidated hosted OKeh's February 1924 visit to the Windy City while temporarily located at 216 North Michigan. Back again in its remodeled facilities a few months later, Fearn's company was the sole OKeh jobber in the area, and its president became celebrated by company executives in New York for his splendid achievements in the development of the label's business. In 1925 an "elaborate and scientifically constructed recording laboratory" was permanently installed on the fourth floor of Consolidated's facilities, thereby eliminating the necessity for transporting recording equipment from New York as in the past.[10]

Godbolt, *The World of Jazz in Printed Ephemera and Collectibles* (Secaucus, NJ: Wellfleet Press, 1990), 34. For a brief history of electric recording, see Allan Sutton and Kurt Nauck, *American Record Labels and Companies: An Encyclopedia, 1891-1943* (Denver: Mainspring Press, 2000), xvi-xvii.

[9] *TMW* 14/12 (15 December 1918), 90; 19/6 (15 June 1923), 73; 19/10 (15 October 1923), 58; E. A. Fearn entry, *1920 Census—United States* (City of Chicago, E. D. 1692); and E. A. Fearn obituary, *Alton [Illinois] Evening Telegraph* (20 July 1953). Native to Illinois, Fearn's family may have spent time in Kansas, where his older brother John was born according to his obituary in *TMW* 21/4 (15 April 1925), 132.

[10] *TMW* 19/6 (15 June 1923), 104; 19/11 (15 November 1923), 112-14; 20/1 (15 January 1924), 120; 20/2 (15 February 1924), 120-21; 20/5 (15 May 1924), 120; and 21/6 (15 June 1925), 115.

Louis and Lil

Meanwhile Louis Armstrong had fallen in love with the Creole Band's pianist Lillian Hardin. After hastily obtaining divorces from their respective mates—Louis from Daisy Parker, still in New Orleans, and Lil from singer James M. Johnson—the couple married on 5 February 1924 and spent their honeymoon playing one-nighters with the Oliver band on an extended tour throughout the Midwest.[11] On their return to Chicago in June, Lil coaxed her husband into leaving Oliver, with whom he was playing second cornet, to seek a more suitable showcase for his burgeoning talent. Armstrong briefly joined Ollie Powers's band at the Dreamland as the singer's first (and only) cornetist before accepting an offer in September from Fletcher Henderson at the Roseland Ballroom in New York City.[12]

Louis traveled to New York alone with his wife following later, but her mother's illness forced Lil's return to Chicago around the first of the year while Armstrong remained with Henderson.[13] Ever ambitious for her husband who "wasn't anxious to be a star,"[14] Lil had noticed the absence of Armstrong's name from Henderson's billing. Purchasing a house at 421 East 44th Street, on Chicago's South Side, she laid plans for enticing Louis home and sought out Bill Bottoms, the owner of the Dreamland:

> So I went to the Dreamland and I said, "I want to put a band in, I want to bring my husband back from New York, and I want him to be featured, I want $75 a week for him, and I want his name out there in front." I had him [Bill Bottoms] to make a sign, "Louis Armstrong, the World's Greatest Trumpet [*sic*] Player."[15]

[11] *Chicago Defender* (9 September 1922), 5, and (16 February 1924), 9; Louis Armstrong, *Louis Armstrong: In His Own Words*, ed. Thomas Brothers (New York: Oxford University Press, 1999), 64-65, 86, 91; and Lil Armstrong, "Satchmo and Me" (Riverside RLP 12-120). Documents of Armstrong's divorce from Daisy are posted online at www.cookcountyclerkofcourt.org. For the Midwest tour, see Walter Allen and Brian Rust, *"King" Oliver*, rev. Laurie Wright (Chigwell, Essex: Storyville, 1987), 38-41; and Louis Armstrong, *In His Own Words*, 62-64.

[12] Lil Armstrong, "Satchmo and Me"; *Chicago Defender* (21 June 1924), 9; and Max Jones and John Chilton, *Louis: The Louis Armstrong Story, 1900-1971* (Boston: Brown, Little, 1971; reprinted New York: Da Capo Press, 1988), 94. Armstrong refused Henderson's first attempt to hire him in New Orleans several years earlier; see Louis Armstrong, *Swing That Music* (New York: Longmans, Green, 1936; reprinted New York: Da Capo Press, 1993), 34-35; and Fletcher Henderson, "Henderson 'Had to Get Louis' for Roseland Ork," *Down Beat* 17/14 (14 July 1950), 4.

[13] Louis Armstrong, *Swing That Music*, 80.

[14] Lil Armstrong, "Satchmo and Me."

[15] *Ibid.*

Lil won her contract and issued a demand for her husband's immediate return, to which she finally received a reluctant wire of assent.[16]

In early October 1925, Lil's Syncopators—without Louis—celebrated the re-opening of the Dreamland, closed for a year due to liquor violations, to a favorable review in the *Chicago Defender*:

> William Bottoms, the popular proprietor of "our own" Dreamland Café, has secured the services of Mrs. Lillian Armstrong, the pianist, who has gotten together six first-class musicians and formed a jazz band. She calls it Lil's Dreamland Syncopators. For a small unit they can't be beat, and they play a whole lot better than some of the "star" cabaret bands. They are versatile, playing well the performers' accompaniments, and their dance music seems to lift you off your feet. Their rendition of jazz is pleasing, not that vulgar mush kind that invites immoral dancing, and it is well for the place, as it keeps an atmosphere of class in the place. These seven jazz hounds make as much music as ten or twelve persons as every one is playing his part, not merely holding the instrument. . . .[17]

Armstrong, having vomited on his leader's "nice clean tuxedo shirt" from overzealous partying on his last night in New York, arrived in Chicago in early November to assume the cornet chair of his wife's Syncopators, to earn his unprecedented salary, and to begin living up to his advertised reputation as the "world's greatest jazz cornetist."[18] (See Illustration 2.1.)

The Dreamland was familiar to the Armstrongs, especially Lil, who

[16]*Ibid.* Armstrong's hesitation in leaving New York may have been his infatuation with a Cotton Club dancer named Fanny. See Robert Goffin, *Horn of Plenty: The Story of Louis Armstrong*, trans. James Bezou (New York: Allen, Towne and Heath, 1947; reprinted New York: Da Capo Press, 1977), 204-05.

[17]*Chicago Defender*, City Edition (31 October 1925), 6; and Wesley Neff, "Little Mitch: A Biography of George Mitchell," *Jazz Information* 2/16 (November 1941), 35. Besides Lil, the other Syncopators were George Mitchell, cornet; Joe Waler, alto sax; Jimmy Strong, clarinet/tenor sax; Sudi Renard, bass; and Baby Dodds, drums. Although he played regularly with Oliver, the seventh player could have been trombonist Edward "Kid" Ory; see Edward "Kid" Ory and Lester Koenig, "The Hot Five Sessions," *The Record Changer* (July-August 1950), 17. The *Defender* (31 October 1925), 6, also announced that Strong had recently arrived in Chicago from Los Angeles and (without mentioning Lil's band) was playing with Dave Peyton. In Ann Banks, ed., *First Person America* (New York: Alfred A. Knopf, 1980), 227, Bud Jacobson recalled Baby Dodds at the Dreamland with Armstrong, but his recollection is neither confirmed nor denied by Dodds's autobiography: Warren "Baby" Dodds and Larry Gara, *The Baby Dodds Story, as Told to Larry Gara*, rev. ed. (Baton Rouge: Louisiana State University Press, 1992). Mitchell remembered Armstrong playing second to his lead, but Armstrong, *In His Own Words*, 94, claimed to have replaced Lil's cornetist. Elsewhere, however, Armstrong in *Swing That Music*, 83, reported that Lil's band had eight pieces, perhaps validating Mitchell's memory.

[18]Louis Armstrong, *In His Own Words*, 94; *Chicago Defender*, City Edition (21 November 1925), 6.

Illustration 2.1.
Ad for Lil Armstrong's
Dreamland
Syncopators

From *Chicago Defender* (28 November 1925), 6.

had played there almost continuously with various bands from 1918 until 1922. Bill Bottoms, among the most successful black entrepreneurs on the South Side in the early 1920s, opened the Dreamland in 1917; from that time until its sale nine years later frequent closings succeeded ever grander re-openings. Lil and Joe Oliver were present in late 1920 at one of the grandest, described by a reporter for the *Chicago Whip*:

> In the large dome in the center of the ceiling hangs a beautiful bunch of green foliage, in which blaze red, white, and blue incandescent electric lights. On the outer edge of the dome are several dozen incandescent lights, with the initial "D." Hanging from the ceiling there are four lights covered with shades, hand painted. Gold decorations is [*sic*] the color scheme and on the floor is a new Brussels carpet. In the center is a glass flooring, five feet square, under which brilliant lights burn with stunning effect. On each table is an electric shade. The new addition is

the balcony which can be reached at the four corners of the room. At the west end is placed the special balcony for the New Orleans Jazz Band under the direction of Professor Joe Oliver.[19]

The Dreamland was a "black and tan"—an establishment catering primarily to blacks but also to whites. Such a clientele could sometimes result in a volatile mixture, as in December 1923, when a white gunman caused a "near riot" over an alleged racist slight.[20] At 3520 South State Street, the cabaret was located in the center of "The Stroll," the South Side entertainment district that ran full blast twenty-four hours a day and where a trumpet held in the air would reputedly "play itself."[21] Patrons came to dance, dine, and be entertained by elaborate revues headlined by the most illustrious names in black show business—Alberta Hunter, Bert Williams, Bill "Bojangles" Robinson. As described in the quoted newspaper report, the Syncopators needed to demonstrate enough versatility to negotiate complex written arrangements for accompanying the floor shows as well as to supply the latest pop and jazz tunes for dancing.

The Hot Five Idea

Lil speculated that the OKeh representative responsible for the Hot Five sessions was Tommy [T. G.] Rockwell, who came to Chicago from the West Coast around the time of the first Hot Five recordings.[22] But Rockwell's new position as manager of the recording department for Columbia's local branch would seem to preclude his hiring Armstrong for a rival company. Later, however, after moving to OKeh as director of recording (despite a reputed "tin ear") in the spring of 1927, as an OKeh executive in New York in 1929, and, from 1929 to 1931, as Armstrong's first manager, Rockwell exerted considerable influence on Louis's career.[23]

Rockwell, incidentally, caused the only reported occurrence of domestic violence between the Armstrongs. While still at Columbia he

[19] *Chicago Whip* (13 November 1920).

[20] *Chicago Defender* (8 December 1923), 1.

[21] William Howland Kenney, *Chicago Jazz: A Cultural History, 1904-1930* (New York: Oxford University Press, 1993), 14-15.

[22] Lil Armstrong, "Satchmo and Me."

[23] Lil Armstrong, "Satchmo and Me"; *TMW* 21/11 (15 November 1925), 134; *TMW* 22/5 (15 May 1927), 108; and James Lincoln Collier, *Louis Armstrong: An American Genius* (New York: Oxford University Press, 1983), 179, 203-05. Rockwell's move to OKeh was likely connected with Columbia's purchase of OKeh-Odeon from Heineman's General Phonograph Corporation.

asked Lil to record several tunes written by the couple. It was understood that Armstrong, as an exclusive OKeh artist, would not play on the sessions. The band, recording as the New Orleans Wanderers and the New Orleans Bootblacks on back-to-back dates in July 1926, consisted of Hot Five personnel except for George Mitchell (in place of Louis) on cornet and the addition of Joe Clark on alto saxophone. When the records were released in the fall of 1926, Armstrong's name was prominently displayed next to his compositions as if he had played them. This led to an argument climaxed by Louis's slapping his wife—accusing her of having known about the misrepresentation all along.[24]

Nor can Chicago saxophonist Bud Jacobson's claim to have persuaded E. A. Fearn to record an all-star quintet under Armstrong's direction be taken seriously.[25] As a retailer and promoter, Fearn could indeed sign up OKeh artists, but his being significantly influenced by Jacobson, then only nineteen and one of the white Chicagoans hanging out with members of the Austin High Gang, begs credibility. Jacobson and his bunch, however, haunted the Dreamland when Armstrong was there, and he and a friend were "the only two whites" at the OKeh Cabaret and Style Show, which featured an appearance by the Hot Five in June 1926.[26]

Hot Five banjoist Johnny St. Cyr thought that Fearn hired Armstrong directly:

> Having recorded on numerous occasions with King Oliver for the OKeh label, Louis became well known to Mr. Fern [*sic*] who was the recording engineer [*sic*] for that company at the time. . . . Mr Fern insisted that Louis record only his own compositions, and persuaded him to sign a five year contract, which Lil and I had advised Louis not to do.[27]

[24]William Russell, interview (1 Jul 1959) of Lillian Armstrong in Chicago (New Orleans: Tulane Jazz Archive). George Mitchell tells a similar story in Wesley Neff, "Little Mitch," 35. Lil considered the Wanderer recordings to have been the first jazz sessions to use written arrangements: "Perdido Street Blues" was entirely written out, even the solos. Of the eight titles released by the Wanderers and Bootblacks, "Gate Mouth" and "Mixed Salad" were Louis's according to copyright deposits in the Library of Congress; see David Chevan, *Written Music in Early Jazz* (Ph.D. dissertation, City University of New York, 1997), 278-81, 495. The domestic conflict may also have concerned the issue of composer credit. In the Armstrong Archive's uncatalogued Fearn collection, both a letter from Columbia and a copyright certificate name Louis as the composer of "Perdido Street Blues," a piece copyrighted by Lil.

[25]Ann Banks, ed., *First Person America*, 227.

[26]Max Jones and John Chilton, *Louis*, 114; *TMW* 19/11 (15 November1923), 114; and William Russell, *New Orleans Style*, ed. Barry Martyn and Mike Hazeldine (New Orleans: Jazzology, 1994), 70.

[27]Johnny St. Cyr, "The Original Hot Five," *Second Line* 5/9-10 (September-October 1955), 1.

Louis, in a 1951 interview, implied similar circumstances: "The minute Mr Fern (the President [*sic*] of the OKeh Company) gave me the go sign, I hit the phone and called the Musician's Union, and asked permission to hire Edward "Kid" Ory [trombone], Johnny St. Cyr [guitar-banjo], and Johnny Dodds [clarinet]."[28] Ory, on the other hand, credited Richard "Myknee" Jones, OKeh's Race Division manager in Chicago since mid-1923, to have arranged the Hot Five dates.[29] Because Jones could not have negotiated with OKeh on his own, his supervisor Fearn—perhaps with additional pressure from Lil, Jones's good friend—presumably hired the personnel.[30]

Regardless of such speculations about a Chicago contract with OKeh, the initial agreement must have been formalized in New York City. Ory in California remembered receiving a letter from Louis, with Henderson still, announcing an offer to play at the Dreamland and to record for OKeh. The money Armstrong mentioned sounded so attractive that Ory broke up his band and hurried to the Windy City, arriving "a few weeks" before Louis.[31] From New York City OKeh also wired Richard Jones to prepare Armstrong to record with Bertha "Chippie" Hill in Chicago, which the cornetist did on 9 November within days of his arrival.[32]

Armstrong's first recordings in New York City had been made with Henderson's Band for Columbia, Pathé, and Vocalion, but others there soon demanded his services—particularly Clarence Williams on his series of Blue Fives for OKeh. The Blue Five served mainly to promote tunes from Williams's publishing house and to back up vocal features by his wife Eva Taylor. Armstrong capably fulfilled his role of providing a strong lead on the recordings and made the most of his opportunities for brief hot solos.

[28]Louis Armstrong, *In His Own Words*, 130.

[29]Christopher Hillman and Roy Middleton, *Richard M. Jones: Forgotten Man of Jazz* (Tavistock, England: Cygnet Publications, 1997), 8.

[30]Edward "Kid" Ory, "The Hot Five Sessions," 17; Johnny St. Cyr, "Jazz As I Remember It, Part Four: Chicago Days," *Jazz Journal* 20/1 (January 1967), 15; Max Jones and John Chilton, *Louis*, 114; and James Lincoln Collier, *Louis Armstrong*, 169-70. The relationship between OKeh and Consolidated Talking Machine remains unclear. In the *Chicago Defender* (6 November 1926), 8, Jones is called the "Western Recording Manager" for Consolidated Music Publishing House, OKeh's publisher of convenience for Consolidated Talking Machine Co. The *Defender* (19 February 1927), 6, announces his resignation of the "dictatorship of the race record department," and the *Defender* (7 May 1927), 7, places him back with OKeh, now a subsidiary of Columbia.

[31]Edward "Kid" Ory, *ibid.*

[32]Christopher Hillman and Roy Middleton, *Richard M. Jones*, 10. On Hill, see "Driver Kills Chippie Hill," *Down Beat* 17/12 (16 June 1950), 12; and Daphne Duval Harrison, *Black Pearls*, 232-34.

Born in Louisiana, Clarence Williams moved to New Orleans shortly after the turn of the century and knew Armstrong as a youngster. Proficient as a pianist but more talented as a businessman, he formed, in 1915, a music publishing company with Armand J. Piron in New Orleans and eventually established profitable branches in Chicago and New York City. Armstrong and Williams may not have been closely associated; the two engaged in a long-standing feud over "I Wish I Could Shimmy Like My Sister Kate," which Piron copyrighted in 1919, Williams published in 1922, and Armstrong later claimed as his own creation.[33] In New York, though, Williams offered welcomed employment and an opportunity for Armstrong to record for OKeh. Williams had been an exclusive artist and local talent scout for the record label since 1923.[34]

The critical link between Louis Armstrong and OKeh, nonetheless, appears to have been Ralph Peer, OKeh's director of production and, after December 1925, the company's general sales manager. Peer entered the recording business as a teenager by working for his father, a Columbia dealer in Independence, Missouri, and eventually landed a position with the Columbia organization in Kansas City. After brief service in the Navy towards the end of World War I, Peer returned to his old job in Kansas City; shortly thereafter he was hired by his former Columbia boss, who had in the meantime joined OKeh in New York City. Rising quickly to a position of authority in sales, Peer was the first in the record industry to act on the implications of the "Crazy Blues" phenomenon.

Claiming to have coined the term "race record," Peer began a separate number series and catalogue for these recordings, which he was to do later for "hillbilly" music as well. Soon he was scouring the country for race and hillbilly artists with Hibbard and his portable recording studio in tow.[35] Peer recalled Lil's appeals for work on her husband's behalf:

> I used to go to Chicago frequently [on sales trips] while I was with OKeh. I would go out late at night to the Royal Gardens [where] I

[33]David A. Jasen and Gene Jones, *Spreadin' Rhythm Around*, 287-88. For a colorful account of Piron and "Sister Kate," see Sidney Bechet, *Treat It Gentle*, 2nd ed. (New York: Hill and Wang, 1960; reprinted New York: Da Capo Press, 2002), 119-22; for Armstrong's version, see Ernie Anderson, "Louis Armstrong, A Personal Memoir," *Storyville* 148 (1 December 1991), 125-27; for the latest retelling, see Thomas Brothers, *Louis Armstrong's New Orleans* (New York: W. W. Norton, 2006), 228-30.

[34]*TMW* 19/8 (15 August 1923), 56.

[35]*TMW* 21/12 (15 December 1925), 120; Lillian Borgeson, interview (January-May 1958) with Ralph Peer (Chapel Hill: Southern Folklife Collection, University of North Carolina); and Ronald Foreman, *Jazz and Race Records*, 92.

> got acquainted with Armstrong and his wife [who] came up to me and said "Louis has an offer to go to New York [with Henderson's Orchestra]. Could you give us recording work there?". . . so we used a pickup orchestra with Louis Armstrong on trumpet. . . . Whenever we needed a New York trumpet player our first choice would be Louis Armstrong. So this went on for a year or so and finally [Lil] came to see me again and said, "[Louis] can't stand it in New York." And I said, "Well, now if he goes back to Chicago, I will do this for you. We will create an Armstrong orchestra so that we can give you some work." . . . [He] went back to Chicago and we sent a recording outfit out to an old warehouse there . . . and rented a floor. . . . I got the best musicians that you could get . . . because I like Louis. . . . I okeyed the musicians, all of whom I knew. . . . I'd really set up the dates around Louis. I really did it to get him enough money so he could pay his way up there . . . that was the beginning of Louis Armstrong.[36]

It seems reasonable to speculate further that Peer had some say in the name and instrumentation of Armstrong's new "orchestra" by either requesting or requiring that it be modeled on the commercially successful drum-less and bass-less Blue Five of Clarence Williams. Peer's self-serving account, nevertheless, is probably a distortion. His decisions, crucial no doubt to the formation of the Hot Five, were likely made in collaboration with E. A. Fearn and Richard M. Jones, with whom he must share credit for "the beginning of Louis Armstrong."

Hot Five Personnel

Because Armstrong's contract permitted him to choose his own personnel, he turned to musicians he knew best.[37] Trombonist Edward "Kid" Ory (1886-1973) was born in LaPlace, Louisiana, about twenty miles northwest of New Orleans near the shore of Lake Ponchartrain.[38] As a boy he began organizing bands—first with homemade instruments—and moved to New Orleans permanently on his twenty-first birthday, bringing down the members of his Woodland Band a month or so later. When his

[36]Lillian Borgeson, interview with Ralph Peer.

[37]The biographical sketches of Hot Five personnel are abstracted from my articles: "Johnny Dodds in New Orleans," 405-40, and "The Genesis of King Oliver's Creole Jazz Band," 283-303.

[38]John McCusker, "Ory Baptismal Certificate," *The Jazz Archivist* (December 1994), 23.

original musicians returned home, Ory replaced them with local players. Featuring Joe "King" Oliver on cornet around the time of World War I, Ory's band was among the busiest and best in the city. When in early 1919 Oliver left for Chicago, Ory replaced him with Armstrong, but the group folded before the end of the year with Ory's move to Los Angeles for health reasons and his failure to entice fellow musicians to accompany him to the West Coast.

Assembling a fresh ensemble of New Orleans and other southern expatriates in California, Ory moved from Los Angeles to Oakland in 1920 for a regular job at the Creole Café. While gigging in and around Oakland, he negotiated a six-month contract with the Pergola Dancing Pavilion in San Francisco for "King" Oliver's Creole Jazz Band in mid-1921. In June 1922 the enterprising musicians and music entrepreneurs, brothers John Spikes and Benjamin "Reb" Spikes, invited Ory's band back to Los Angeles to record some of their published songs. Ory, concerned that his band would not be heard to enough advantage backing up blues singers on the Spikes brothers' songs, lobbied them to record some instrumentals, his own "Ory's Creole Trombone" among them.[39]

Initially resisting an offer to join Oliver in Chicago, Ory leapt at the chance to record with his old friend Armstrong. The trombonist implied that the Hot Five comprised the Dreamland band after Louis's return, but this recollection is improbable because Dodds and St. Cyr already held regular jobs and Ory himself joined Oliver's Dixie Syncopators at the Plantation on the South Side shortly after setting foot in the Windy City.[40]

Johnny Dodds (1892-1940) had been one of Ory's first replacements in New Orleans for Woodland clarinetist Lawrence Duhé, who later took the progenitor of "King" Oliver's Creole Jazz Band to Chicago in 1917. A Crescent City native from the "uptown" black district as opposed to the "downtown" Creole district, Dodds became Ory's regular clarinetist from

[39]Floyd Levin, "Kid Ory's Legendary Nordskog/Sunshine Recordings: A Seventy Year-Old Controversy," *New Orleans Music* 2/4 (April 1991), 7-23. Levin reports on page 18 that Nordskog's son, Robert, was able, "by vivid memories of related events, to establish definitively the year of the Ory recordings as 1921—not 1922 as most discographies indicate." An entry in the *Chicago Defender* (27 May 1922), 8, however, settles the matter: "Last week the Spikes Brothers, who are beginning to manufacture recordings and piano rolls, sent to Oakland for 'Kid' Ory's Famous Creole Jazz Band to make their first records." In addition, according to the *Chicago Defender* (24 June 1922), 8, the Spikes Brothers presented their first "artist in public demonstration" on 2 June at the Gaumet Auditorium in Los Angeles, where Ory's group was billed as the band "which made the first records for the Spikes Bros." They played "Ory's Creole Trombone," "Maybe Some Day," and "Too Sweet Blues."

[40]Before Oliver, Ory played briefly with Carroll Dickerson and Doc Cooke. Ory also said that he "worked with Louis at the Dreamland for a while" during the early Hot Fives; see William Russell, *New Orleans Style*, 180-81. See also this chapter, note 17.

Sidney in Fate Marable's band around the winter of 1918 and continued in Ory's band when the young cornetist replaced Oliver. Oliver summoned Dodds to Chicago in 1921 to replace Duhé in his Creole Band, but Johnny left Oliver in a dispute over money before the Midwest tour of 1924.

Illustration 2.2.
Louis Armstrong's Hot Five: Exclusive OKeh Record Artists (Without Instruments)

Courtesy of the Hogan Jazz Archive, Tulane University

Illustration 2.3.
Louis Armstrong's Hot Five: Exclusive OKeh Record Artists (With Instruments)

Courtesy of the Hogan Jazz Archive, Tulane University

During that year he began a long-term residency at Kelly's Stables on the near North Side that lasted throughout the Hot Five period.[41]

Johnny St. Cyr (1880-1966), a "downtown" Creole born in New Orleans, was active in several bands and pick-up groups, principally in the red-light district known as Storyville, before joining Ory about the same time as Dodds. With Ory for barely more than a year, St. Cyr left to gig on his own, reverting to plastering as a day job when musical opportunities were limited. He spent the summers and off-seasons of 1918 through 1920 on the riverboats with Armstrong in Marable's band before heading to Chicago on his own in 1923. Not intending to remain, St. Cyr moved in with "King" Oliver temporarily, sat in with Oliver's Creole Band "to catch their style,"[42] and played on the Oliver recordings for Gennett, Columbia, and OKeh in October 1923. When his Creole Band apprenticeship ended, St. Cyr found a steady job with Charles "Doc" Cooke and remained with him until the summer of 1929, playing for white dancers at Harmon's Dreamland on the West Side during the winters and at Riverside and White City amusement parks during the summers.[43]

Displaying natural talent and considered a prodigy by friends and relatives, Memphis-born Lil Armstrong (1898-1971), née Lillian B. Hardin, studied piano privately with several teachers and spent an abortive year at Fisk University in Nashville before moving with her family to Chicago in 1917. There she attracted attention at a local music store by easily sight-reading and assertively plugging pop and jazz tunes of the day. The store manager recommended Lil to Lawrence Duhé, whose band had been recruited from the Crescent City to Chicago in 1917 to accompany Mabel Elaine's vaudeville act. Elaine left the show soon after Lil was hired to replace guitarist Louis Keppard; the band eventually found regular work at the DeLuxe Gardens on the South Side.

Duhé had moved across the street from the DeLuxe to the Dreamland by the time Oliver arrived to replace Thomas "Mutt" Carey on cornet and to displace Duhé as leader. After about six months on the job Oliver was blamed by Dreamland's management for falling revenues and was duly released. Lil stayed on with his successor, Clarence Jones's Jolly Jazzing Jeopards, whose soft and dreamy music in turn failed to please. This led

[41]Gene Anderson, "Blues for You Johnny: Johnny Dodds and His 'Wild Man Blues' Recordings of 1927 and 1928," *Annual Review of Jazz Studies* 8 (1996), 42.

[42]Johnny St. Cyr, "Jazz As I Remember It, Part Four: Chicago Days," 14.

[43]See also St. Cyr's autobiography, "Jazz as I Remember It, Parts 1-3," published serially in *Jazz Journal* 19 (October-November 1966).

to Oliver's reinstatement six months later and the grandest of re-openings, recounted above. Lil went to the West Coast with Oliver but returned to Chicago after six months to work with May Brady, once again at the Dreamland—where Oliver brought Louis to meet her in late 1922, shortly after the cornetist's arrival in Chicago. She rejoined Oliver, now playing at the Lincoln Gardens (formerly the Royal Gardens), and doubled after-hours at the Edelweiss Gardens in a band with Freddie Keppard.[44]

Louis Armstrong's early life in New Orleans—his birth in poverty, his employment as a child by a sympathetic Jewish family, his remanding to the local Colored Waif's Home as a teenager, and his idolization of Joe Oliver as mentor, teacher, and surrogate father—is familiar enough to obviate retelling. Perhaps still not universally known are his birth date of 4 August 1901, rather than 4 July 1900 as he had long contended, and his "adoption" of his cousin Flora's illegitimate child, Clarence Miles. Louis grew fond of the infant, born in 1915; when Flora died soon after, the baby came to live with Louis and his mother Mayann. On Louis's marriage to Daisy Parker a few years later, the boy joined the newlyweds at their dilapidated second-story apartment in New Orleans. During a rainstorm, the toddler slipped off one of the apartment's outside balconies and incurred a head injury that left him mentally impaired for life. Ever after, Clarence lived with, was looked after, or was provided for by Louis. This charitable decision put a strain on more than one of Armstrong's four marriages.[45]

Another biographical detail—Armstrong's middle name of "Daniel," bestowed in *Time* magazine's 21 February 1949 cover story[46]—may be more credible than previously thought. The cornetist could not account

[44]Lil Armstrong, "Satchmo and Me"; *Chicago Defender* (26 August 1922); Lil Armstrong, "Lil Tells of 1st Time She Met Louis," *Down Beat* 17 (14 July 1950), 18; Laurence Bergreen, *Louis Armstrong: An Extravagant Life* (New York: Broadway Books, 1997), 177-90; James L. Dickerson, *Just for a Thrill: Lil Hardin, First Lady of Jazz* (New York: Cooper Square Press, 2002), 1-113; and Louis Armstrong, *In His Own Words*, 66-67.

[45]For Armstrong's birth date, see Gary Giddins, *Satchmo*, 48-49; for Armstrong's early life and career, see his autobiographies, *Satchmo: My Life in New Orleans* (New York: Prentice Hall, 1954; reprinted New York, Da Capo Press, 1986); *Swing That Music*; "The Armstrong Story" and "The Satchmo Story" in *Louis Armstrong, In His Own Words*, 47-76, 11-126; and William Howland Kenney, "Negotiating the Color Line: Louis Armstrong's Autobiographies," *Jazzin' Mind: Essays on the History and Meaning of Jazz*, ed. Reginald T. Buckner and Steven Weiland (Detroit: Wayne State University, 1991), 38-59.

[46]"Louis the First," *Time* LIII/8 (21 February 1949), 52-58.

for the name that "came out of clear skies,"[47] but New Orleans historian Tad Jones, the discoverer of Armstrong's baptismal certificate, traced Louis's forebears to his paternal great-great-grandfather—a slave named Daniel Walker of Richmond, Virginia, bought in New Orleans for about $600 in 1818. Also named Daniel, Walker's son married Catherine, who co-sponsored Armstrong at his baptism. The name "Daniel," which does not appear on Louis's baptismal certificate, may yet be found, if it exists, on his still unlocated birth certificate.[48]

Thirty-two years later, Armstrong vividly remembered the day he left New Orleans to join "King" Oliver in Chicago—8 August 1922—and the details of his first encounter with the Creole Jazz Band at the Lincoln Gardens. Between then and the group's appearance at the Convention of Applied Music Trades the following June, Armstrong performed nightly at the Gardens as Oliver's second cornet, astounding visiting musicians with his and Oliver's uncanny duet-breaks. In early April the band boarded a train for Richmond, Indiana, to make nine historic sides for the Gennett label, among them Armstrong's first recorded solo on "Chimes Blues" (see Example 9.14).

[47]Max Jones and John Chilton, *Louis*, 48.

[48]Ralph Blumenthal, "Digging for Satchmo's Roots in the City That Spawned Him," *New York Times* (15 August 2000), E:1, col. 4. See also Thomas Brothers, "Louis Armstrong: The 'Saints' and the 'Boys,'" *Musica Oggi: Louis Armstrong verso il ventunesimo secolo* 21 (2001), 5. Armstrong's baptismal certificate is reproduced in Gary Giddins, *Satchmo*, 48.

Into the Studio

The Hot Five recordings were usually made in the morning between the completion of members' regular or doubled gigs and their heading home for a few hours sleep. St. Cyr's job with Doc Cooke, for example, lasted from eight until midnight after which he doubled at the Apex Club with Jimmy Noone from one until six a.m. Armstrong, during much of the Hot Five period, was featured with Erskine Tate at the Vendome Theater from seven until eleven every evening before doubling at the Dreamland or Sunset Café from midnight until three or four in the morning.[1]

"Kid" Ory described the rather informal scheduling of recording dates and the procedures at the studio in the following account:

> Our recording sessions would start this way: the OKeh people would call up Louis and say they wanted so many sides. They never told him what numbers they wanted or how they wanted them. Then Louis would give us the date, and sometimes he'd call me and say I'm short of a number for this next session. Do you think you can get one together? . . . We would get to the studio at nine or ten in the morning. . . . In the beginning we made records acoustically. . . . Then later, of course, we made records electrically. When we'd get in the studio, if we were going to do a new number, we'd run over it a couple of times before we recorded it. . . . We spoiled very few records, only sometimes when one of us would forget the routine or the frame-up, and didn't come in when he was supposed to.[2]

In a 1950 interview with Nesuhi Ertegun for *Down Beat,* the trombonist elaborated:

> We usually made eight sides at one session, and we made them so quickly that the OKeh people were amazed. . . . Most of the other bands took all day to make a couple of sides. We would make eight in three hours. Often we didn't know the tunes when we got to the studio; one of us would suggest a melody, we'd run through

[1]William Russell, *New Orleans Style,* ed. Barry Martyn and Mike Hazeldine (New Orleans: Jazzology, 1994), 71; Louis Armstrong, *Swing That Music* (New York: Longmans, Green, 1936; reprinted New York: Da Capo Press, 1993), 85.

[2]Edward "Kid" Ory and Lester Koenig, "The Hot Five Sessions," *The Record Changer* (July-August 1950), 17, 45.

> it once and then we'd record it. We never used any kind of arrangement. All we needed was a lead sheet and everybody would figure out his own part.[3]

Reeds, brass, piano, and banjo played into separate horns for acoustic recordings, but clarinetist Dodds could not play "hot" without loudly tapping his right foot, under which Fearn was obliged to place a pillow to keep from ruining the cuts. The band members were so acclimated to each other's playing that they soon came to rehearse and time the numbers in the studio, thereby eliminating tests and often managing to cut a master on the first take.[4] Both Ory and St. Cyr recalled the Hot Five sessions as happy, relaxed, and fun and remembered Louis as a "wonderful" leader who respected his sidemen and put the band before his personal acclaim. Most importantly for posterity's sake, OKeh avoided trying to "expert" the musicians, allowing them almost complete artistic freedom in the studio.[5]

On 12 November 1925, the first three Hot Fives were cut in OKeh's portable studio at the Consolidated Talking Machine Company. Even if "no earthshaking jazz" may have resulted,[6] the band performed with the confidence expected from players who had known each other personally and professionally for years. Not surprisingly, the musical style recalled both the players' New Orleans origins and "King" Oliver's recordings of two years earlier. Ensemble playing with frequent breaks dominated the first two numbers, and the leader animated his sidemen with hometown hokum in the third. Although the youngest of the group at twenty-four, Armstrong exerted his musical authority by means of his swinging leads, innovative solos, and hot breaks.

[3]Edward "Kid" Ory and Nesuhi Ertegun, "Louis Was Just a Little Kid in Knee Pants," *Down Beat* 17/14 (14 July 1950), 8. Ory exaggerated the number of sides per session, which was usually four, although the Hot Five recorded six sides on 26 February 1926.

[4]Johnny St. Cyr, "The Original Hot Five," *Second Line* 5/9-10 (September-October 1954), 1-2; William Russell, interview (1 July 1959) with Lillian Armstrong (New Orleans: Hogan Jazz Archive, Tulane University).

[5]Edward "Kid" Ory, "The Hot Five Sessions," 45.

[6]Gunther Schuller, *Early Jazz: Its Roots and Musical Development* (New York: Oxford University Press, 1968), 98.

"My Heart"*

Table 3.1. Structural Outline of "My Heart" [E♭ Major]

SECTION	INSTRUMENTATION	BARS
Introduction	Parallel Clarinet, Cornet, Trombone	2
Chorus 1	Ensemble / Cornet Break	30 / 2
Verse	Ensemble / Trombone Break / Ensemble	7 / 1 / 8
Chorus 2	Stop-time Clarinet Solo / Clarinet Break	14 / 2
	Piano Solo / Cornet Break / Trombone Break	14 / 1 / 1
Chorus 3	Ensemble / Trombone Break	14 / 2
	Ensemble / Cornet Break / Ensemble	8 / 4 / 4
Tag	Cornet / Ensemble	1 / 1

"My Heart," the first Hot Five number waxed, had been copyrighted by Lil five years earlier as a waltz titled "My Heart Will Lead Me Back to You."[7] Revised into a fox-trot and refitted with a bluesy clarinet solo, "My Heart" begins with an arranged or prepared introduction—a descending, syncopated arpeggiation of the tonic triad.

The first chorus (Example 3.1 on the following page) illustrates the "guidelines" of collective improvisation as worked out by early New Orleans bands exemplified by Oliver's. Against the cornet's lead or relatively unadorned version of the melody, the clarinet plays an obbligato above in shorter note values while the trombone supplies a quasi bass line or obbligato below in longer note values. With counterpoint being the prevailing texture, rhythmic and melodic independence of the instruments is paramount. Hence, unisons and parallelisms are avoided, and registers kept separate. There should be little or no "dead space"; long durations in one part should be filled in by another part, giving the impression of a constant stream of eighth notes from beginning to end. Two- and four-bar phrases, sixteen-bar verses, and thirty-two-bar choruses are the norm with breaks occurring as cadences in the final two measures of sixteen-bar sections. Blue notes, particularly as lowered thirds and sevenths, are endemic to the tone system but tend to be used more sparingly in popular

[7]Max Jones and John Chilton, *Louis: The Louis Armstrong Story, 1900-1971* (Boston: Little, Brown, 1971; reprinted New York: Da Capo Press, 1988), 258. The original copyright deposit (see Table A1.1) is lost. The label copy for "My Heart" is reproduced in Jim Godbolt, *The World of Jazz in Printed Ephemera and Collectibles* (Secaucus, NJ: Wellfleet Press, 1990), 35. In Warren "Baby" Dodds and Larry Gara, *The Baby Dodds Story, as Told to Larry Gara*, 2nd ed. (Baton Rouge: Louisiana State University Press, 1992), 10, Dodds remembered that, in New Orleans, "We used to take waltz tunes and change them into four-four time."

songs than in blues numbers.[8] Apart from the G♭'s in the cornet melody of "My Heart" (Example 3.1, mm. 2, 4, 18, and 20), the only other prominent blue notes are the D♭'s in Dodds's break (Example 3.3, m. 15, on page 29).

Invoking the above criteria, Ory's part is the least satisfactory among the "front line" players. For much of first half of the chorus his repeated quarter notes on the beat duplicate the function of the rhythm section; not until bar 8 does he begin to animate the ensemble with a contribution of greater independence. In the second half of the chorus where his quarter-note passages are somewhat less frequent and less repetitious, however, he provides a more effective foil for the cornet and clarinet.

Example 3.1. First Ensemble Chorus of "My Heart"

[8]Gunther Schuller, *Early Jazz*, 94.

Example 3.1 Continued.

Dodds fulfills his ensemble clarinet role faithfully—diverging from his contrapuntal duties only to play in octaves with Ory (m. 15). Frequent on-the-beat dissonances (minor seconds or ninths and major seconds) with the lead (in mm. 2, 4, 9, etc.) are mitigated or absolved by their brevity and convincing voice-leading. And typically, in contrast to the lead, Dodds unifies his part with recurring arpeggiated figures and triplet motives (mm. 4, 6, 9-10, 13, etc.).

Armstrong's assertive lead exhibits several trademarks: the dramatic "rip" to a high note on weak beats (mm. 16 and 31-32), the descending line followed by an ascending leap of a seventh (mm. 18 and 27-28), and the shake (m. 16).[9] The absence of Lil's copyright deposit prevents any determination of how closely Armstrong's lead follows the original melody, but in those pieces for which deposits exist he tends to embellish the melody mildly in his exposition and to vary it increasingly thereafter.[10] Successive leads thus resemble a series of solos of building excitement and complexity that conclude with an "out chorus" in the high register, as is the case in "My Heart." While Ory duplicates much of what he played in the first chorus and Dodds simplifies his earlier effort, Armstrong retains only one bar from his former lead while adding triplets, an extensive arpeggio, and additional rips (Example 3.2, mm. 5, 7, and 9). After Ory's break, Armstrong begins the final half of the third chorus on a high B♭ for a rousing conclusion.

Dodds's solo in "My Heart" is his first on record entirely in the low or chalumeau register of the clarinet, a type of solo that would become his speciality. All of his recorded solos with Oliver's Creole Band were played in the upper register—seldom, if ever, dropping below the "break" (between written B♭ and B♮ above middle C). Because of the changes of embouchure and breath support necessary for "crossing the break," its negotiation seemed to be a problem for Dodds, who avoided it, in solos at least, by restricting himself exclusively to one register or another.

Although brief, Dodds's "My Heart" solo is impressive (Example 3.3). Giving the lie to critics of his "extremely weak rhythm,"[11] he demonstrates his command of a formidable technique and a secure sense of time at a challenging tempo—one complicated, moreover, by a syncopated stop-time accompaniment. For variety Dodds typically repeats note patterns on different beats (*e.g.*, the cambiata-like figure, C - B♭ - F♯ - G, in m. 2, beats

[9]*Ibid.*, 94, 97. To these, Schuller adds a three-note short-short-long figure (see Example 9.4, m. 1, of Armstrong's solo). Armstrong plays a rip in his first recorded solo (Example 9.14, m. 12). Jeffrey Magee, in *The Music of Fletcher Henderson and His Orchestra in the 1920s* (Ph.D. dissertation, Columbia University, 1992), 315-25, lists five other "formulaic phrases" from the cornetist's Henderson period that persist into his later playing: (1) a syncopated opening or lead-in preceding a three- or four-note "stabilizing figure" (Example 3.10, beginning of Armstrong's solo); (2) a syncopated double leap of a third or fourth (Example 4.8, m. 1); (3) an ascending chromatic triplet figure followed by a descending broken chord (Example 9.14, chorus 2, mm. 9-10); (4) a descending leap to the raised supertonic followed by the mediant and tonic (Example 9.15, chorus 1, m. 1); and (5) a string of eighth notes oscillating between two pitches a half- or whole-step apart (Example 6.11, m.15). See also H. David Caffey, "The Musical Style of Louis Armstrong, 1925-1929," *Journal of Jazz Studies* 3/1 (Fall 1975), 72-96; and Richard Domek, "Musical Organization and Trademarks in the Maturing Solos of Louis Armstrong," *Jazz Research Papers* (Manhattan, KS: NAJE, 1996), 32-47.

[10]Armstrong was already known in New Orleans for playing a "figurated" lead; see Brian Harker, "Louis Armstrong and the Clarinet," *American Music* 21/2 (Summer 2003), 138.

[11]André Hodeir, *Jazz, Its Evolution and Essence*, trans. David Noakes (New York: Grove Press, 1956; reprinted New York: Da Capo Press, 1975), 52-53.

Example 3.2. First Half of the Third Ensemble Chorus of "My Heart"

Example 3.3. Dodds's Solo in "My Heart"

2-3; m. 3, beats 1-2; and m. 4, beats 3-4) or replaces the melody with arpeggios for a harmonically-based improvisation.[12] He complements this rhythmic and harmonic variety with those of gesture and melody. After the opening E♭ octave leap defining the solo's range, he fills this musical space with ascending and descending arpeggiated figures of varying complexity and changes of direction: the first (mm. 1-4), down-up-down in three bars; the second (mm. 5-8), down-up-down in four bars with chromaticism; the third (mm. 9-12), up-down-up-down in four bars with triplets; and the fourth (mm. 13-16), up-down in four bars with a blue-note break.

The drums were a staple in New Orleans jazz bands and, because Armstrong's later small ensembles all had them, one must presume that the decision to forego their inclusion in the Original Hot Five was not his. Their function in these recordings is chiefly assumed by the banjo. In "My Heart," as in the rest of the Hot Fives, St. Cyr, regardless of tempo, supplies a quadruple metrical "feel" by emphatically strumming chords four times in each measure. A competent player with a good ear, he plays solos only twice in thirty-three numbers while providing the occasional introduction, interlude, modulation, or break.

Lil's left hand with sporadic help from Ory contributes what bass the group has at its disposal. Thus, her "heavy" playing, which she said she learned from "Jelly Roll" Morton as a young girl,[13] serves the Hot Five well. Often criticized for lack of imagination and swing, Lil, nevertheless, solos frequently on the early Hot Fives and supplies numerous interludes or transitions on later ones. Her "My Heart" solo contains two syncopated break-like passages that resurface in her later work (Example 3.4).

Example 3.4. Lil's Break-like Passages in "My Heart"

[12]See also mm. 13-14 of Gunther Schuller's transcription of Dodds's solo in "Brown Bottom Bess" in *Early Jazz*, 202.

[13]Lil Armstrong, *Satchmo and Me: Lil Armstrong's Own Story* [recorded memoir] (Riverside RLP 12-120, ca. 1950-1959).

"Yes! I'm in the Barrel"

Table 3.2. Structural Outline of "Yes! I'm in the Barrel"

SECTION	INSTRUMENTATION	BARS	KEY
Introduction	Muted Cornet over Vamp	19.5	D Min
Chorus 1	Ensemble	20	F Maj
Verse	Ensemble	16	D Min
Blues Strain 1	Clarinet Solo	12	F Maj
Blues Strain 2	Clarinet Solo	12	F Maj
Chorus 2	Ensemble / Trombone Break	6 / 2	F Maj
	Ensemble / Cornet Break / Ensemble	4 / 4 / 4	F Maj

The formal complexity of Armstrong's composition "Yes! I'm in the Barrel," copyrighted in 1923 as "I Am in the Barrel, Who Don't Like It?," is somewhat unusual for Hot Five personnel, who tended to favor simple structures for reasons of expediency and lack of rehearsal time. In a 1951 interview for *Esquire*, Armstrong explained that the title came from an old New Orleans idiom:

> Whenever one of those gambling guys would get busted in a gambling game . . . they would pawn their best clothes to pay off their gambling debts. Quite naturally they would have to go back to their old raggedy clothes until they got lucky and get the good ones out of pawn again. So that's why we used the expression, "Yes! I'm in the barrel." Yes, I too was in the barrel lots of times.[14]

The copyright deposit (see Appendix 1) comprises an introduction of four bars in F major, a sixteen-bar verse in D minor, a twenty-bar chorus in F major, and a two-bar tag. The alternation of minor and relative major is maintained on the recording, which expands the introduction and switches the verse and chorus. Differences between the deposit and the recording, however, reflect a high degree of musical sophistication. The decision to switch the verse and chorus, for example, must have been a consequence of changing the introduction from a preview of the verse to a meditation on the D minor triad. After the lengthy D minor introduction, the contrast of the F major chorus may thus have been deemed more musically

[14]Louis Armstrong, *Louis Armstrong: In His Own Words*, ed. Thomas Brothers (New York: Oxford University Press, 1999), 132.

appropriate than sixteen more bars in the same key.[15] Considerations of length and variety most likely prompted the insertion of blues choruses, which could have been suggested by Lil, whose popular song "Sweet Lovin' Man" was recorded by "King" Oliver's Jazz Band in 1923 with two blues choruses for clarinet solo as additions to the copyright deposit.[16]

Perhaps in honor of his mentor Oliver, famous for his "eccentric playing," Armstrong lays down a rare muted solo over a minor vamp as an introduction, which amounts to a temporal exploration of the D minor triad over a two-octave range (Example 3.5).[17] Louis's blue fifth (A♭) in bars 6 and 17 foreshadows the chorus's blue thirds and their enharmonic counterparts, G♯'s. The rhythmic notation is approximate; over the rigid vamp Armstrong places the notes everywhere but squarely on the beat, all at a fairly brisk tempo. Yet, despite Armstrong's set-up for the chorus a half bar early, the ensemble seamlessly adjusts to the two skipped beats.

Example 3.5. Armstrong's Introduction to "Yes! I'm in the Barrel"

Armstrong's lead closely adheres to his copyright deposit, in which the melody emphasizes the chordal third by means of an applied leading tone—G♯ - A for the F harmonies, E - F for the D harmonies, and (on the recording) C♯ - D for the B♭ harmonies (see note 9, item 4). Prominent accentuation of the third, the excursion into D minor (mm. 3-4 and 11-12), and the melody's triadic construction link it strongly to the introduction (see Example 3.6).

15David Chevan, *Written Music in Early Jazz* (Ph.D. dissertation, City University of New York, 1997), 292-93.

16For a copyright history of "Sweet Lovin' Man" and copies of its deposits, see David Chevan, *Written Music in Early Jazz*, 249-51, 468-70. A recording of the tune by the New Orleans Rhythm Kings three months before Oliver's did not include the blues choruses.

17Armstrong never used a mute on his recordings with Oliver but played frequently with one on his recordings with Henderson in New York. "Yes! I'm in the Barrel" is his only muted Hot Five/Seven solo. On Armstrong's muted solos and work in minor keys, see Edward Brooks, *Influence and Assimilation in Louis Armstrong's Cornet and Trumpet Work, 1923-1928* (Lewiston, NY: Edwin Mellon Press, 2000), 30-39, 159-62.

Example 3.6. Comparison of Armstrong's Copyright Deposit for "I Am in the Barrel, Who Don't Like It?" with His Recorded Lead in "Yes! I'm in the Barrel"

The pitch G♯, used either to embellish A or as a blue third to replace A, is central to the melodic structure. The opening two bars of the chorus embellish A, forming subphrase "a" in the twenty-bar melody, which is divided into two eight-bar periods and a truncated period of four bars. Subphrase "c" with a blue third ends the consequent phrase in the first period and begins the consequent phrase in the second. Subphrase "a′" echoes the rhythm and shape of "a," and the final sub-unit "a - a′" summarizes the D minor and F major conflict of the piece (see Table 3.3 on the following page). The chorus therefore balances the predictability of regularly recurring material "a" with irregularly recurring "c," related "a′," and contrasting material "b," "d," and "e." Such a procedure approaches what Beiderbecke called the "correlated chorus," whose invention he attributed to Armstrong: "play two measures, then two related, making four measures, on which you played another four measures related to the first four, and so on . . . to the end of the chorus."[18]

[18]Leon "Bix" Beiderbecke, quoted in Richard M. Sudhalter and Philip R. Evans, *Bix: Man & Legend* (New Rochelle, NY: Arlington House, 1974), 100-01.

Table 3.3. Phrase Structure of "Yes! I'm in the Barrel"

PERIOD 1				PERIOD 2			
Antecedent		Consequent		Antecedent		Consequent	
a	a′	b	c	a	d	c	e
1-2	3-4	5-6	7-8	9-10	11-12	13-14	15-16

PERIOD 3	
Antecedent	Consequent
a	a - a′
17-18	19-20

Beyond the subphrase level, the first period's antecedent "a - a′" prolongs the chordal third by filling in the musical space a fourth above the mediant (A) and a fifth below. Its consequent "b - c" prolongs the dominant (C) and fills in its musical space up to the tonic (F)—the period's melodic climax—followed immediately by the first appearances of a blue seventh (E♭). While the virtual absence of the subdominant (B♭) and of the leading tone (E) give Armstrong's melody a pentatonic flavor, there is nothing primitive or folk-like about his tune, which exhibits classic ingredients of sound melodic construction.

Interestingly, Armstrong's slight departures from the deposit are all structural "improvements." The blue third (m. 8) adds color to the melody, and the lead's antecedent phrase "a - d" of the second period strengthens the prolongation of D by means of a tonicization. The shape and rhythm of the lead's bars 13-14—a syncopated emphasis on the blue seventh, descent of a major ninth to its octave, dramatic upward leap of a major seventh, and arpeggiation of the tonic triad with a blue third—are the quintessence of tension and repose in microcosm when compared with what Armstrong originally composed.

After an ensemble verse in minor, Dodds blows two blues choruses in the relative major. The piece concludes with a chorus in major featuring a two-bar trombone and a four-bar cornet break. The whole resembles formal schemes from the Oliver Band repertory without corresponding to any particular one, while being, because of its extensive emphasis on relative minor and major keys, more tonally advanced than anything Oliver recorded.[19]

[19]"King" Oliver's 1923 recordings are exclusively in major, and modulations are exclusively to the subdominant, *e.g.*, from E♭ to A♭.

The tritone descent from D to A♭ (m. 2) of Dodds's solo (Example 3.8 on the following page) recalls his first recorded solo on "Canal Street Blues" with "King" Oliver's Creole Jazz Band on 5 April 1923 (Example 3.7). A set-piece like Armstrong's solo on "Chimes Blues" (provided later as Example 9.14), "Canal Street," nevertheless, serves as a template for Dodds's blues solos in general, which typically amount to expansions of tonic harmony with a diatonic / blue third and a blue seventh (F - A♭ / A♮ - C - E♭). In "Yes! I'm in the Barrel" Dodds favors the major third (A) in the first chorus and the blue third (A♭) in the second. Except for the B♭'s in bars 5-6, Dodds avoids an unequivocal reference to the subdominant harmony at the equivalent location in the second chorus by repeatedly sounding the F and A♭ common to the tonic (F) and subdominant seventh (B♭7). Given its rhythmic variety, this kind of melodic redundancy proves crucial to the solo's coherence, which features a repeated F - G - F neighbor figure occurring at equal intervals on different beats or portions thereof for a striking hemiola effect (chorus 2, mm. 5-7).

Example 3.7. Dodds's Solo in "Canal Street Blues"

Dodds's manipulation of melodic shape contributes an additional unifying element to his solo. After the tonic seventh arpeggiation of the first three bars of the first chorus, the next four fill in the arpeggiation stepwise from the blue seventh down to the tonic. The last five bars fill in the sixth between the tonic and the A below with the blue third in bar 11 counterbalancing the blue third in bar 2. The second chorus begins on the fifth of the tonic triad rather than the third and quickly descends stepwise to a prolonged tonic. Its last five bars summarize earlier material by filling in the entire melodic range of a diminished twelfth from high E♭ down to A before recapitulating the A♭ / A♮ conflict central to the solo in its penultimate bar. While each chorus exhibits a symmetry and balance of its own, the melodic shape of the second chorus complements the first, thus integrating them into one solo of twenty-four bars rather than two solos of twelve bars apiece.

Example 3.8. Dodds's Solo in "Yes! I'm in the Barrel"

“Gut Bucket Blues”*

Table 3.4. Structural Outline of “Gut Bucket Blues” [C Major]

SECTION	INSTRUMENTATION	BARS
Introduction	Banjo	12
Chorus 1	Ensemble	12
Chorus 2	Ensemble	12
Chorus 3	Piano solo	12
Chorus 4	Trombone solo	12
Chorus 5	Clarinet solo	12
Chorus 6	Cornet solo	12
Chorus 7	Ensemble	12
Tag	Cornet / Ensemble	1 / 1

The third cut of the first Hot Five session was created at the studio in response to Fearn's request for a blues to round out the set. Because Armstrong complained that all their blues sounded alike, St. Cyr suggested beginning with a banjo solo:

> So we made a short rehearsal and cut the number. When Mr. Fern [sic] asked, "What shall we name it?," Louis thought for a while and then said, "Call it 'The Gut Bucket.'" Louis could not explain the meaning of the name. He said it just came to him. But I will explain it. In the fish markets in New Orleans the fish cleaners keep a large bucket under the table where they clean the fish, and as they do this they rake the guts in this bucket. Thence "The Gut Bucket," which makes it a low down blues.[20]

The simple structure of "Gut Bucket Blues" heralds the organization of later Hot Fives—a string of ensemble and solo choruses increasingly showcasing Armstrong. In "Gut Bucket," however, every player solos—each urged by the leader to "whip it" or "do that thing."[21] But in the studio

[20]Johnny St. Cyr, “The Original Hot Five,” 2.

[21]Armstrong’s voice was first heard on “Everybody Loves My Baby,” Fletcher Henderson’s recording of 22 November 1924, on which he improvises three rhythmically spoken breaks: “Ow brother, don’t play me that / Ah, now you come to do it / Oh, that’s it, boy.” The breaks hardly qualify as “scatting,” which Gary Giddins claims in his liner notes to *The Complete Hot Five and Seven Recordings*, Vol. 1 (Sony Music Entertainment, 2003).

when it came time for Dodds to introduce "Papa Dip,"[22] he froze in front of the horn, ruining several takes before finally turning the line over to Ory.[23]

The formal simplicity of "Gut Bucket Blues" belies its refined musical content. St. Cyr's introductory solo, one of his most extensive on record, reveals deft technique and a nicely crafted melodic line spiced with chromaticism rising to a prominent blue seventh (B♭) in measure 3. A passing diminished chord (m. 6) and a series of secondary dominants (mm. 8-9) before arriving (m. 10) at the dominant (G) constitute a few embellishments of the standard blues progression (Example 3.9). St. Cyr's progression differs, in fact, from the one followed during the remainder of the piece: C - F7 - C - C7 / F7 - F7 - C - A7 / G7 - F7 - C - C.

Example 3.9. St. Cyr's Introduction to "Gut Bucket Blues"

Incidentally, the copyright deposit of "Gut Bucket Blues" offers no compositional insights. Submitted several months after the recording, it is a descriptive lead-sheet incorrectly transcribed by Lil from the recording or from memory (see Appendix 1).[24] The introduction has thirteen bars instead of twelve, and bars 1-2 and bars 5-6 of the first ensemble chorus alone resemble Armstrong's recorded cornet lead. The second ensemble chorus, solo choruses, and Armstrong's solo tag are not included. Only the final ensemble chorus and a few bars of the introduction actually duplicate the recording.

[22]According to Louis Armstrong, *Satchmo: My Life in New Orleans* (New York: Prentice-Hall, 1954; reprinted New York: Da Capo Press, 1986), 235, "Papa Dip," a variation of "Dippermouth," was one of his earliest nicknames. Lil recorded "Papa Dip" with her New Orleans Wanderers on 13 July 1926 and copyrighted the tune six days later.

[23]Bill Rand, interview (ca. 1953) with Louis Armstrong for WERE Radio (Cleveland), Cassette 26 (New York: Louis Armstrong Archives, Queens College).

[24]Although listed in the Music Division's catalogue, the copyright deposit for "Gut Bucket Blues" cannot presently be located. The author thanks David Chevan for providing the photocopy reproduced in Appendix 1.

Interestingly, Lil's version of St. Cyr's solo improves the structure of the original by inserting the fifth (G) in its arpeggiation of the C7 harmony, thereby delaying the seventh (B♭) until its usual appearance in bar 4. On the recording St. Cyr reaches B♭ prematurely in measure 3, making a two-bar prolongation of C7 necessary before the move to the subdominant (F) in bar 5 (see Chapter 9, note 29). Lil's inclusion of the C7 prolongation from the original (or her interpolation of an arpeggiation on G) produced the introduction's extra bar.

Example 3.10. Comparison of Solos in "Gut Bucket Blues"

On the recording, however, the series of solos after the two ensemble choruses provides a study in motivic development (Example 3.10).[25] Lil

[25]William Russell, "Play That Thing, Mr. Johnny Dodds," *Jazz Information* (23 August 1940), 11, includes a transcription of Dodds's "Gut Bucket" solo. For purported evidence of "King" Oliver's influence on Armstrong's "Gut Bucket" solo, see Edward Brooks, *Influence and Assimilation*, 62.

introduces a descending five-note motive (C - A - G - D♯ - E) in bars 1-2, which she repeats twice in bars 2-3, the second time inverted. Blue notes (E♭'s) occur frequently as the seventh of the subdominant (F7) but not as the third of the tonic (C), and she refers to the implied A7 from bar 8 of St. Cyr's introduction, a harmonic detail overlooked or ignored by succeeding soloists. In comparison, Ory's chorus is less complex, more "primitive." Avoiding blue notes entirely, he repeats literal statements of Lil's motive, disregarding the E♭ / E♮ dissonance with the sounding F7 (mm. 2 and 5-6). Dodds, on the other hand, develops the motive rhythmically (mm. 1 and 3) and melodically (mm. 7-8). Except for bar 2, Dodds's blue notes are sevenths of the subdominant harmony (mm. 6 and 10).

Concluding the set of solos, Armstrong's performance can be heard as an extension of his predecessors' efforts and a wry reflection on Ory's in particular. Beginning like the trombonist with a motivic statement, he "corrects" Ory's missed or ignored F7 changes (mm. 2 and 5-6).[26] Then, after stating Lil's motive in the second half of measure 6 as Ory had done, Armstrong elects to leave the D♯ unresolved, thus transforming the pitch into a blue third (E♭) against tonic harmony (m. 7)—a clever thwarting of a voice-leading expectation (D♯ - E) introduced by St. Cyr in his opening solo and repeatedly reinforced by all other soloists.

Armstrong's tag following the final ensemble chorus (Example 3.11) summarizes and synthesizes "Gut Bucket Blues" rhythmically, melodically, and harmonically. Beginning with a characteristic rip up to high note on a weak beat and combining syncopated and unsyncopated rhythms, he recapitulates the blue third and blue seventh, the A - E♭ tritone, and the piece's E♭ / E♮ conflict. Such details of nuance and creativity distinguish Armstrong early on from his Hot Five colleagues and serve as a prelude to his increasing musical dominance of the later recordings.

Example 3.11. Armstrong's Solo Tag in "Gut Bucket Blues"

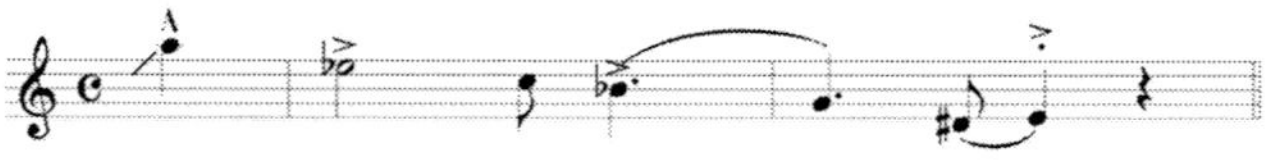

[26]Gunther Schuller, *Early Jazz*, 83, points out Armstrong's heightened sense of harmonic sensitivity in comparison to that of his musical colleagues in "Chimes Blues," his first recorded solo (Example 9.14).

Dreamland to the Vendome

In December 1925 Armstrong began doubling with Erskine Tate at the Vendome Theater a few blocks north of the Dreamland on the Stroll.[27] Besides supplying music for the silent pictures, Tate's crack fifteen-piece orchestra played a mixture of light classics, pop tunes, and jazz before and between shows. The concerts were often a bigger draw than the films.

> This week the Vendome Orchestra put over a unique novelty presentation. . . . Director Tate took Clarence Williams' "Royal Garden Blues," partitioned it for each section of the orchestra, who were hid in different parts of the house. Each unit had its solo part. The drum gave the old familiar minstrel roll-off and then the march to the pit by these music masters, ending the scene with hot jazz. When it was apparently over . . . Charlie Harris came strutting down the aisle playing "All Alone" on his oboe and he was all alone.[28]

Blowing "King" Freddie Keppard off the bandstand at the Dreamland and thrilling the Vendome patrons with high F's,[29] Armstrong soon became a celebrity: "Louis Armstrong was featured at the Vendome last Sunday night. He played 'The Sugar Foot Stomp.' In it he fluttered, he cried, he raved, and the band raved with him."[30] Trumpeter "Doc" Cheatham describes his own reception by the Vendome crowd when substituting for the World's Greatest Jazz Cornetist:

> When Louis was there, the minute that spotlight hit Louis on "Poor Little Rich Girl," the people were screaming so much you couldn't hear what he was playing half the time. So when the spotlight hit me, I jumped up and started playing, and the house screamed and screamed. After a while you could hear the diminishing of the

[27] *Chicago Defender* (12 December 1925), 7. For a history of the Vendome, see George Hoefer, "Chicago Jazz Landmark Being Razed," *Down Beat* 17/2 (27 January 1950), 2.

[28] *Chicago Defender* (20 February 1926), 7.

[29] Lil Armstrong, *Satchmo and Me.*

[30] *Chicago Defender* (20 March 1926), 6. According to Max Jones and John Chilton, *Louis*, 237; and Brian Harker, *The Early Musical Development of Louis Armstrong, 1901-1928* (Ph.D. dissertation, Columbia University, 1997), 259-62, Armstrong's big number was Mascagni's *Cavalleria Rusticana*, of which he probably played a transposition of the first violin part from the "Intermezzo." For the influence of opera on Armstrong's playing, see Joshua Berrett, "Louis Armstrong and Opera," *The Musical Quarterly* 76/2 (1992), 216-41.

Illustration 3.1. OKeh Ad for "Gut Bucket Blues"

From *Chicago Defender* (6 March 1926), 6.

> screams. Came right down to nothing, and I'm up there playing like a fool. Well, I'll tell you, it took me years to get over that. I did the best I could with it. I didn't do a lousy job, but I was no Louis Armstrong.[31]

In the mid-1920s the cylindrically-bored trumpet with its bright and brilliant tone quality began to eclipse the conically-bored cornet as the jazz instrument of choice. Armstrong reported that he began switching from cornet to trumpet with Tate, probably performing on both in live circumstances. Because the evidence from recordings and publicity photographs is inconclusive, however, the change to trumpet may not have become permanent until a year or two later.[32]

[31] "Doc" Cheatham, quoted in Bill Crow, *Jazz Anecdotes* (New York: Oxford University Press, 1990), 209.

[32] Max Jones and John Chilton, *Louis*, 237. James Lincoln Collier, in *Louis Armstrong: An American Genius* (New York: Oxford University Press, 1983), 360, states that it is "generally felt" that the Hot Sevens in May 1927 were Armstrong's first recordings on trumpet, but Armstrong discographer Hans Westerberg, in *Boy from New Orleans* (Copenhagen: JazzMedia, 1981), 31, would postpone the change

"Come Back Sweet Papa"

Table 3.5. Structural Outline of "Come Back Sweet Papa" [C Major]

SECTION	INSTRUMENTATION	BARS
Introduction	Ensemble (minus Sax) / Trombone Break	1 / 1
	Cornet Break / Ensemble	2 / 2
Chorus 1	Sax Solo / Sax Break	14 / 2
	Sax Solo / Ensemble	14 / 2
Chorus 2	Ensemble (Minus Clarinet)	8
	Ensemble / Trombone Break	6 / 2
	Ensemble / Cornet Break	14 / 2
Verse	Ensemble	16
Chorus 3	Piano Solo	16
	Ensemble / Cornet Break / Ensemble	8 / 4 / 4
Tag	Ensemble	2

The second Hot Five recording session on 22 February 1926 yielded only one side, "Come Back Sweet Papa" by Paul Barbarin and Luis Russell.[33] Armstrong was a Barbarin family friend in New Orleans and corresponded with Isidore Barbarin, Paul's father, after coming to Chicago to join Oliver.[34] Paul had played drums with Oliver before Armstrong's arrival but returned to the Crescent City in 1923 to join a band at Tom Anderson's led by Russell, a pianist who had moved to New Orleans from Panama four years earlier. At the time of the Hot Fives, both Barbarin and Russell were members of "King" Oliver's Dixie Syncopators at the Plantation Café across the street from the Dreamland.[35] After "Come Back Sweet Papa" the Barbarin-Russell collaboration would later produce "I've Got That Thing" (with Walter Pichon) and "Freakish Light Blues" (for the Oliver band).

"Come Back Sweet Papa" has long been extolled as the quintessential demonstration of the invidious comparison between Armstrong and his band mates—chiefly Dodds. Hodeir complains:

to 1928; see Chapter 8, note 23. On the possibility of his playing trumpet on a session with Henderson in 1925, see Richard Hadlock, *Jazz Masters of the Twenties* (New York: Macmillan, 1965), 23.

[33]Another Barbarin composition, "What I Like about Loving Is More of It," may have been recorded at the same session but rejected; see John R. T. Davies and Laurie Wright, "The Other Take," *Storyville* 29 (1 June 1970), 172-73.

[34]Louis Armstrong, *In His Own Words*, 42-43.

[35]John Chilton, *Who's Who of Jazz* (1972), 4th ed. (New York: Da Capo Press, 1985), 19, 287.

> In respect to swing, Louis cannot in any case be compared with his sidemen in the early Hot Five, whose rhythm is extremely weak. Listen to Johnny Dodds's alto solo in "Come Back Sweet Papa." Isn't it an excellent sample of not getting the notes in the right place, rich in rhythmic faults and anti-swing if anything ever was? Now listen to the next chorus, in which Louis is perfect; he seems to want to give his clarinetist a lesson in swing. . . . A bit further on, Dodds and Armstrong play the verse in sixths; hence, they ought to play exactly together. Does Dodds try to make his part fit in with Louis's? He almost never succeeds. . . . Compared to Armstrong's, Kid Ory's break invites the same remark; rhythmically, it's the difference between night and day. . . . Some of [Dodds's] phrase endings in the ensembles of "Come Back Sweet Papa" and "Big Fat Ma" are spoiled by his playing in unison or octaves with the cornet part; such contrapuntal platitudes must be deplored. Note that it would have been quite simple for him to avoid them, since Louis wisely sticks right to the theme. . . . Do [jazz fans] really think that Dodds has a good tone on the alto in "Come Back Sweet Papa"?[36]

The criticism of Dodds's rhythm is overly harsh; "anti-swing" it may be in comparison to Louis's, but seldom faulty and never weak. Notation alone cannot convey the ineffable concept of swing, which depends as much on timbre and articulation as on the temporal placement of pitches, but Example 3.12 (on the facing page) shows Armstrong's rhythm to be more varied and unpredictable than that in Dodds's two solos.[37] He seldom repeats the same rhythmic combination, but when he does, it always involves different pitches; Dodds tends to repeat patterns of pitches and rhythms (mm. 9-12 in the alto sax and mm. 8-9 and 11-12 in the clarinet).

The greatest enemy of swing in the Dodds saxophone solo is his persistent maintenance of the halting short-to-long rhythm of the melody in almost every measure; Armstrong, who employs nothing lengthier than a dotted quarter, plays mostly long-to-short rhythms that propel the music

[36]André Hodeir, *Jazz, Its Evolution and Essence*, 52-53, 55, 60.

[37]Dodds's clarinet solo is taken from the first half of the first chorus (mm. 23-38) of a retitled "Come Back Sweet Papa" recorded by the Chicago Footwarmers on 2 July 1928 for OKeh as "Get 'Em Again Blues." Dodds's alto sax solo is from the first half of the first chorus (mm. 7-22), and Armstrong's lead is from the first half of the second chorus (mm. 39-54).

from one bar to the next. As on the saxophone, Dodds's phrasing on the clarinet is similarly "square." He begins each measure on the downbeat and invariably divides four-bar phrases into two-bar subphrases, and his pickups or anticipatory notes before phrases for variety or emphasis are minimal and infrequent. Armstrong, however, avoids becoming enslaved by the downbeat, and his lengthy pickups provide an overlapping or eliding effect, as if the next phrase begins before the present one ends. His pickup to the second phrase (mm. 5-8), for example, starts on the second beat of bar 4, and his pickup to the third phrase (mm. 9-12) starts on the second half of the first beat of bar 8. Armstrong's subphrases are also less clearly delineated than Dodds's. In "Come Back Sweet Papa" Louis's C♯ in bar 2 tonicizes the D in bar 3, and the dotted-quarter-eighth rhythm on the second half of measure 6 drives the line to the downbeat of measure 7, obliterating a two-bar segmentation of the four-bar unit.

Example 3.12. Comparison of Dodds's Alto Sax Solo on "Come Back Sweet Papa" with Armstrong's Lead and Dodds's Clarinet Solo in "Get 'Em Again Blues"

Generally overmatched by Armstrong as a soloist, Dodds is fully the cornetist's equal as an ensemble player. Hodeir's faulting of Dodds for not fitting his part perfectly with Armstrong's lead betrays the critic's ignorance of early New Orleans jazzmen's heterophonic or polyphonic approach to accompaniment as others have rightly observed.[38] Ending phrases in unison or octaves with the ensemble lead is, in fact, a rarity for Dodds, who normally cadences on the chordal third.

Hodeir takes a "cheap shot" in scorning Dodds's alto saxophone playing. In early 1926 the clarinetist was still a relative novice on the instrument he took up while in residency at Kelly's Stables. "Baby" Dodds, drummer of the group that included Natty Dominique on trumpet, recalled:

> But when he began playing saxophone we poked so much fun at him he refused to continue. He never took lessons on the sax but got one to use in the band. Dominique and I used to tell him he wasn't doing so well on it. Of course, he was doing alright but we wouldn't say so. We just didn't like a sax in our outfit and wanted to hear John play clarinet.[39]

As the emerging replacement for the clarinet in jazz bands of the time, the saxophone may have been chosen for its "hipness factor." Barbarin himself might have requested the instrument, considering its only other Hot Five appearance is heard on the drummer's "Don't Forget to Mess Around." Dodds's relative level of comfort on the saxophone and clarinet is graphically illustrated in Example 3.12: he duplicates the melody on the former but improvises something completely different on the latter.

The other members of the quintet, of course, contribute to the musical substance of "Come Back Sweet Papa." Lil provides one of her most spirited solos, displaying an agile left hand and ending with a break from "My Heart" (Example 3.4, mm. 13-14). Ory's "tailgate" style suits the piece admirably (see Chapter 4, note 51). Variations of his break outlining a dominant seventh reappear in subsequent Hot Fives, and he energizes the third chorus with a secondary rag passage that shows up again in "Muskrat Ramble" (Example 4.16, mm. 7-8). In the verse Armstrong adds flutter-tonguing to his repertoire of timbres; his breaks are characteristically flamboyant and expressive, but his leads in this piece uncharacteristically remain bound by the melody.

38 G. E. Lambert, *Kings of Jazz 10: Johnny Dodds* (London: Cassell, 1961), 67-68.

39 Warren "Baby" Dodds and Larry Gara, *The Baby Dodds Story*, 54-55.

CHAPTER 4

Initial Hits

While the first two Hot Five sessions laid the groundwork and charted the direction of their successors, the third was to make jazz history and Armstrong a star—ironically more for his singing than his playing. He had sung tenor in quartets on the streets of New Orleans as a boy, but as a teenager his voice had already developed its distinctive gravelly timbre: "He could sing real well too, even though his voice was coarse," recalled his Colored Waif's Home bandleader, Peter Davis.[1]

"Even though singing was more *into* [his] Blood than the trumpet,"[2] Louis had to wait until the Creole Band's *Schwanengesang*—its 1924 tour of the Midwest—before Oliver let him take vocals, which the customers went for "in a big way."[3] Later in New York, Henderson displayed the same resistance to Armstrong's entreaties with the same result: "About three weeks after he joined us," Henderson remembered, "he asked me if he could sing a number. I know I wondered what he could possibly do with the big fish horn voice of his, but finally I told him to try it. He was great. The band loved it, and the crowds just ate it up."[4] While the "dicty" Henderson occasionally permitted Armstrong to sing before live audiences, he was generally embarrassed by Louis's vocal efforts and allowed none to be recorded.[5] Armstrong, in a flash of qualified pride, allowed that his "vocalizings" were "nothing to write home about. *But.* It [*sic*] *was* Different."[6] Certain of his own abilities, Louis sang early in the series and often; of the thirty-three Hot Five recordings, he took vocal solos on fourteen.

[1]Peter Davis, quoted without documentation in Will Friedwald, *Jazz Singing: America's Great Voices from Bessie Smith to Bebop and Beyond* (New York: Charles Scribner's Sons, 1990), 26. Armstrong's raspy voice may have been caused by vocal nodes according to James Lincoln Collier, *Louis Armstrong: An American Genius* (New York: Oxford University Press, 1983), 239.

[2]Louis Armstrong, *Louis Armstrong: In His Own Words*, ed. Thomas Brothers (New York: Oxford University Press, 1999), 64.

[3]*Ibid.*, 63.

[4]Fletcher Henderson, quoted without documentation in James Lincoln Collier, *Louis Armstrong*, 133.

[5]Dan Morgenstern, "Louis Armstrong and the Development and Diffusion of Jazz," *Louis Armstrong: A Cultural Legacy*, ed. Marc H. Miller (Seattle: University of Washington Press, 1994), 103.

[6]Louis Armstrong, *In His Own Words*, 64.

"Georgia Grind"

Table 4.1. Structural Outline of "Georgia Grind" [E♭ Major]

Section	Instrumentation	Bars
Introduction	Ensemble	4
Chorus 1	Ensemble	12
Chorus 2	Lil's Vocal Solo	12
Chorus 3	Lil's Vocal Solo	12
Chorus 4	Trombone Solo	12
Chorus 5	Louis's Vocal Solo	12
Chorus 6	Louis's Vocal Solo	12
Chorus 7	Clarinet Solo / Ensemble	8 / 4

According to the latest edition of Rust's *Jazz and Ragtime Records*, the Hot Five, at their third session on 26 February 1926, was the first to record Spencer Williams's "Georgia Grind," which was copyrighted seven months later.[7] Its title reportedly refers to a particularly lascivious dance.[8] Its form resembles "Gut Bucket Blues"—an introduction followed by several blues choruses.

Of Louis's voice little need be said; it is instantly recognizable and the analogue of his playing, as he seems to acknowledge: "To me, scat singing is just like playing an instrument."[9] There is little "bluesy" about Lil's shrill solo, which repeats the melody as determined by comparison with other contemporary recordings.[10] Armstrong, on the other hand, avoids the

[7]Other contemporary recordings were made by Duke Ellington's Washingtonians (March 1926), Caroline Johnson (April 1926), Edmonia Henderson (21 July 1926), Perry Bradford's Georgia Strutters (8 August 1926), and Tom Morris and His Seven Hot Babies (17 August 1926). The "Georgia Grind" recorded later by the State Street Ramblers and the Memphis Night Hawks is a different piece. The composer of numerous jazz standards, such as "Tishomingo Blues," "Everybody Loves My Baby," and "Basin Street Blues," Williams was the band and orchestra director for Clarence Williams, with whom he wrote "Royal Garden Blues," in New York around this time; see Jeffrey P. Green, "Spencer Williams: Composer," *Storyville* 123 (February-March 1986), 89.

[8]In his *A Life in Jazz*, ed. Alyn Shipton (New York: Oxford University Press, 1986), 48, Danny Barker calls the Georgia Grind an "old-time dance step" in the same category as the cakewalk, turkey trot, and shimmy. He may, however, have been referring to a dance connected with the 1915 rag of the same name by Ford T. Dabney.

[9]Louis Armstrong, *In His Own Words*, 133. On Louis's singing as the counterpart of his playing, see Gunther Schuller, *Early Jazz: Its Roots and Musical Development* (New York: Oxford University Press, 1968), 100; Hugues Panassié, *Louis Armstrong* (New York: Charles Scribner, 1972), 54-55; and Dan Morgenstern, "Louis Armstrong and the Development and Diffusion of Jazz," 106.

[10]As noted above, these include Duke Ellington's Washingtonians (March 1926), Caroline Johnson accompanied by Tom Morris (April 1926), Edmonia Henderson accompanied by Jelly Roll Morton (21 July 1926), and Tom Morris and His Seven Hot Babies (17 August 1926).

melody entirely (Example 4.1). Like his introduction to "Yes! I'm in the Barrel," his solo is almost entirely based on the tonic triad but with emphasis on the blue third (G♭). The tonic (E♭) often paired with the submediant (C) against tonic harmony (mm. 14-16), the blue third embellished by upward slides (mm. 5, 12, 21-22), the tonic embellished by a fall-off (m. 7), and the cadential tonic embellished by a scoop—all are characteristic of Bessie Smith, with whom Armstrong recorded in New York.[11] As in his cornet playing, Armstrong's rhythms dance around the beat and play havoc with the natural accents. Here he highlights the words, "Georgia Grind," with expressive syncopations in contrast to the

Example 4.1. Lil's and Louis's Vocal Solos in "Georgia Grind"

[11]Gunther Schuller, *Early Jazz*, 231-32.

metrical rhythms of the rest of the text. Each repetition of the title phrase is given a unique treatment, and none conform to the natural accents of the meter (GEOR-gia GRIND) save the last one, which is in turn rescued from conventionality by the aforementioned scoop.

Ory repeats the melody in the first half of his solo and his first-chorus ensemble part in the second half (Example 4.2). Dodds, perhaps further inspired by Ory's smears (mm. 3-4), heightens his approach to the tonic seventh (D♭) in bar 4 with a spectacular melismatic descent from the upper C, which had been presaged by similar passages in the introduction and first chorus (see Example 4.3). In characteristic fashion he exploits the enharmonicism of the raised supertonic (F♯) and blue third (G♭), replacing the former with the latter after the first four measures, and navigates a convincing return to tonic harmony (mm. 4-7) through voice-leading by half-step—D♭ - C - C♭ (blue third of A♭) - B♭.

Example 4.2. Ory's Solo in "Georgia Grind"

Example 4.3. Dodds's Solo in "Georgia Grind"

"Heebie Jeebies"*

Table 4.2. Structural Outline of "Heebie Jeebies" [A♭ Major]

SECTION	INSTRUMENTATION	BARS
Introduction	Piano / Trombone	6 / 2
Chorus 1	Ensemble	18
Verse	Ensemble	12
Chorus 2	Clarinet Solo	18
Chorus 3	Louis's Vocal Solo	18
Chorus 4	Scat Solo / Vocal Solo	12 / 6
Chorus 5	Ensemble (Minus Cornet) / Ensemble	8 / 10
Coda	Speech / Ensemble	7 / 1

"Heebie Jeebies," featuring the second Armstrong vocal recorded at the third recording session, became the Hot Five's first commercial hit, reportedly selling a phenomenal 40,000 copies in just a few weeks.[12] The tune's composer, violinist Boyd Atkins, had played with Armstrong on the riverboats and was later a member of Armstrong's Stompers at the Sunset Café. The secret of the otherwise ordinary song's popularity was its scat chorus, which Armstrong claimed to have improvised after dropping a page with the words:

> Because the day we recorded "Heebie Jeebies," I dropped the paper with the lyrics—right in the middle of the tune. . . . And I did not want to stop and spoil the record which was moving along so wonderfully. . . . So when I dropped the paper, I immediately turned back into the horn and started to scatting . . . just as nothing had happened. . . . When I finished the record I just knew the recording people would throw it out. . . . And to my surprise they all came running out of the controlling booth and said—"Leave that in."[13]

[12]Louis Armstrong, *Swing That Music* (New York: Longmans, Green, 1936; reprinted New York: Da Capo Press, 1993), 85; and James Lincoln Collier, *Louis Armstrong*, 173.

[13]Louis Armstrong, *In His Own Words*, 132. For an analysis of this story as a "touchstone legend of origin," see Brent Hayes Edwards, "Louis Armstrong and the Syntax of Scat," *Critical Inquiry* 28/3 (Spring 2002), 618-49.

Apocryphal or not, the story was repeated with minor variations by Louis for the rest of his life. St. Cyr and Ory essentially confirmed Armstrong's account—the banjoist adding that "Heebie Jeebies" was an instrumental for which Armstrong composed the lyrics in the studio; he scatted after dropping the music, having not had the time to memorize the words.[14]

Armstrong did not invent scatting, but he made it popular.[15] After the release of "Heebie Jeebies" in May 1926, the recording reportedly "took all of Chicago by storm," and for months thereafter "you would hear cats greeting each other with Louis's riffs when they met around town: 'I got the heebies' one would yell out, and the other would answer 'I got the jeebies,' and the next minute they were scatting in each other's face."[16] Musicians were "sticking their heads out of windows trying to catch colds to sound like Louis."[17] Beiderbecke went wild over the tune:

> That morning, as soon as we grabbed those cats out of their pads and played "Heebie Jeebies" for them, they all fractured their wigs. "Ha! Ha! Ha!" Bix kept chuckling as the record played over and over, and his long bony arms beat out the breaks, flailing through the air like the blades of a threshing machine. He never did get over Louis's masterpiece. Soon as it was over he grabbed it from the machine and tore out of the house to wake up everybody he knew around Hudson Lake and make them listen to it.[18]

An interesting article (containing no mention of Armstrong) entitled "How the 'Heebie Jeebies' Reached Apex of Popularity and Developed a New Dance" in the trade journal *Talking Machine World* describes the lengths to which OKeh would go to capitalize on the song's success:

[14]Johnny St. Cyr, "The Original Hot Five," *Second Line* 5/9-10 (September-October 1954), 1; and Edward "Kid" Ory and Lester Koenig, "The Hot Five Sessions," *The Record Changer* (July-August 1950), 17. The published arrangement of "Heebie Jeebies" that came out later in 1926 attributed the words and music to the composer.

[15]Armstrong acknowledged that he used to scat in his boyhood quartet in New Orleans in his 5 May 1970 interview by William Russell in the Tulane Jazz Archive. For a history of recorded scatting before Armstrong, see Will Friedwald, *Jazz Singing*, 16-19, 28.

[16]Mezz Mezzrow and Bernard Wolfe, *Really the Blues* (New York: Random House, 1946; reprinted New York: Citadel Press, 1990), 120.

[17]Earl Hines, quoted without documentation in Gary Giddins, *Satchmo* (New York: Doubleday, 1988), 87.

[18]Mezz Mezzrow and Bernard Wolfe, *Really the Blues*, 122.

Last Spring, in the OKeh record laboratories of the Consolidated Talking Machine Co., Chicago, OKeh record distributor, a record was made under the title "Heebie Jeebies," with a "skat" chorus. The recording proved to be a popular one, and was sold to dance lovers throughout the country. Late in October the Consolidated Music Publishing House, headed by E. A. Fearn, also president of the Consolidated Talking Machine Co., published "Heebie Jeebies" in sheet music form.

Through the cooperation of Floyd Du Pont, nationally known producer of musical comedies and revues, a dance step was devised to suit the rhythm of the song. A professional dancer, Miss Tinah Tweedie, was the first individual to publicly appear in a performance of the "Heebies Jeebies" dance, and the event caught the eye of the *Chicago Evening American*, which published a strip of pictures showing Miss Tweedie executing the various steps, and accompanied the illustrations with instructions, enabling the reader to learn the dance. Other newspapers quickly adopted the idea. Underwood & Underwood photographed Miss Tweedie, and illustrations of how the dance is done were quickly syndicated throughout the United States, often appearing in the rotogravure sections of leading metropolitan newspapers within recent weeks. On one occasion Miss Tweedie was photographed as she danced on the cornice of a thirty-eight-story building in Chicago's "loop," or business district, to music received by an Operadio portable set, while the photographer clung to a flagpole as he snapped the picture [photograph included].

Sensing the publicity value of the "Heebie Jeebies" dance as a drawing card, ballroom and cabaret managers throughout the country are now planning contests and revues built around the popular step. In Chicago alone the Mid-Nite Frolics, Samovar, and seven other night clubs are staging "Heebie Jeebies" revues, the dance being featured as the main attraction on the program. In each case special programs are placed on the tables, listing the names of the entertainers, while on the back cover detailed instructions and illustrations of the various steps are printed. Café patrons are advised by the program that the "Heebie Jeebies" record is obtainable on OKeh records and that the sheet music is published by the Consolidated Music Publishing House. On the back cover of the sheet music edition of the number, instructions and illustrations posed by Miss Tweedie are also included, while a picture of Paul Ash [the "Rajah of Rhythm"], Chicago's idol of jazz, occupies the front cover.

During the week ending November 6 the "Heebie Jeebies" dance occupied center stage at the Oriental Theatre, owned by Balaban & Katz. The stage setting resembled a hall of fame, with all of the old-fashioned and modern dances, from the minuet and polka down to the Charleston, listed upon one side, as already members of the hall of fame, while on the other side of the stage, the "Black Bottom" and "Heebie Jeebies" were listed as applicants. Paul Ash sat as judge, dressed in the gown and wig of an old English member of the bench. To decide the controversy between Miss "Heebie Jeebies" (Miss Tweedie) and Miss "Black Bottom," Ash suggested that they each call in six witnesses and have them execute their particular dances. The clashing factions both finished their separate dances, and then did them simultaneously. Ash, still puzzled as to who was the victor, left the verdict to the audience. The question still apparently could not be decided, so both the "Heebie Jeebies" and "Black Bottom" were allowed to enter the Hall of Fame.

Another instance which shows the rapid rise of the dance to popularity within a space of a few weeks is the adoption of the name "Heebie Jeebies" by a shoe manufacturer, a maker of hats, and a local restaurant owner who has applied the name to a sandwich. The dance, hard on the heels of the "Black Bottom," is making a strong bid for popularity honors, and both the OKeh record and the Consolidated sheet music version have been in tremendous demand as a result.[19]

[19] *TMW* 22/11 (15 November 1926), 128. Contemporary recordings were made by Ethel Waters (29 July 1926), Alberta Hunter (13 September 1926), the Goofus Five (24 September 1926), Fess Williams and His Orchestra (1 October 1926), Original Indiana Five (October 1926), and Red Nichols' Red Heads (11 November 1926). Recordings by the Boswell Sisters and Chick Webb, among others, persisted into the 1930s. The "Heebie Jeebies" recorded by Lovie Austin and Her Blues Serenaders in April 1925 is a different piece from Atkins's. Butterbeans, of the vaudeville team Butterbeans and Susie, danced the "Itch" to "Heebie Jeebies" as the climax of his act; see Marshall Stearns and Jean Stearns, *Jazz Dance: The Story of American Vernacular Dance* (New York: Macmillan, 1968; reprinted New York: Da Capo Press, 1994), 27. For Paul Ash, see Charles A. Sengstock, *That Toddlin' Town: Chicago's White Dance Bands and Orchestras, 1900-1950* (Urbana: University of Illinois Press, 2004), 150-53.

The published sheet music provides a rough transcription of Louis's scat chorus, of which an edited version appears in Example 4.4.[20] Collier claims that the chorus of "Heebie Jeebies" was "lifted" from the second strain of the rag "Heliotrope Bouquet" by Scott Joplin and Lewis Chauvin.[21] There are indeed striking similarities between the two but no identical measures. It is thus left to the reader to decide on the extent of borrowing (Example 4.5 on the following page).

Example 4.4. Armstrong's Scat Chorus in "Heebie Jeebies"

Replete with trademark arpeggios, triplet passages, and stiff phrasing, Dodds's solo in "Heebie Jeebies" is nonetheless a nicely constructed harmonic variation. A motivic passage associated with A♭ harmony emerges at analogous places in the melody (mm. 3-4 and 11-12) and appears independently (mm. 7-8). Dodds further extracts the passage's ascending leap of a minor sixth (C - A♭) as a separate motive in bars 8-9 (F - D♭) and bars 14 and 16 (A♮ - F). The downbeat of harmonic changes most often finds Dodds on the chordal third rather than the tonic or fifth, and his movement to the chordal third at the final cadence by means of parallel melodic tritones (D♮ - A♭ and D♭ - G, both resolving to C, in mm. 15-18) may have already become a jazz cliché. Curiously, Dodds's accent on beat four of measure 8 corresponds to a similar articulation in "Heliotrope Bouquet," but there are no other overt connections between the ragtime tune and his improvisation.

[20]The example retains the scat syllables of the original, changes dotted-eighth-and-sixteenth rhythms to swing eighths, and corrects certain pitches.

[21]James Lincoln Collier, *Louis Armstrong*, 172.

Example 4.5. Comparison of the Melody of "Heliotrope Bouquet" with the Published Melody of "Heebie Jeebies" and Dodds's Solo in "Heebie Jeebies"[22]

Because of the popularity of "Heebie Jeebies" and the efforts by OKeh to promote it, a cursory look at the handling of its mechanical royalties might be instructive for illustrating music business practices at the time. In his colorful way Armstrong imagined that Boyd Atkins "must have made a nice little taste, meaning that the tune made quite a bit of 'loot,' meaning OKeh sold lots of records and made lots of 'dough,' meaning money."[23] Composers, according to the Copyright Act of 1909, were eligible for a

[22]The melody of "Heliotrope Bouquet" has been transposed from its original key of G major, and its rhythm rewritten from the original two-four meter for ease of comparison. The lyrics and melody of "Heebie Jeebies" are taken from the sheet music; the harmonies are based on the recording.

[23]Louis Armstrong, *In His Own Words*, 132.

royalty of two cents on each tune recorded per recording sold,[24] but in practice, indeed, many musicians opted for immediate cash, as Armstrong recalled by means of a delightful mixed metaphor:

> [the record companies] would either buy the tune outright or ask us if we dared to collect the royalties. . . . P.S. Of course you don't have to make any guesses as to our decisions . . . Aye? . . . Sure . . . Our slogan was, A bird in hand gathers no moss. "Got No Blues" got a nice little "Taste" for us. . . . We split the royalties [*recte* flat fee]. . . . Of course, it wasn't enough to make one "Hump Back" for carrying it. . . . But, as we New Orleans musicians used to express it—it did beat a blank (meaning) the money came in handy. . . . And it was more than we had. . . . Yea man. . . .[25]

Documents in the uncatalogued Fearn materials of the Armstrong Archives flesh out the copyright history of "Heebie Jeebies." As of 1 September 1926 Consolidated Music Publishing House (CMP), OKeh's subsidiary publishing company, owned the rights to "Heebie Jeebies," probably paying Atkins $50.00, the amount Percy Venable received for "Big Butter and Egg Man" (see below). CMP copyrighted an orchestration of the piece by Richard M. Jones and Charles M. Cooke on 16 July 1926 and an arrangement for piano and ukelele by Rube Bennett on 22 October 1926. In October CMP began selling piano rolls to various companies for two cents per roll and granted Bell Record Corporation (a distributor to W. T. Grant stores) exclusive copyright privileges in return for two cents per record sold. In January 1927 CMP granted Canadian distribution rights to Brunswick-Balke-Collender Company in exchange for royalties of the amount and in the manner described by the Canadian Copyright Act.

Revenues were clearly rigged in favor of the recording companies and their allied publisher, like CMP, whose representatives routinely pressured composers to sign over their copyrights. Product markups were high; each OKeh record, which cost twenty cents to make, sold for the standard price

[24]William Lichtenwanger, "Music and Copyright Law in the United States," *Music Publishing & Collecting: Essays in Honor of Donald W. Krummel*, ed. David Hunter (Urbana: University of Illinois Press, 1994), 83-84.

[25]Louis Armstrong, *In His Own Words*, 136. "Got No Blues" copyright, claimed by CMP, assigns composer credit to Lil (see Appendix 1). Jelly Roll Morton signed over his rights to the Melrose Brothers at their insistence; see Alan Lomax, *Mister Jelly Roll: The Fortunes of Jelly Roll Morton, New Orleans Creole and "Inventor of Jazz"* (1949), 2nd ed. (Los Angeles: University of California Press, 1973; reprinted Los Angeles: University of California Press, 2001), 187-88.

of seventy-five cents.[26] Beyond income from piano rolls, arrangements, orchestrations, and distribution rights, CMP could collect two cents for every copy of "Heebie Jeebies" made by other record companies,[27] of which between 1926 and 1931 there were at least ten. Composer royalty obligations, when they could not be avoided, were entirely dependent on the companies to calculate, collect, and distribute and thus subject to manipulation and abuse.

Ralph Peer, OKeh's general sales manager during the Hot Fives, devised a contract for "hillbilly" and "race" music that became an industry model. For a fixed "talent fee" per side (originally $25.00) all rights were assigned to OKeh; the composer was guaranteed a one-half cent royalty per side sold.[28] "Talent fees" might actually be treated as an advance. The Fearn materials, cited above, contain a 12 December 1926 letter from Percy Venable, certifying that he received $50.00 for "Big Butter and Egg Man" and assigned royalties "that may accrue to my credit" for that amount to CMP. The song, released 4 January 1927, must not have sold well because in a letter dated 27 January 1927 Venable promised to repay the money by 4 February 1927 or to relinquish his rights.

[26]William Howland Kenney, *Recorded Music in American Life: The Phonograph and Popular Memory, 1890-1945* (New York: Oxford University Press, 1999), 121.

[27]*Ibid.*, 118.

[28]Russell Sanjek and David Sanjek, *American Popular Music Business in the 20th Century* (New York: Oxford University Press, 1991), 21.

"Cornet Chop Suey"*

Table 4.3. Structural Outline of "Cornet Chop Suey" [F Major]

SECTION	INSTRUMENTATION	BARS
Introduction	Cornet Solo / Ensemble	3 / 1
Verse	Ensemble	16
Chorus 1	Ensemble / Cornet Break / Ensemble	6 / 2 / 8
	Ensemble / Cornet Break / Ensemble	4 / 4 / 8
Chorus 2	Piano Solo	32
Patter Chorus	Stop-Time with Cornet Solo	16
Chorus 3	Ensemble / Cornet Break / Ensemble	6 / 2 / 8
	Ensemble / Cornet Break / Ensemble	4 / 4 / 8
Coda	Ensemble / Cornet	4 / 4

Armstrong remembered that he composed "Cornet Chop Suey" on Lil's back steps, perhaps in tribute to the New Orleans cutting contests between Henry Rena, Buddy Petit, Joe Johnson, and himself in which fast fingers were decisive.[29] The copyright deposit date of 18 January 1924 (Appendix 1) coincides roughly with that of "Yes! I'm in the Barrel" and thus during the couple's tenure with "King" Oliver.[30] As an instrumental showcase "Cornet Chop Suey" intimates that, even while playing second to Oliver's lead, Armstrong imagined himself a virtuoso soloist, a view encouraged or possibly conceived by his future wife. This vision became a reality with the Vendome Theater Orchestra and was now to be represented in the Hot Five repertory for the first time. (See the OKeh ad as Illustration 4.1 on page 60.) If Armstrong blurred the distinction between solo and lead in the first Hot Fives, he pushed the concept to its limit in "Cornet Chop Suey." The other members of his front line are effectively overpowered or pushed aside, making the piece, save for the chorus by unaccompanied piano, an extended cornet solo.

As such, the piece represents a break with the New Orleans small group tradition by going far beyond early instrumental features like "High

[29]Louis Armstrong, *In His Own Words*, 132-33. Lil was probably living with her mother at 3320 Giles on Chicago's South Side. The title alludes to Armstrong's affection for Chinese food according to James Lincoln Collier, *Louis Armstrong*, 173.

[30]Louis may have performed the piece with Oliver—see Dan Morgenstern, "Louis Armstrong," *The Oxford Companion to Jazz*, ed. Bill Kirchner (New York: Oxford University Press, 2000), 107—or, even more likely, with Tate—see Louis Armstrong, *In His Own Words*, 127-28.

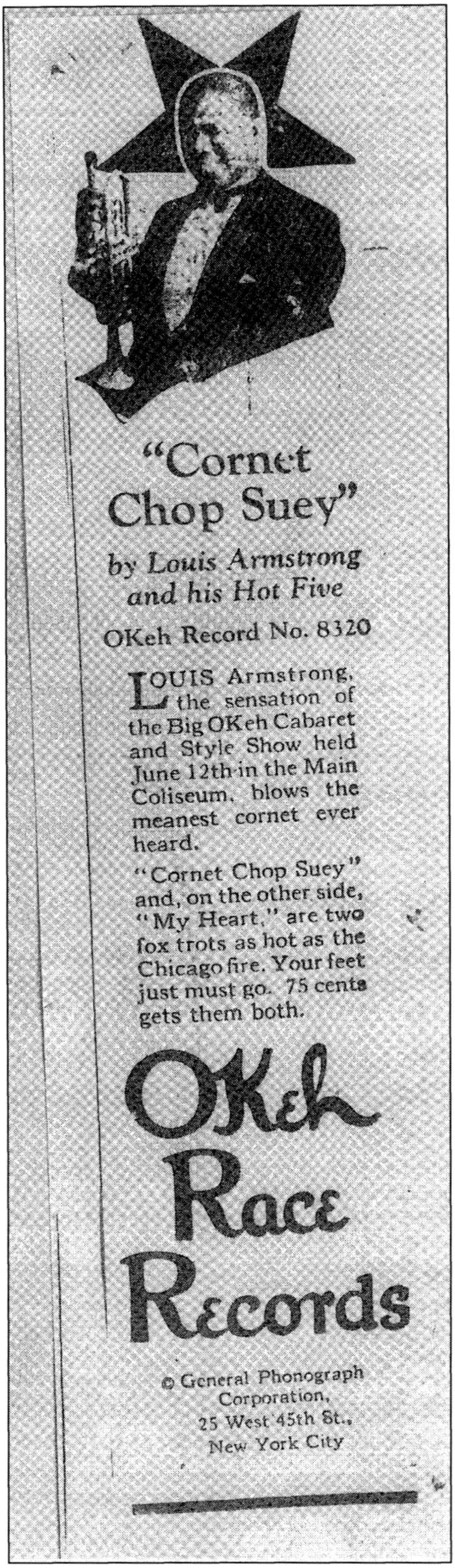

Illustration 4.1.
OKeh Ad for
"Cornet Chop Suey"

From *Chicago Defender* (3 July 1926), 6.

Society" for clarinet and "Ory's Creole Trombone," in which the ensemble functioned as the foil for the soloist. "Cornet Chop Suey," which inspired an oil painting,[31] became a test-piece for generations of aspiring jazz musicians—many of whom crashed and burned on its formidable terrain.

More than one writer has noticed allusions to Dodds's "High Society" obbligato (Example 4.6) in Armstrong's "Chop Suey" solos, a connection made credible by Sidney Bechet's reporting that Louis could play the challenging clarinet solo as a boy in New Orleans.[32] On the basis of this and other similarities, Brian Harker argues persuasively that arpeggios, running eighth notes, expanded range, technical virtuosity, and the blurred distinction between solo and lead evident in Armstrong's Hot Five style in general and in "Cornet Chop Suey" in particular are, in fact, adopted "clarinetisms."[33]

Example 4.6. Bars 1-16 of Dodds's Clarinet Obbligato on "King" Oliver's Recording of "High Society Rag"

[31]"Cornet Chop Suey," a 1938 oil painting by Misha Reznikoff, is reproduced in Marc H. Miller, "Louis Armstrong: A Cultural Legacy," *Louis Armstrong: A Cultural Legacy*, 46.

[32]Sidney Bechet, *Treat It Gentle*, 2nd ed. (New York: Hill and Wang, 1960; reprinted New York: Da Capo Press, 2002), 92. The clarinet solo was first recorded by Johnny Dodds with "King" Oliver's Jazz Band (including Armstrong) on 22 June 1923. See James Lincoln Collier, *Louis Armstrong*, 173. For Armstrong's references to "High Society" in his solos, see Edward Brooks, *Influence and Assimilation in Louis Armstrong's Cornet and Trumpet Work, 1923-1928* (Lewiston, NY: Edwin Mellon Press, 2000), 134-37.

[33]Brian Harker, "Louis Armstrong and the Clarinet," *American Music* 21/2 (Summer 2003), 137-58.

The copyright deposit (see Appendix 1) and the recording are so similar that one might imagine Armstrong's reading from it in the studio, although he more likely was relying on his prodigious memory.[34] The differences between the two, if small, are not inconsequential. As in "Yes! I'm in the Barrel," Armstrong's improvised alterations to the copyrighted melody are typically more interesting than the original. The first four bars of the chorus provide a telling illustration. In the deposit the phrase is repeated verbatim every eight measures for a total of eight times (counting the repeat of the chorus), but on the recording Armstrong eschews exact duplication. The first time through the chorus (mm. 21-52) he lightly alters the first two bars from the deposit (mm. 21, 29, 37, and 45), while more dramatically varying the second two; the second time (mm. 101-132) he drastically varies the first two measures (mm. 101, 109, 117, and 125), while lightly varying the second two from earlier repetitions (see Example 4.7).[35]

Arriving almost exactly at the golden section of "Cornet Chop Suey," the sixteen-bar stop-time "patter" provides the highlight of the piece[36] and furnishes another fine illustration of Beiderbecke's "correlated chorus" (see Example 4.8 on page 64). In the first eight measures each two-bar subphrase after the first amplifies its predecessors while retaining a basic organization around the tonic triad (F - A - C). The first subphrase (mm. 1-2) states the "thesis" most clearly, concisely, and explicitly. Subphrases two (mm. 3-4), three (mm. 5-6), and four (mm. 7-8) all begin with a variation on the tonic-to-dominant oscillation of the first: subphrase two, with an interpolated D and off the beat; subphrase three, with an inversion

[34]The incorrect quarter rest in the first measure of the chorus and similar locations elsewhere apparently indicates a staccato articulation: Lawrence Gushee, "The Improvisation of Louis Armstrong," *In the Course of Performance: Studies in the World of Musical Improvisation*, ed. Bruno Nettl (Chicago: University of Chicago Press, 1998), 298. Having been issued in E♭, E, and F, the correct key of "Cornet Chop Suey" remains in dispute. Consensus presently favors F, but E♭ has its respected adherents; see Phil Schaap, liner notes to Sony's *Complete Hot Five and Hot Seven Recordings*, 29. Because the recording key matches the deposit key in "Yes! I'm in the Barrel," the key of "Cornet Chop Suey" may well be its deposit's key of F. OKeh recordings were meant to be played at 80 rpm rather than 78 (about a quarter step sharp), and Louis played the piece in F in subsequent recordings, according to Randy Sandke in notes accompanying his full transcription: Louis Armstrong, *Cornet Chop Suey as Recorded by Louis Armstrong and His Hot Five*, transcr. Randy Sandke, ed. David Baker (Washington, DC: Smithsonian Institution, National Museum of American History, 2000).

[35]For additional discussion of comparisons between the recorded and copyrighted versions of "Cornet Chop Suey," see David Chevan, *Written Music in Early Jazz* (Ph.D. dissertation, City University of New York, 1997), 295-302.

[36]The golden section occurs in bar 86.5 (140 x 0.618), and the patter chorus occurs at bar 84 (see Chapter 6, note 4). "Patter" in music of the 1920s represents an interlude, usually falling between choruses and differing in character from the rest of the work. For more on the term, see David Chevan, *Written Music in Early Jazz*, 302-05; and James Dapogny's "Performance Notes" accompanying Randy Sandke's full transcription of "Cornet Chop Suey."

Example 4.7. Comparison of Bars 21-24 of Armstrong's Copyright Deposit for "Cornet Chop Suey" with the Hot Five Recording

of the initial pitches; and subphrase four, with the interpolated but relocated D from subphrase two. Subphrase two introduces legato articulation, stepwise motion, new pitches, and an expanded range while its serpentine shape, focus on the dominant (C), and general downward direction supply further contrast to subphrase one. Subphrase three, while retaining the articulation of subphrase two, expands the range further, adds D♭ as an embellishment of the dominant, and reintroduces the rip, upward direction, and explicit tonic arpeggiation of subphrase one. Subphrase four abandons the legato articulation and expansive ranges of subphrases two and three and reverts to the pivotal shape of subphrase one while reestablishing the tonic on the lower octave intensified by a blue third.

Measures 9-16 elaborate on measures 1-8 but in four-bar—rather than two-bar—units. Phrases five (mm. 9-12) and six (mm. 13-16), respectively, combine aspects of both subphrases one and two by retaining certain characteristics, eliminating others, and adding a few that are new. The dominant-tonic reiteration (m. 1) develops into the reiteration of the tonic triad (mm. 9-11), and the embellishment of the fifth (G) of the dominant with an F♯ (m. 4) is replaced with an embellishment of the third

(E) of the dominant with a D♯ (m. 12). The blue seventh (E♭) of bar 13 and the implied secondary dominant-seventh (G - B - D - F) of bar 15 offset the blue thirds of measures 6 and 8.

Example 4.8. Armstrong's Stop-Time Chorus "Cornet Chop Suey"

The balance of repetition, variation, and motivic expansion in these remarkable sixteen measures are characteristic of fine composition in general and not unworthy of Mozart or Beethoven. Unlike the rest of "Cornet Chop Suey," Armstrong plays the stop-time chorus almost note-for-note. Ironically, the only relative weakness in the performance, the awkward repetition of F - A♭ (mm. 7-8), is its departure from the lead sheet.

The single formal portion missing from the copyright deposit is the coda, which may have been improvised on the spot or played with little preparation in the studio. Spontaneous or not, it balances the introduction beautifully, recalling its essentials while changing them ingeniously. The upper-neighbor triplet idea in the introduction is transformed into a lower-neighbor secondary rag, dividing three groups of four eighth notes into four groups of three.[37] Reverting to common time halfway through the antepenultimate measure, Armstrong, unintentionally perhaps, ends on an arpeggiated tonic of the relative minor (D) and with a syncopation in contrast to the introduction's modal and metrical clarity (Example 4.9).

[37]Winthrop Sargeant, *Jazz, Hot and Hybrid* (1938), 2nd ed. (New York: E. P. Dutton, 1946; reprinted New York: Da Capo Press, 1975), 60.

Example 4.9. Comparison of Armstrong's Introduction and Coda of "Cornet Chop Suey"

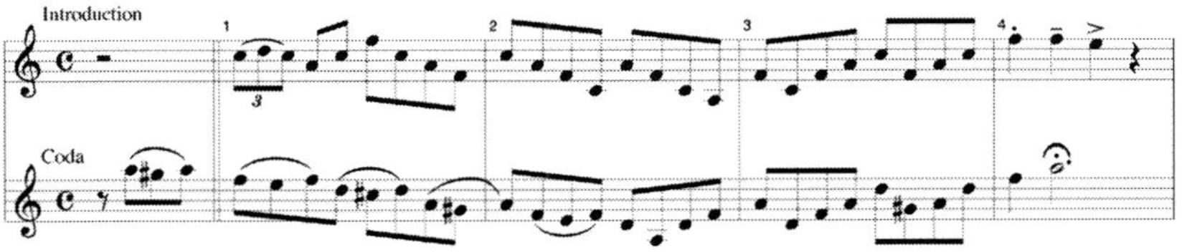

Schuller calls Lil's solo "embarrassing" but, perhaps, "pedestrian" or "unimaginative" might be fairer.[38] She simply plays the melody with little drive and some rushed pyrotechnics based on the second of her break-like passages from "My Heart" (Example 3.4) in bars 13–16 (mm. 65-68 of the full transcription). And her unvarying repetition of the phrase examined in Example 4.7 implies the presence of a lead sheet.

The foregoing begs the question of the role that memorization and precomposition play in the supposedly spontaneous act of improvisation. Armstrong was known to blow multiple but widely varying choruses of a tune or to play divergent solos on successive takes, while treating others, apparently prepared in advance or conditioned by means of repeated live performances, as set-pieces unchanged for years.[39] In the recording of "Cornet Chop Suey" he combined the processes of memory (or, perhaps, composition) and inspiration. The role of memory aside, he described his approach to improvisation as that of theme and variations of increasing abstraction: "The first chorus I plays the melody. The second chorus I plays the melody round the melody, and the third chorus I routines"[40]

Despite OKeh's Truetone technology, the acoustically recorded Hot Fives suffer from balance decisions favoring Armstrong. His full sound often dominates the ensemble to such an extent that the other players can barely be heard. This imbalance has led to suggestions that his sidemen were intimidated by the Armstrong onslaught, with Dodds cited as his chief victim.[41] His relative musical shortcomings aside, Dodds is poorly

[38]Gunther Schuller, *Early Jazz*, 99.

[39]Stanley Dance, *The World of Earl Hines* (New York: Scribner's, 1977; reprinted New York: Da Capo Press, 1983), 50; James Lincoln Collier, *Jazz: The American Theme Song* (New York: Oxford University Press, 1993), 32-33; and Jeffrey Magee, *The Music of Fletcher Henderson and His Orchestra in the 1920s* (Ph.D. dissertation, Columbia University, 1992), 326-31. On Armstrong's memory, see Nat Shapiro and Nat Hentoff, *Hear Me Talkin' to Ya: The Story of Jazz as Told by the Men Who Made It* (New York: Rinehart, 1955; reprinted New York: Dover Publications, 1966), 49.

[40]Quoted in Richard M. Sudhalter and Philip R. Evans, *Bix: Man & Legend* (New Rochelle, NY: Arlington House, 1974), 192. For differing interpretations of this quotation, see James Lincoln Collier, *Louis Armstrong*, 287, and Lawrence Gushee, "The Improvisation of Louis Armstrong," 320.

[41]André Hodeir, *Jazz, Its Evolution and Essence*, trans. David Noakes (New York: Grove Press, 1956; reprinted New York: Da Capo Press, 1975), 60.

served by the recording technology of the time and sounds more like Armstrong's equal on the later electric recordings. Armstrong's sound and indeed his musicianship were irrepressible from the beginning. During the first recordings of "King" Oliver's Creole Jazz Band for Gennett in 1923 he was forced to stand much further from the horn than his band mates to avoid overpowering his mentor, and his solos on the Fletcher Henderson recordings are instantly identifiable by their drive and swing.[42]

[42]Lil Armstrong, *Satchmo and Me: Lil Armstong's Own Story* [recorded memoir] (Riverside RLP 12-120, ca. 1950-1959; and Jeffrey Magee, *The Music of Fletcher Henderson*, 126-97.

“Oriental Strut”*

Table 4.4. Structural Outline of “Oriental Strut”

Section	Instrumentation	Bars	Key
Introduction	Ensemble / Rhythm Vamp	4 / 4	D Min
Verse	Ensemble / Rhythm Vamp / Ensemble	6 / 2 / 8	D Min
Chorus A1	Ensemble	16	F Maj
Chorus B1	Trombone Solo	16	F Maj
	Clarinet Solo / Banjo Break	14 / 2	F Maj
Chorus B2	Cornet Solo / Ensemble / Cornet Break	12 / 2 / 2	F Maj
	Cornet Solo / Ensemble	8 / 8	F Maj
Chorus B3	Ensemble / Banjo Break	14 / 2	F Maj
	Ensemble	16	F Maj
Tag	Ensemble	4	F Maj

The lack of distinction between solo and lead exhibited in Armstrong's playing extended perversely to his sidemen in Johnny St. Cyr's "Oriental Strut": both Ory's and Dodds's solos here resemble lead-like statements of the melody. As in "Cornet Chop Suey," the highlight of "Oriental Strut" is Armstrong's stop-time solo, which begins like its predecessor and shares its arpeggiated construction (Example 4.10 on the next page).

In a recent article, Brian Harker identifies this chorus as a transition between Armstrong's move from tune-based to harmony-based solos. With Henderson in New York (1924-1925), his solos were largely dependent on pre-existent melodies, although his degree of paraphrase ranged from playing the original with little change to improvising a new one almost independent of the original. In the early Hot Fives Armstrong picks up on the latter stage of solo construction and concomitantly begins integrating arpeggiated breaks into the solo itself, which with Henderson he kept normally distinct. This integration of melodic paraphrase with break-like material encouraged building solos on harmonies alone and the development of a "unified solo style." Aspects of such a style, which comes to predominate in the later Hot Fives recordings, first emerge in Armstrong's stop-time solo in "Oriental Strut." Here, by beginning more than half the measures of his solo with the comparable note in the melody, Armstrong uses its pitches as a scaffolding on which to drape his "wide-ranging arpeggios"—a technique facilitated by the stop-time's similarity to the breaks.[43]

Example 4.10. Comparison of the Melody with Armstrong's Stop-Time Solo in "Oriental Strut"

Lacking the clichés of a pentatonic melody or Chinese gong, there is little Asian about "Oriental Strut," whose ostinato oom-pah-pah rhythm of the introduction and verse strikes one as more Native-American than Far-Eastern. It is, moreover, a flawed performance: Armstrong fluffs several notes in his solo, Dodds misses a change in his solo (m. 22), and both Ory

[43]Brian Harker, "'Telling A Story': Louis Armstrong and Coherence in Early Jazz," *Current Musicology* 63 (1999), 50-65. Gunther Schuller, *Early Jazz*, 103, holds similar views: "Louis's solo conception developed in exact proportion to the degree his solos departed from the original tune. His later solos all but ignored the original tune and started with only the chord changes given." For Lawrence Gushee, "Improvisation of Louis Armstrong," 312-17, Armstrong would not "cut himself loose completely from the tune" until his move to the pop repertoire during the 1929-1932 period.

and Dodds sound lost during the stop-time. Indeed, although not joining the accompaniment of Louis's solo until bar 4, Ory misses bar 6 entirely, the third beats of bars 10 and 22, and the fourth beat of bar 11. Dodds, who chooses to lay out during most of the section, enters early (m. 17) and attempts a sustained accompaniment (mm. 18-19 and 22-23) only to come in a measure late at the re-entry of the ensemble (m. 25).

Yet the number's novelty, energy, and Armstrong's perceived genius transcended these imperfections for contemporary musicians according to trumpeter Joseph "Wingy" Manone:

> Jack [Teagarden] . . . was gone on . . . a tune called "Oriental Strut." . . . Jack thought that was the end. He decided nobody else could ever top that, and said we ought to put it away someplace to preserve it for posterity. . . . Jack and I drove out on the mesa with it. We dug a big hole and laid that record away, and as far as I know it is still there today.[44]

[44]Joseph "Wingy" Manone, quoted without documentation in Mike Pinfold, *Louis Armstrong: His Life and Times* (New York: Universe Books, 1987), 53.

"You're Next"

Table 4.5. Structural Outline of "You're Next"

SECTION	INSTRUMENTATION	BARS	KEY
Introduction	Piano Solo	4 / 4	F Min
Verse	Cornet Solo	16	F Min
Chorus 1	Ensemble / Banjo Break	14 / 2	A♭ Maj
	Ensemble / Banjo Break / Ensemble	8 / 4 / 4	A♭ Maj
Chorus 2	Piano Solo	16	A♭ Maj
	Clarinet Solo / Clar. Break / Clar. Solo	8 / 4 / 4	A♭ Maj
Chorus 3	Ensemble / Trombone Break / Ensemble	4 / 4 / 4	A♭ Maj

There is little extraordinary about the solos and ensemble playing in "You're Next," leading to the probable conclusion that Lil's tune was hastily prepared at the studio with the players reading from the lead sheet later submitted for copyright (Appendix 1). Lil's bombastic introduction (not provided on the deposit) corroborates her training as a classical pianist (Example 4.11). Later she pursued this interest by obtaining a teacher's certificate from the Chicago Musical College. There she studied with Dutch pianist-composer Louis Victor Saar, who presented her in a public recital of compositions by Mozart, von Weber, Chopin, Debussy, and Scriabin.[45] Although Lil's introduction to "You're Next" might strike one's ear as incongruous, pretentious, or even ironic today, its intent at the time

Example 4.11. Lil's Introduction to "You're Next"

[45] *Chicago Defender* (9 June 1928), 6, and (25 May 1929), 6. Lil claimed to have beaten Jelly Roll Morton in a "cutting contest" as a teenager by playing Bach, Chopin, and [MacDowell's?] *Witches' Dance* in "Lil Armstrong Reminisces about Early Chicago Days," *Down Beat* 18/11 (1 June 1951), 12.

may well have been to legitimize a music thought to be disreputable by Chicago's influential black establishment, of which her mother, Dempsey Miller, was a card-carrying member.[46]

Example 4.12. Comparison of the Copyrighted Melody with Armstrong's Solo on the Verse of "You're Next"

Armstrong's solos on verses generally follow the melody more closely than on choruses, for which he seems to hold his creative powers in reserve. So it is with "You're Next" (Example 4.12). However, his treatment of the opening two phrases, identical on the copyrighted lead, demonstrates his aversion to exact repetition, as has already been shown in "Cornet Chop Suey" and will be encountered repeatedly in later Hot Fives. By avoiding G in these passages he actually reduces the pitch content from the original and relies, instead, on varying the rhythm. After beginning bar 5 on an afterbeat tonic as he had in bar 1, he changes—except for the F dotted-quarter in bar 7—the rhythm and pitch on every beat compared to what he had played in the first four measures. By replacing relative inactivity or simplicity with relative activity or complexity, each measure of the second phrase functions as the musical opposite of its first-phrase analogue. The moderately syncopated triadic arpeggio of bar 1, for example, is contrasted with the more highly syncopated and partially chromatic bar 5;[47] the rests of bar 2 are filled by a triplet in bar 6; the

[46]See Thomas J. Hennessey, "The Black Chicago Establishment 1919-1930," *Journal of Jazz Studies* 2/1 (December 1974), 15-45, and James L. Dickerson, *Just for a Thrill: Lil Hardin, First Lady of Jazz* (New York: Cooper Square Press, 2002), 54-55.

[47]The half-valve heard in this passage is Armstrong's first use of the technique on record: Edward Brooks, *The Young Louis Armstrong on Records: A Critical Survey of the Early Recordings, 1923-1928* (Lanham, MD: Scarecrow Press, 2002), 306. Armstrong's grip of his right thumb hooked around the

mediant-tonic repetitions of bar 3 are replaced by a lone tonic in bar 7; and the half note in bar 4 is balanced by a ripped, syncopated upper F and a descending arpeggio in bar 8.

Example 4.13. Comparison of the Copyrighted Melody with Lil's and Dodds's Solos in "You're Next"

first valve casing and fingers flat across the keys "allowed him to invent the seamless half-valve gliss" and "gave him his signature vibrato and 'shake'" according to Randy Sandke, "The Trumpet in Jazz," *The Oxford Companion to Jazz*, ed. Bill Kirchner (New York: Oxford University Press, 2000), 616-17.

Lil's "You're Next" solo, like all of her Hot Five solos, strings together stock patterns of eighth notes in a limited number of repeated rhythms that outline the melody (Example 4.13). If her husband's arpeggios signify an inclination towards harmony, Lil's continuously figurated lines imply an inclination towards melody. Yet her preferred types of syncopation—between rather than within beats—are more the stuff of ragtime than jazz. The fills or break-like passages (mm. 3-4 and 15-16) can be traced to bars 7-8 of her earlier "My Heart" solo (Example 3.4).

Dodds's half-chorus solo contains numerous idiosyncracies—the blue note (mm. 16-17); the triplet passage (m. 18); the leap of a minor sixth (mm. 19-20); the melodic tritones (mm. 18, 27-29); the lipped glissando (m. 30); the ubiquitous arpeggios; and the emphasis on the harmonic third on downbeats. The solo's reiteration of A♭ and its notably restricted range of a minor sixth for most of its length (narrowing to a minor third in bars 21-23) make it one of Dodds's more conventional efforts. His break outlining a D diminished seventh (mm. 25-26), however, is harmonically more compelling than St. Cyr's before and Ory's after, whose similar breaks remain within the given chord change. In all three the blue seventh (C♭) acts as a leading tone to the third (C) of the tonic (A♭), but Dodds's interpolation of a D♮ allows for a leading tone to the fifth (E♭) of the tonic as well (Example 4.14).

Example 4.14. Comparison of St. Cyr's, Dodds's, and Ory's Breaks in "You're Next"

"Muskrat Ramble"*

Table 4.6. Structural Outline of "Muskrat Ramble" [A♭ Major]

SECTION	INSTRUMENTATION	BARS
Chorus A1	Ensemble	16
Chorus B1	Ensemble	16
Chorus B2	Trombone Solo	16
Chorus B3	Cornet Solo	16
Chorus B4	Clarinet Solo	16
Chorus A2	Ensemble	16
Chorus A3	Ensemble	16
Tag	Trombone / Ensemble	1 / 1

The final cut of this session became, along with "Heebie Jeebies," the most frequently recorded of the Hot Fives and the group's only tune to approach the status of a "jazz standard."[48] Confusion over the title has long ago been put to rest. "Muskat" appeared on the recording's initial release, but "Muskrat" is indeed the name found on the copyright deposit (see Appendix 1). The original label copy, now in the Sony Archives, has "Muskat" crossed out and "Muskrat" pencilled in.

Although "Kid" Ory claimed composer credit, the origin of the tune remains obscure:

> Ory says he originally conceived ["Muskrat Ramble"] in Los Angeles, revising it out of an exercise in a saxophone study book: "I wrote it back around 1921 when I was playing in a taxi dancehall at Third and Main in Los Angeles. It had no name then. Lil Armstrong gave it that title at the record session." But Louis Armstrong told Dan Morgenstern in *Down Beat* [15 July 1965, 18] . . . "I wrote Muskrat Ramble. Ory named it, he gets the royalties. I don't talk about it." On the other hand, Sidney Bechet once remembered "Muskrat Ramble," or at least its second

[48]Brian Rust in *Jazz and Ragtime Records, 1897-1942,* 2 vols. (Denver: Mainspring Press, 2002) lists a dozen post-Hot Five recordings of "Heebie Jeebies" and an equal number of "Muskrat Ramble." The former, however, were essentially limited to the late 1920s and early 1930s (see Chapter 4, note 19) while the latter—recorded by marquee bands like Bob Crosby, Roy Eldridge, Lionel Hampton, Woody Herman, Lu Watters—became the theme song of the New Orleans revival during the late 1930s and early 1940s. See also Chapter 10, note 29.

theme, as an old folksong he heard in his youth, "The Old Cow Died and the Old Man Cried" [*Jazz Record* (July 1945)].[49]

"Muskrat Ramble's" ragtime origins are reflected in sixteen-bar choruses, its saw-toothed theme, and hemiola rhythms that echo Joplin's "Maple Leaf Rag" (1899), Sweatman's "Down Home Rag" (1911), Bowman's "Twelfth Street Rag" (1914), and the Original Dixieland Jazz Band's recording of "Tiger Rag" (1917).[50]

Ory's composition of "Muskrat Ramble" (or something like it) years earlier could account for its sounding more arranged than other Hot Fives. Passages such as that in Example 4.15 were likely worked out with his Original Creole Jazz Band in California, as was his other set-piece, "Ory's Creole Trombone" (see below). But whether he composed it or not, "Muskrat Ramble" is a show-piece for the trombonist for whose "tailgate" style of playing it is the ideal vehicle.[51]

Example 4.15. Second Strain Ensemble Excerpt in "Muskrat Ramble"

[49]Martin Williams, *Jazz Masters of New Orleans* (New York: Macmillan, 1967; reprinted New York: Da Capo Press, 1979), 211.

[50]Hugues Panassié, *Louis Armstrong*, 70, also detected characteristics of the French quadrille, one of the possible precursors of ragtime; see Edward Berlin, *Ragtime: A Musical and Cultural History* (Berkeley: University of California Press, 1980), 118.

[51]Ory is the model for an early New Orleans punchy and smeary style of trombone playing, so called from the location of the instrument when parading in a horse-drawn cart.

The existence of the copyright deposit (see Appendix 1) provides the first opportunity in this study to compare Dodds's, Armstrong's, and Ory's solos with an original non-blues melody (Example 4.16).[52] Their solos elucidate three separate approaches to improvisation: each is distinguished by different degrees of melodic and harmonic abstraction. While melodic variation would always be part of each soloist's "bag," harmonic variation would become increasingly an alternate possibility, especially for Louis as previously observed.

Example 4.16. Comparison of the Copyrighted Melody with Solos by Dodds, Armstrong, and Ory in "Muskrat Ramble"

[52]The melody has been transposed from F to A♭, and obvious mistakes of notation have been corrected for purposes of comparison.

Example 4.16 Continued.

The first in the series, Ory's solo can be identified as the most conspicuously formulaic. Introduced by two measures of ensemble stop-time, the first half of his solo (mm. 3-8) is a loosely-related two-bar succession of break-like material, accompaniment figures, and a stock hemiola pattern. The second half (mm. 11-16) begins like the first half, makes a direct reference to the melody (m. 13), and concludes with accompaniment figures. Ory's most lasting contribution to his piece is the two-bar tag, which, like "Oh, play that thing!" in "Dippermouth Blues," has become *de rigeur* in all later performances of "Muskrat Ramble" (Example 4.17).

Example 4.17. Ory's Tag in "Muskrat Ramble"

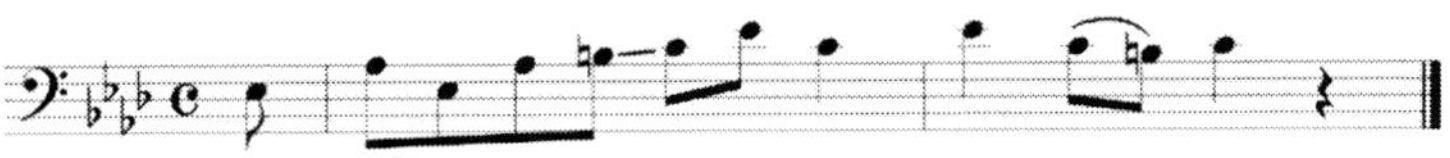

Harker correctly sees Armstrong's solo as his first on record to be harmonically based, albeit not dominated by arpeggios.[53] His solitary nod to the melody is a tangential reference in diminution (mm. 3-4) to its descent from the mediant to the leading-tone, C - B♭ - A - G (mm. 2-5), although he borrows the figure in bar 6 from his second ensemble strain (Example 4.15). Otherwise the solo pursues its own design by subdividing the two parallel eight-bar phrases of the melody into smaller, asymmetrical units. Beginning with a one-bar quarter-note "statement" on the chordal ninth / seventh, Armstrong answers it with four bars of a wide-ranging new melody that conclude with a second statement on the chordal seventh / fifth (m. 5). He restores order with a two-bar subphrase (mm. 6-7), then opens the second phrase of the melody with a lengthy ripped high G that

[53]Brian Harker, "'Telling a Story,'" 60, 65. Blues solos are somewhat of an exception. Because of the simplicity and repetitiveness of blues melodies, players tended to concentrate on blues harmonies for their improvisations, which often relied on recurring stock patterns for coherence (see Examples 3.7, 3.10, and 9.14).

begins a three-bar subphrase (mm. 9-11), followed by a two-and-a-half-bar subphrase (mm. 12-14.5) and completed by another two-and-a-half-bar subphrase (mm. 14.5-16).

As an extension of their arpeggiated and obbligato accompaniments, harmonically-based solos were much more the norm for clarinets than the other front-line instruments in New Orleans jazz bands. Dodds's "Muskrat Ramble" solo—like his earlier Hot Five solos—avoids the original tune, which he replaces with arpeggios and running passages built on or around the third of the harmonic changes. His avoidance of the melody, however, does not amount to the rejection of the melody by Armstrong. Dodds quotes the tune (m. 12) and relies on it in other structural ways: his G on the downbeat of bar 2 and D on the downbeat of bar 6 coincide with melodic notes, and his bars 4-5 reshuffle the melody's pitches and voice-leading; Dodds divides the first phrase of the melody into subphrases of 3 + 3 + 2, but he begins the second half of the solo like the first, and his phrasing of bars 9-16 matches the original. While the solos do differ considerably, Dodds, last in the parade of soloists, plays an inversion of Ory's secondary rag (m. 7), ends with Ory's E♭ - D - D♭ approach to a cadence on C, and ignores the A♮ of the F7 change (m. 13) as had Armstrong immediately before (despite the cornetist having observed the change in the preceding ensemble passage).

CHAPTER 5

Early Fame

On 27 February 1926, the day after the third Hot Five recording session, Armstrong was one of fourteen featured celebrities at an OKeh Race Record Artists Night Entertainment and Dance held in the Coliseum North Annex. The *Talking Machine World* published the following details in its account:

> The carnival . . . was opened by Ex-Mayor William Hale Thompson, who gave an opening address that was timely and effective. Subsequent to Mr. Thompson's address, the OKeh artists who were present gave the public which crowded the Coliseum an adequate idea of their distinctive talents. . . . A Charleston contest followed the program, subsequent to which the guests danced to the music of Cooke's Dreamland Orchestra. . . . One of the features of the carnival was the recording of OKeh records on the Coliseum stage, under the supervision of Chas. Hibbard, recording chief of the General Phonograph Corp.'s laboratories in New York. . . . The process of recording was carried out in detail on the stage and the finished records were played shortly after the original recording, to the keen enthusiasm of the thousands of music lovers who were present.[1]

The event had been organized to promote OKeh records by E. A. Fearn, who presided and introduced the guests.

Unfortunately, neither the *TMW* report, cited above, nor another news story appearing after the event in the *Defender* mention the "stuff" that Armstrong was predicted to do in a 6 February *Defender* article: "Louis Armstrong . . . the world's greatest jazz cornetist will do his stuff. Chicago has gone wild over Louie and his cornet work. People of all nationalities come nightly to the South Side to hear Louie flutter on his cornet at [the] Dreamland."[2] That "his stuff" could have included a Hot Five performance of "Gut Bucket Blues," the recently-released recording cited beneath Armstrong's picture in the *Defender* advertisement of 20 January, is obliquely supported by the 6 February article that also proclaimed that

[1] *TMW* 22/3 (15 March 1926), 108. Charles "Doc" Cooke's orchestra was in residence at Paddy Harmon's Dreamland, located on Chicago's West Side.

[2] *Chicago Defender*, City Edition (6 February 1926), 6. This is the last mention in the *Defender* of Armstrong at the Dreamland.

"King" Oliver's band would "shoot hot jazz" and Richard M. Jones's Three Jazz Wizards would play their "recording arrangement" of "Spanish Shawl."[3]

The four-month period before the next Hot Five session was one of transition for Armstrong. Henpecking by Lil at the Dreamland and teen-age adulation by Alpha Smith at the Vendome weakened his marriage.[4] At some point during this period or slightly before, the Dreamland was shut down once again, presumably for liquor violations, leaving Armstrong with only his nightly job at the Vendome. When the cabaret reopened in April, a band led by Erskine Tate's pianist, Teddy Weatherford, had replaced Lil's Syncopators. Meanwhile Armstrong had begun doubling with Carroll Dickerson at the Sunset Café a few blocks away from the Dreamland. There he saw his name up in lights for the first time: "Louis Armstrong, World's Greatest Trumpet [*sic*] Player."[5]

The success of his first race record extravaganza prompted Fearn to organize a second, whose promotion stimulated his "Barnumism" to new heights (see Illustration 5.1). When the doors opened at the Coliseum on South Wabash for the OKeh Cabaret and Style Show at 8:00 p.m. on 12 June, nearby streets were filled with "a seething mass of humanity" for whose control extra details of police and firemen were "rushed to the scene." Public dancing, various contests, and race vaudeville and recording stars entertained the crowd from 9:00 p.m. until the style show at 2:00 a.m., followed by the obligatory Charleston contest at 3:00 a.m. Of the twenty-five thousand predicted, an estimated twenty thousand attended; of the twenty-one orchestras (ensembles) advertised, fifteen participated. Publicized as a benefit for the black musicians' union, Local 208, to whom the "entire proceeds will be turned over," the largest amount of revenue, ticket sales at $1.10 each, actually went to Fearn's Consolidated Talking Machine Company, with the union getting only the money from "program space selling, check room privileges, confections, etc." Nevertheless, it was presumed, the union "profited handsomely."[6]

[3] *Ibid.*

[4] Max Jones and John Chilton, *Louis: The Louis Armstrong Story, 1900-1971* (Boston: Little, Brown, 1971; reprinted New York: Da Capo Press, 1988), 109.

[5] *Chicago Defender* (3 April 1926), 6; (17 April 1926), 6; and Louis Armstrong, *Swing That Music,* (New York: Longmans, Green, 1936; reprinted New York: Da Capo Press, 1993), 84. Ory contended that Armstrong left the Dreamland in a dispute over money; see William Russell, *New Orleans Style*, ed. Barry Martyn and Mike Hazeldine (New Orleans: Jazzology, 1994), 181.

[6] *Chicago Defender* (12 June 1926), special supplement; (19 June 1926), 6; and *TMW* 22/6 (15 June 1926), 6, 18.

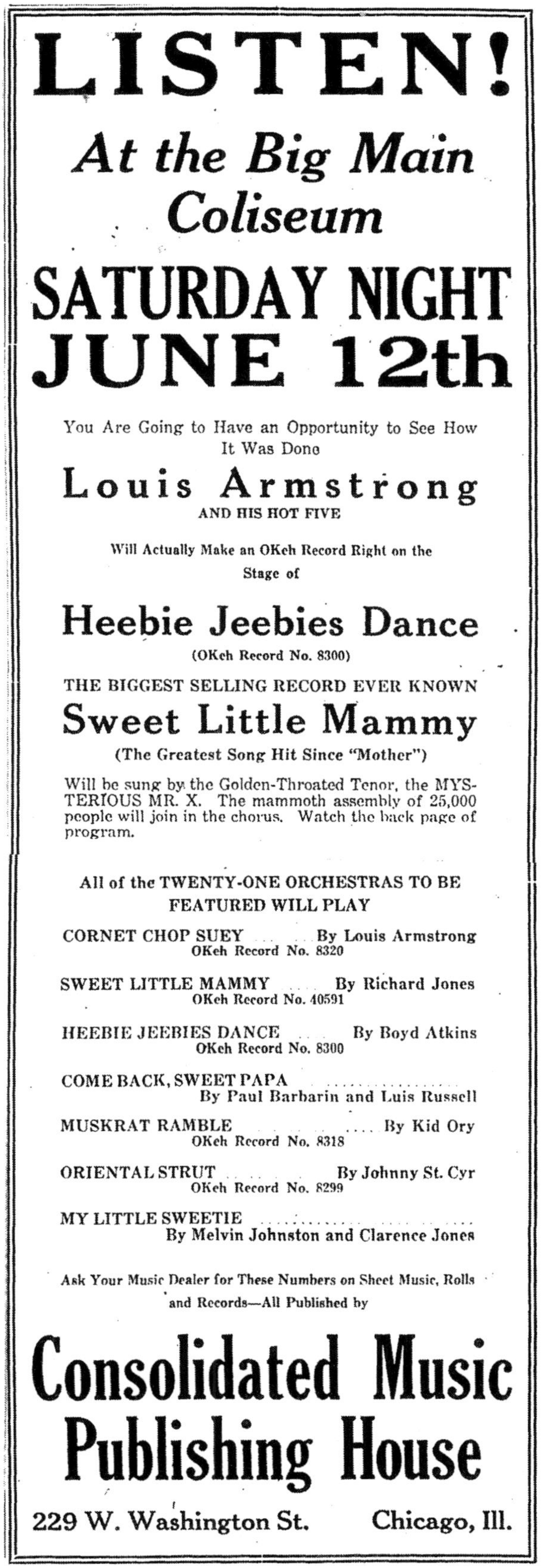

Illustration 5.1.
Ad for OKeh Cabaret and Style Show

From *Chicago Defender* (12 June 1926), Music Edition Extra: 2.

The recording of "Heebie Jeebies"—"right on the stage"—proclaimed in the *Chicago Defender* apparently did not take place, and it is unlikely that "all twenty-one orchestras to be featured" played the latest Hot Five recordings as advertised.[7] But the Hot Five, in its only documented public appearance, "broke up the big ball on June 12 with their hot playing" and "nearly brought the house down at the Chicago Coliseum show of OKeh Race Stars."[8]

The quartet of numbers cut at the Hot Five's fourth session on 16 June, four days after the Cabaret and Style Show, has been largely ignored. The chief reason for posterity's indifference to these pieces is undoubtedly their lack of cornet solos: Armstrong supplied vocal solos on three of them and a slide-whistle solo on a fourth. Yet in Armstrong's day these moves made astute commercial sense and were almost certainly stimulated by the phenomenal success of his singing on "Heebie Jeebies" and by the strong attraction to novelty and hokum during the 1920s.

The basic similarity of the pieces allows them to be discussed as a group. None are perfectly executed. Armstrong fluffs his rip in the final chorus of "I'm Gonna Gitcha," and Dodds botches the Charleston rhythms of "Don't Forget to Mess Around." Ory stumbles on his break in "Don't Forget to Mess Around" and struggles with articulation and embouchure control in his solos in "Droppin' Shucks" and "Who'sit." Conversely, Armstrong's "psalmodic" vocals induce novelty,[9] and Dodds's several well-crafted clarinet solos sustain interest. Lil turns in solid but heavy-handed solos on "Droppin' Shucks" and "Who'sit," while on the latter St. Cyr tastefully backs up the Armstrong-Dodds duet. Also worth noting are Armstrong's nimble triplets in "Don't Forget to Mess Around" and "Droppin' Shucks," his exciting breaks at the end of "Who'sit," and, in "I'm Gonna Gitcha" and "Droppin' Shucks," his expanded range—to a high written D, his highest recorded pitch so far.[10]

[7]Advertisement for OKeh Race Record Night, *Chicago Defender* (12 June 1926), special supplement.

[8]*Chicago Defender* (19 June 1926), 6, and (14 August 1926), 6.

[9]André Hodeir, *Jazz, Its Evolution and Essence*, trans. David Noakes (New York: Grove Press, 1956; reprinted New York: Da Capo Press, 1975), 61. On the African elements of Armstrong's "speechlike vocal delivery," see Benjamin Givan, "Duets for One: Louis Armstrong's Vocal Recordings," *The Musical Quarterly* 87 (Summer 2004), 189-91.

[10]Edward Brooks, *The Young Louis Armstrong on Records: A Critical Survey of the Early Recordings, 1923-1928* (Lanham, MD: Scarecrow Press, 2002), 330.

"Don't Forget to Mess Around"

Table 5.1. Structural Outline of "Don't Forget to Mess Around" [A♭ Major]

SECTION	INSTRUMENTATION	BARS
Introduction	Ensemble / Cornet Break	1 / 1
	Ensemble / Cornet Break / Ensemble	1 / 1 / 4
Chorus 1	Ensemble	32
Verse	Ensemble	16
Chorus 2	Sax Solo / Sax Break / Sax Solo	14 / 2 / 16
Chorus 3	Louis's Vocal Solo	32
Chorus 4	Clarinet Solo / Clarinet Break	14 / 2
	Ensemble	8
	Trombone Break / Cornet Break / Ensemble	2 / 2 / 4

Comparing the recording to the copyright deposit of "Don't Forget to Mess Around (When You're Doing the Charleston)" (see Appendix 1) provides few revealing insights. Besides expanding the introduction to eight bars, placing the verse after the first chorus, and modifying a few pitches of the melody (B♭ instead of an A in mm. 5 and 21 and a G♮ instead of a G♭ in mm. 9 and 11), the Hot Five reproduces the deposit at the studio session. Although not registered on the copyrighted lead sheet almost three months before the recording, the lyrics were clearly not an afterthought: "voice" is indicated at the start of the verse.

Despite the Charleston rhythms, the lyrics actually promote a popular dance, the "Mess Around," which emerged in the early 1910s.[11]

Verse

Way down south in New Orleans;
There's a gal down there called the Charleston Queen.
Oh how she could Charleston,
You ought to see her Charleston.
Uncle Jack, the Jazzbo King,
Taught her a brand new dance;
And after she learned this great dance,
This is what she said:

[11]Marshall Stearns and Jean Stearns, *Jazz Dance: The Story of American Vernacular Dance* (New York: Macmillan, 1968; reprinted New York: Da Capo Press, 1994), 106-07.

Chorus

Don't forget to mess around
While you're doin' the Charleston, Charleston;
First thing you do,
Now when you rear back,
Grab your gal,
And then you Eagle Rock,
But don't you stop at all.

Oh, Uncle Jack, the old dancin' fool,
Wouldn't do that Charleston, Charleston.
When he learned
Of that brand new dance,
Such a prance.
Now he clean forgot his age
When he danced this brand new rage.
Don't forget to do your stuff
When you dance that dance called Messin' Around.[12]

Dodds sounds more confident on the saxophone here than in "Come Back Sweet Papa" and even attempts a break during his sax solo in "Don't Forget to Mess Around." In these fourth-session tunes he recycles several characteristic one- or two-bar licks that appear in ensemble passages and solos alike—often as breaks or in the portion of the phrase where breaks are expected. His clarinet solo in "Don't Forget to Mess Around," for example, contains at least three such licks (Example 5.1). The figure in bar 4 is the most ubiquitous, occurring in the introduction (m. 7), the first chorus (mm. 5 and 21), and the final ensemble chorus (mm. 21 and 31); a variation also shows up in the first chorus (m. 4) of "Droppin' Shucks." The break-like passage (mm. 9-10) is first heard at the same location in the first chorus, and Dodds plays a version of bar 16 in bar 27 of his solo in "I'm Gonna Gitcha" (Example 5.4 on page 89).

If Armstrong's "task" in his early Hot Five solos was to integrate melodic paraphrase with arpeggios, Dodds's problem was the reverse. The clarinetist's fourth-session solos, typical of his output in general, are all highly arpeggiated, sometimes relentlessly so, and make only passing

[12]Lyrics from the OKeh recording by Alberta Hunter (26 September 1926). The "Eagle Rock" dates back to religious dances in an eponymous black Baptist church after the Civil War; see Marshall Stearns and Jean Stearns, *Jazz Dance*, 26-27. Armstrong, who omits the verse, contradicts the song's "message" by ending with the line, "When you dance, don't mess around."

reference to the melody—if at all. One wonders if Dodds can think melodically and harmonically simultaneously. In his clarinet solo for "Don't Forget to Mess Around," he not only ignores the melody but also the Charleston rhythms, its most conspicuous feature; in his saxophone solo he plays the Charleston rhythms but duplicates the melody.

The circumstances surrounding the arrangement of "Don't Forget to Mess Around" recorded for Paramount by Austin's Musical Ambassadors in February 1926, a month before Barbarin sent in the copyright deposit, are unknown. Except for the lack of a vocal chorus, the Ambassadors' format of the tune and their melodic deviations from the copyright deposit (*e.g.*, no G♭ in bar 11 of the chorus) match the Hot Five recording of four months later.

Example 5.1. Comparison of the Copyrighted Melody with Dodds's Solo in "Don't Forget to Mess Around"

"I'm Gonna Gitcha"

Table 5.2. Structural Outline of "I'm Gonna Gitcha" [F Major]

SECTION	INSTRUMENTATION	BARS
Chorus 1	Ensemble	16
	Ensemble / Clarinet, Cornet, Trombone Break	4 / 2
	Ensemble	8
Verse	Ensemble	16
Chorus 2	Clarinet Solo	16
	Clarinet Solo / Clarinet Break / Clarinet Solo	4 / 2 / 8
Chorus 3	Louis's Vocal Solo	16
	Vocal Solo / Vocal Break	4 / 2
	Vocal Solo / Clarinet Break	7 / 1
Chorus 4	Clarinet Solo / Clarinet Break	6 / 2
	Ensemble / Trombone Break	6 / 2
	Ensemble / Cornet Break	4 / 2
	Ensemble	8

Lil's copyright deposit for "I'm Gonna Gitcha" is strikingly similar to the separate recordings of "I'm Gonna Get You" by Mamie Smith and by Trixie Smith in 1922.[13] Not only do their verses (mm. 1-16) share many of the same rhythms, their melodic structure (a - a' - b - a'') is identical, and their b phrases (mm. 9-12) are constructed of a two-bar sequence (Example 5.2 on the next page). The form of the deposit's truncated chorus differs from the earlier recordings, but Lil must have had Mamie's or Trixie's song in mind when setting the title (m. 17). (See Illustration 5.2 on page 88.)

If the lyrics of "Droppin' Shucks" could have been meant for Lil, the lyrics of "I'm Gonna Gitcha" could have been meant for Alpha Smith, with whose family Louis and Clarence briefly lived. Yet, the couple would not be free to marry until Lil, whom Armstrong at the time accused of consorting with a Chicago pimp, finally agreed to a divorce in 1938.[14]

Hey mama! I'm gonna bet you that I'm gonna get you.
I'm gonna get you some sweet day,

[13]"I'm Gonna Get You" by Porter Grainger and Bob Ricketts was recorded by Mamie Smith and Her Jazz Hounds for OKeh (ca. 10 December 1922) and by Trixie Smith for Black Swan (ca. November-December 1922). Despite the "Getcha" of Lil's copyright deposit, the word became "Gitcha" on OKeh label copy and thus its official title.

[14]Louis Armstrong, *Louis Armstrong: In His Own Words*, ed. Thomas Brothers (New York: Oxford University Press, 1999), 96-98.

And don't think you can give me the air.
And I'm gonna race you, I'm gonna chase you,
I'm gonna follow you everywhere.
Don't you believe you can give me the air.
Oh, you can take a man out and throw the cat out,
But when you are right
You can't treat sweet papa with the same old jive.
I'm gonna feel 'ya, I'm gonna steal ya,
I must have you mama some sweet day.
Nothin' doin' baby, you just can't get away.

Example 5.2. Comparison of the Melody of Mamie Smith's "I'm Gonna Get You" with Lil's Copyrighted Melody of "I'm Gonna Gitcha"

The parallel chromatic dissonances in the first chorus ensemble break of "I'm Gonna Gitcha" (Example 5.3), its most striking feature, had to have been worked out in advance. There is little other evidence, however, of arranged elements—aspects of which become increasingly prominent in later Hot Fives.

Example 5.3. Ensemble Break in "I'm Gonna Gitcha"

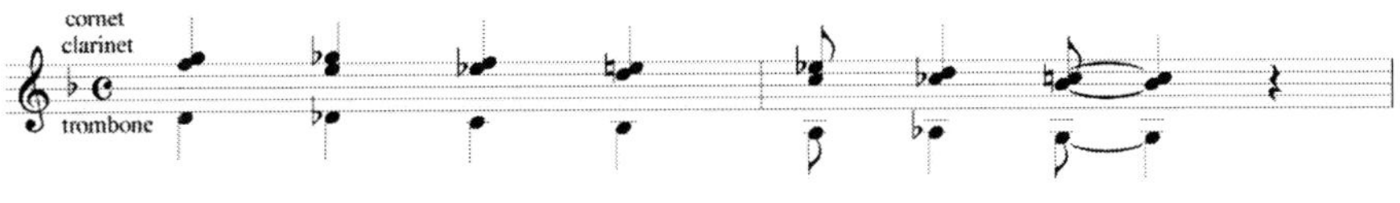

Illustration 5.2.
OKeh Ad for
"I'm Gonna Gitcha"

From *Chicago Defender*
(4 August 1926), 6.

Dodds's "I'm Gonna Gitcha" solo reinforces the notion that he tended to improvise either harmonically or melodically but not with a balance of both (Example 5.4). While it could be argued that on the unfamiliar saxophone he "plays it safe" by sticking close to the melody, such a constraint is removed here in one of his least creative Hot Five efforts. Dodds's only excursions beyond the original tune are the break-like passages (mm. 7 and 15), which he had already played in the verse (m. 13) and in the first chorus (m. 15) and would reuse in the final chorus (mm. 12 and 29). The figure, which falls easily and naturally under a clarinetist's fingers, proves to be a favorite of Dodds, who finds frequent use for it in "Droppin' Shucks" and later Hot Five solos and breaks (Example 6.9, m. 9; Example 7.6, m. 59; and Example 7.11, m. 25).

Example 5.4. Comparison of the Copyrighted Melody with Dodds's Solo in "I'm Gonna Gitcha"

Illustration 5.3.
OKeh Ad for
"Dropping Shucks"

From *Chicago Defender,*
(11 September 1926), 6.

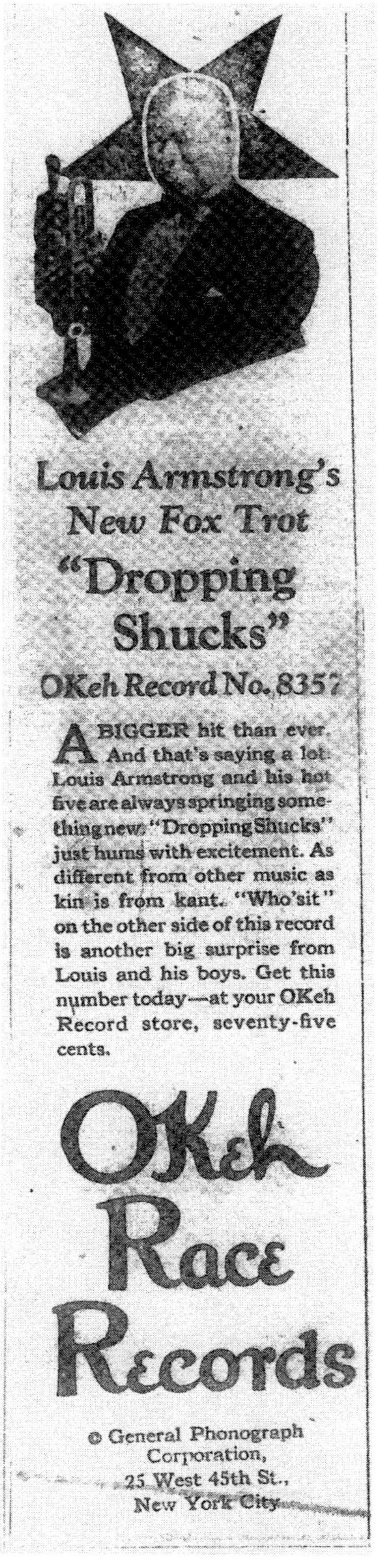

"Droppin' Shucks"

Table 5.3. Structural Outline of "Droppin' Shucks"

SECTION	INSTRUMENTATION	BARS	KEY
Verse	Ensemble	16	A Maj
Chorus 1	Ensemble	16	F Maj
Chorus 2	Piano Solo / Banjo Break / Piano Solo	8 / 4 / 4	F Maj
Chorus 3	Vocal Solo / Vocal Break / Vocal Solo	8 / 4 / 4	F Maj
Interlude	Vocal Solo (Speech / Singing)	8 / 4	F Maj
Chorus 4	Clarinet Solo / Clarinet Break / Clarinet Solo	8 / 4 / 4	F Maj
Chorus 5	Trombone Solo / Tromb. Break / Tromb. Solo	8 / 4 / 4	F Maj
Chorus 6	Ensemble	8	F Maj
	Trombone Break / Cornet Break / Ensemble	2 / 2 / 4	F Maj

Although Lil wrote the music for "Droppin' Shucks," the lyrics, which eerily describe the Armstrongs' marital situation, may have been supplied or adapted by Louis. (See Illustration 5.3.)

Sweet mama, you been droppin' shucks on me,
Now I'm gonna drop 'em on you.
I caught you with your sweet man the other night,
And I know you was untrue.
So hey, sweet mama, way last fall,
That you come and find another mule in your stall.
You been droppin' shucks on me,
And now I'm gonna drop 'em on you.
Roses are red and violets are blue.
You run and talk but I'm cookin';
What's the matter with you?
You read 'bout your papa sayin' he was it;
This sweet mama I got just won't quit;
You been droppin' shucks on me,
And now I'm gonna throw 'em on you."

Paying homage in bar 3 to the melody of "Droppin' Shucks" (as determined by Armstrong's lead), Dodds's solo is otherwise a harmonic variation like most of his others during this session, differing only in the sheer pervasiveness of its arpeggiation (Example 5.5 on the next page).

The figure in bars 5 and 14—so prominent in "I'm Gonna Gitcha"—reappears in "Droppin' Shucks" in the first chorus (mm. 2 and 10) and in the final chorus (mm. 1 and 13).

Example 5.5. Comparison of Armstrong's Lead with Dodds's Solo in "Droppin' Shucks"

"Who'sit"*

Table 5.4. Structural Outline of "Who'sit" [C Major]

Section	Instrumentation	Bars
Chorus 1	Ensemble	32
Chorus 2	Trombone Solo	32
Chorus 3	Slide Whistle and Clarinet Duet with Banjo	32
Chorus 4	Piano Solo / Clarinet Break	14 / 2
	Clarinet Solo / Clarinet Break	8 / 4
	Clarinet Solo / Cornet Break	2 / 2
Chorus 5	Ensemble / Cornet Break	8 / 4
(Last Half)	Ensemble / Cornet Break	2 / 2

The ensemble passages of the Hot Five's fourth session are precise and invigorating, particularly the final chorus of "Who'sit," which is preceded by a lively clarinet solo and introduced by a suspenseful cornet break on a sustained G followed by a rip (Example 5.6). Opening with a transposition of bar 28 from "I'm Gonna Gitcha" (Example 5.4) in bar 2, built entirely on

Example 5.6. Comparison of the Copyrighted Melody with Dodds's Solo in "Who'sit"

the changes, and delivered at a challenging tempo with commanding technique, Dodds's solo is, indeed, a miniature masterpiece. Particularly impressive is the stop-time break (mm. 11-14), in which two similar one-measure phrases of a filled-in major sixth are answered with a brilliant two-measure arpeggiation extending almost two octaves to the upper limits of the usable clarinet register before ending with the A - A♭ - G pattern with which it began.

Example 5.7. Slide Whistle and Clarinet Duet by Armstrong and Dodds in "Who'sit"

Rather than representing the weakest of the Hot Fives, as Panassié declared,[15] "Who'sit," composed by an otherwise unknown Beatrice Jones,[16] at the very least highlights the session. The nicely constructed, low-register clarinet obbligato to Armstrong's often derided slide whistle solo (Example 5.7) illustrates Dodds's fine ear for counterpoint against a sustained melody, already demonstrated in "High Society" with Oliver's Creole Band (Example 4.6). The low-register obbligato in particular became one of Dodds's trademarks, reaching its apotheosis in "Wolverine Blues" (recorded with "Jelly Roll" Morton on 10 June 1927). In that notable performance the clarinetist plays six thirty-two-bar choruses in two successive takes with virtually no literal duplication.

Dodds's "Who'sit" obbligato is unified by a constantly varied rhythmic motive of an eighth-note triplet followed by two eighth notes (introduced in m. 3), which sometimes occurs in diminution (as in mm. 7 and 10). The momentum flags only in a few spots when rhythms or the relative inactivity of the two parts coincide (as in mm. 12, 14, 18, and 24). The trill (m. 24), a device more at home in a marching band than in a jazz band, is rare for Dodds.

[15]Hugues Panassié, *Louis Armstrong* (New York: Charles Scribner, 1972), 72.

[16]The piece is attributed to Richard M. Jones by John Chilton in his liner notes to *Louis Armstrong: The Hot Fives,* Vol. I (CBS Records CK44049, 1988), but "Beatrice Jones" appears on the copyright deposit (see Appendix 1). It is not known whether she was related to Richard Jones; see Christopher Hillman and Roy Middleton, *Richard M. Jones: Forgotten Man of Jazz* (Tavistock, England: Cygnet Publications, 1997), 80. "Whoosit" on the copyright deposit was transposed into "Who'sit" on the label copy now in the Sony Archives.

The "Worst" of the Hot Fives

The four numbers from the Hot Five session a week later, on 23 June 1926, differ from each other as much as those from the preceding session were the same. Two of them contain spoken dialogue, perhaps inspired by the Hot Five's accompaniment of vaudeville stars Butterbeans and Susie five days earlier.[1] Beyond this similarity and in spite of Schuller's judgment that these pieces "constitute the nadir of Hot Five recording activity,"[2] two are unique in the Hot Five literature, and all vary widely in tempo, mood, style, and key.

"King of the Zulus"*

Table 6.1. Structural Outline of "King of the Zulus" [E Minor]

SECTION	INSTRUMENTATION	BARS
Chorus A1	Ensemble	18
Vamp	Rhythm	2
Chorus B1	Trombone Solo over Vamp	22
Interlude	Speech	
Vamp	Rhythm	2
Chorus A2	Cornet Solo	16
Chorus A3	Cornet Solo	16
Chorus A4	Banjo Solo	16
Chorus A5	Ensemble / Banjo Break	14 / 2
Tag	Banjo / Ensemble	1 / 1

"King of the Zulus," the first piece waxed at that June session, was dedicated to the King of the Zulus of 1926 [Joseph J. Smith], the elected leader of the black parody Mardi Gras parade in New Orleans.[3] The tune is the only Hot Five cast entirely in minor mode and employs only tonic

[1]Clarence Babcock, a Chicago vaudeville personality who played a chitlin'-lover from Jamaica in a "King of the Zulus" sketch, may have happened to be in the studio during the recording.

[2]Gunther Schuller, *Early Jazz: Its Roots and Musical Development* (New York: Oxford University Press, 1968), 102.

[3]Louis Armstrong, recorded commentary on *Satchmo: A Musical Autobiography* (Verve Records 314-543-822-2, 1957; reissued 2001). To his great satisfaction Armstrong himself was crowned King of the Zulus in 1949. Editor's Note: One of his "stepfathers" had been so honored in 1919, and among his proudest childhood memories was seeing his father Willie featured as the Grand Marshall in an Odd Fellows Lodge parade. See Thomas Brothers, *Louis Armstrong's New Orleans* (New York: W. W. Norton, 2006), 77-81.

and dominant harmonies throughout—ostensibly to depict its "primitive" or "jungle" character. It is similar in many respects to "Jelly Roll" Morton's "Jungle Blues" recorded by his Red Hot Peppers almost a year later. The soloists reinforce such a musical portrayal by constructing their solos almost exclusively of tonic triads and dominant seventh chords and by using the melodic progression, B - B♭ (blue fifth) - A - G - (F) - E, as a common cadence formula. Ory's unique twenty-two-bar solo over the minor vamp, one of his most rhythmically inventive, is indeed a double prolongation of this progression (Example 6.1). In the first half of his solo an extended B approached from the tonic below moves through B♭ - A - G - E (mm. 7-9). The second half recalls the first, except that B is approached by an extended tonic from above.

Example 6.1. Ory's Solo in "King of the Zulus"

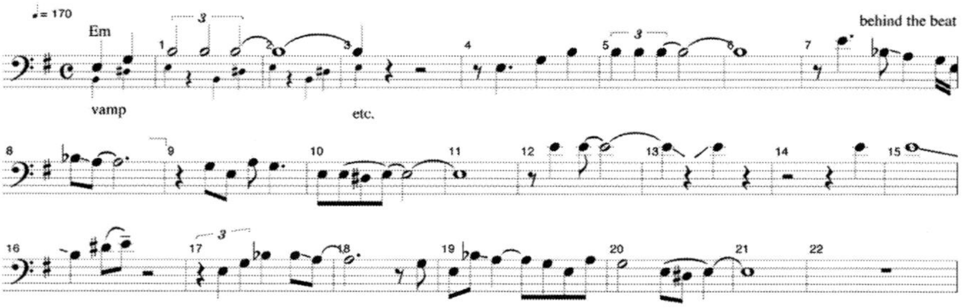

Armstrong appropriates these same structural ideas in his following pair of sixteen-bar choruses. Whereas Ory resolved the notes of the progression directly with no intervening pitches, Armstrong heightens melodic tension by embellishing and delaying their respective resolutions (Example 6.2). At its first appearance he spreads the dominant-to-tonic series over six bars (mm. 4-9), and at its second and third appearances, over three bars each (mm. 13-15 and 29-31). The pitch B on the staff serves as fulcrum for each phrase of the pivotal melody, which generally lies between this pitch and its lower octave for the first chorus and between this pitch and its upper octave for the second.

Armstrong's intuitive application of proportional or golden section relationships imposes a level of coherence beyond the organizational principles implied by Ory's solo.[4] Such relationships strongly suggest that

[4]Known to the Ancient Greeks as the "extreme-mean ratio" and evident in art and architecture since that time, so-called golden proportions are represented by dividing a line so that the ratio of the smaller unit (a) to the larger (b) equals the ratio of the larger unit to the whole: a / b = b / a + b. Although an irrational number like *pi*, the golden section of a line one unit long would be a approximately 0.612 of its length. For an introduction to golden section relationships in music, see Roy Howatt, "Bartok, Lendvai and the Principles of Proportional Analysis," *Music Analysis* 2/1 (1983), 69-95.

Armstrong conceived his solo as a whole rather than as two distinct units and might help explain the dramatic effect of the passage at the end of the first chorus and the beginning of the second (mm. 16-20). At this point in the solo, the excruciatingly long high G is relieved by his climactic rip to a high B, an arpeggiated descent to its lower octave, and the concluding rip to the tonic within the golden section of the combined choruses.[5]

Example 6.2. Armstrong's Solo in "King of the Zulus"

Following the pathos and the drama of Ory and Armstrong, St. Cyr's banjo solo (Example 6.3 on page 100) provides a welcome relief of tension. Uncomplicated rhythmically, harmonically, melodically, and formally, his blue-note-free interlude effectively introduces the final ensemble of cornet and clarinet in counterpoint over a cantus firmus by the trombone. Unfortunately, St. Cyr's arpeggiated break after the ensemble creates the opposite effect of his solo and leads to a ragged, weak, abrupt ending.

Lil's copyright deposit (Appendix 1), filed a month after the recording, appears to be a hastily-written outline of an intended performance rather than a transcription of a finished one. Most likely, the copyrighted lead sheet was used at the studio, where the title of the piece was changed from "Chief Bonco Boo," and its "chitlin' rag" hokum was improvised on the spot.[6] The essential aspects of the recording are present in the deposit,

[5]The golden section is bar 19.7 (32 x 0.618). For another consideration of the golden section in an Armstrong solo, see Gene Anderson, "Blues for You, Johnny: Johnny Dodds and His 'Wild Man Blues' Recordings of 1927 and 1928," *Annual Review of Jazz Studies* 8 (1996), 61.

[6]The vocal banter is transcribed in Frederic Ramsey, Jr., and Charles Edward Smith, *Jazzmen* (New York: Harcourt Brace Jovanovich, 1939; reprinted New York: Limelight Editions, 1985), 133. The

including the blue-note-tinged melodic progression discussed above. The rough approximation of Ory's solo suggests that Lil played it for him before the recording and that the trombonist's memory and imagination produced the final result. She might have done the same for Armstrong, who, nevertheless, plays only four bars before soaring off.

Example 6.3. St. Cyr's Solo in "King of the Zulus"

The Fearn Collection in the Armstrong Archives contains undated lyrics, presumably Lil's, titled "King of the Zulus—Blues":

Verse

Ah ha! Ah ha!
Hail to the King of the Zulu Isle
Where the Zulu Band plays wild.
Ah ha! Ah ha!
Now the band starts playin',
Maids start a-swayin'
To the tune they are playin';
So neat they can't be beat;
Watch them shakin' their feet.

Interlude

King of the Zulus,
Land of those Hulas,
Where the maids shake their bam-bo-las.

vaudeville rather than the musical aspects of "King of the Zulus" led John Chilton in Max Jones and John Chilton, *Louis: The Louis Armstrong Story, 1900-1971* (Boston: Little, Brown, 1971; reprinted New York: Da Capo Press, 1988), 260, to identify it as "probably the Hot Five's poorest recording."

On the Zulu Isle
They shake everything
For their mighty king
Of the Zulus
Cause they love to see him smile.

Chorus
When the king was crowned
They gathered 'round
And they sang their native song
Bo-la-bu, ya-kin-do.
In Zulu that means "I love you."
That same day the king did say
"Dance the Zulu blues away
For the King of the Zulu's blue."[7]

The connection of these lyrics to "King of the Zulus" proves problematic: only the first and fourth lines of the verse fit the melody of the copyright deposit or the recording. Perhaps they were written for publicity. "Hear the story of the famous Zulu King" trumpets a 30 October *Defender* ad announcing the recording's release on Hallowe'en Eve at a King of the Zulus Feast. (See Illustration 6.1 on the next page.)

Although never published, "King of the Zulus" was covered in New York by the Dixie Washboard Band for Columbia in late October and by the New Orleans Blue Five for Victor in early November. The former re-creation is the closer of the two, even down to rough reproductions of Hot Five solos. Although these recordings were made on or before the release of "King of the Zulus" in November (see Appendix 1), the leaders of both bands could boast of OKeh affiliations. Clarence Williams, the pianist-leader of the Dixie Washboard Band, and Tom Morris, cornetist-leader of the New Orleans Blue Five, were or had been exclusive OKeh artists. Williams, in particular, maintained a close affiliation with Chicago OKeh operations—appearing, for example, as a special guest at the OKeh Race Record Artists Night in February—so his access to an advanced pressing of "King of the Zulus" seems more than plausible.

[7]Fearn Collection (New York: Louis Armstrong Archives, Queens College).

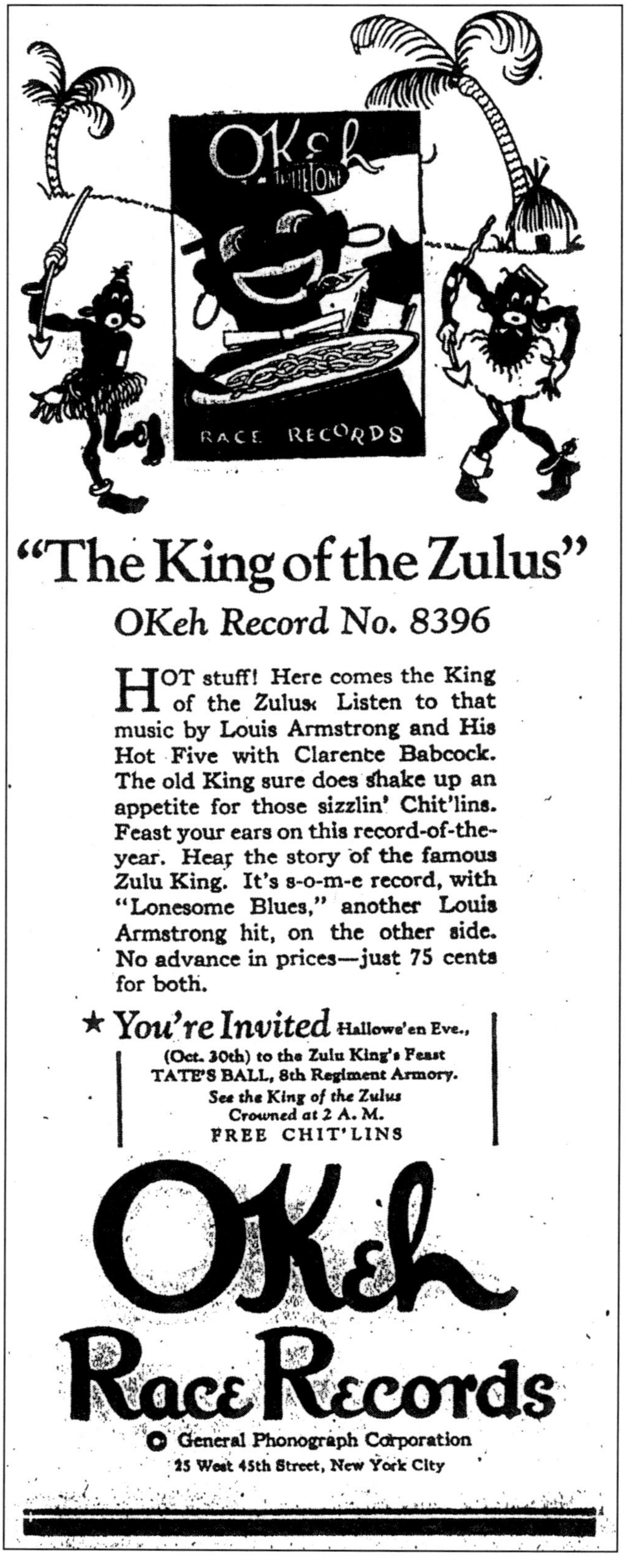

Illustration 6.1.
OKeh Ad for "The King of the Zulus"

From *Chicago Defender* (30 October 1926), 6.

"Big Fat Ma and Skinny Pa"

Table 6.2. Structural Outline of "Big Fat Ma and Skinny Pa" [E♭ Major]

SECTION	INSTRUMENTATION	BARS
Verse	Trombone / Speech / Trombone / Speech	4 / 4 / 4 / 4
Chorus 1	Ensemble	16
Chorus 2	Ensemble	16
Chorus 3	Clarinet Solo	16
Chorus 4	Louis's Vocal Solo	16
Chorus 5	Louis's Vocal Solo	16
Blues Chorus	Trombone Solo	12
Chorus 6	Ensemble	16

Whistling for attention and heralded by Ory's marching-band fanfare, Richard M. Jones exhorts "everybody to fall in line; grab your partner and get back on time" to begin his novelty number "Big Fat Ma and Skinny Pa."[8] But instead of a square dance, the pair's "dance you never saw" of Armstrong's lyrics involves the "cut-out" and the "pigeon-wing" and encourages everyone to "shake that thing."

Now big fat ma and skinny pa start dancin'
Ah, the latest steps with lotta pep so entrancin'
Ah, 'fore she cut-out or he do the pigeon-wing
Everybody starts singin' "Shake that thing!"
When big fat ma and skinny pa did dance, dance.
And big fat ma and skinny pa start dancin'
All the latest steps with lotta pep so entrancin'
Now, lookee here—[this grand old ma?] wants me to know
In every show to shake to start to shakin' some mo'
And big fat ma and skinny pa that's all—hi, hi!

Dodds intersperses the melody with characteristic break-like figures. After several sixteen-bar choruses, Ory turns in a vigorous twelve-bar blues solo that, intended or not, complements the stylistic pastiche of the tune

[8] Although the whistled and spoken introduction has been attributed to Clarence Babcock in most discographies, it is "clearly RMJ" according to Christopher Hillman and Roy Middleton, *Richard M. Jones: Forgotten Man of Jazz* (Tavistock, England: Cygnet Publications, 1997), 42.

but also exemplifies the want of melodic invention for which the trombonist has been often criticized (Example 6.4).[9]

Example 6.4. Ory's Solo in "Big Fat Ma and Skinny Pa"

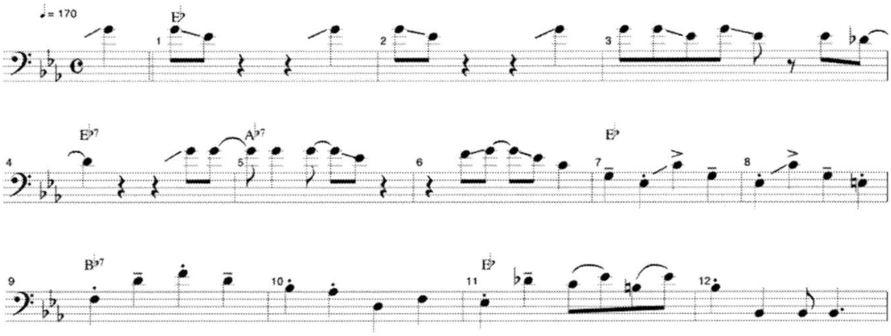

Illustration 6.2. Okeh Ad for "Big Fat Ma and Skinny Pa"

From *Chicago Defender* (23 October 1926), 7.

[9]André Hodeir, *Jazz, Its Evolution and Essence*, trans. David Noakes (New York: Grove Press, 1956; reprinted New York: Da Capo Press, 1975), 61.

"Lonesome Blues"

Table 6.3. Structural Outline of "Lonesome Blues" [B♭ Major]

Section	Instrumentation	Bars
Introduction	Piano	4
Chorus 1	Clarinet Solo	12
Chorus 2	Clarinet Solo	12
Chorus 3	Louis's Vocal Solo	12
Chorus 4	Louis's Vocal Solo	12
Chorus 5	Clarinet Solo / Ensemble	8 / 4

Lil's "Lonesome Blues" is the slowest number recorded by the Hot Five, whose tempos normally fall into the moderate-to-fast fox-trot range. After a portentous four-bar piano introduction, Dodds delivers a yearning solo uncharacteristically devoid of blue notes but boasting a striking melodic gesture (mm. 7-8): an augmented fifth to a major seventh (F♯ to A) against tonic harmony (Example 6.5). The almost exact repeat of the solo and a third repeat of it for the first eight bars of the final chorus prove it to be the actual "lead" or melody.[10] The number may have been concocted at the studio and, under the pressure of time, made as uncomplicated as possible.

Example 6.5. Dodds's Solo in "Lonesome Blues"

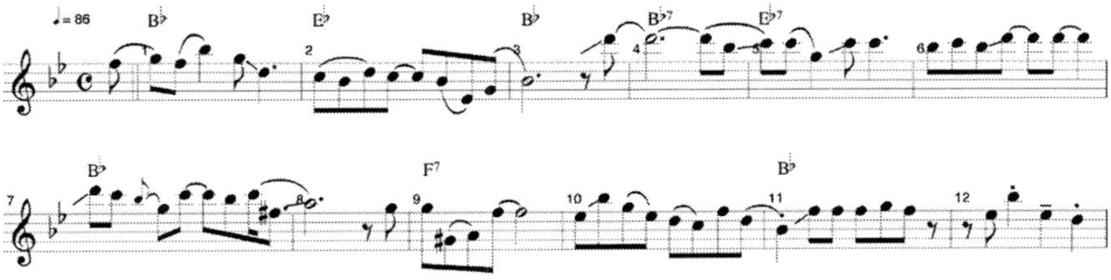

Brooks notices the "lifting" of Dodds's "Lonesome Blues" solo by Paul "Stump" Evans on soprano sax in "King" Oliver's recording of "Snag It" for Vocalion/Brunswick on 17 September 1926.[11] Evans's opening two bars are indeed almost identical to Dodds's solo; the remainder is rhythmically and melodically similar. Evans could not have appropriated the solo from

[10]The B♭ grace note in bar 7 is the melody note rather than the G in Dodds's subsequent statements of the tune.

[11]Edward Brooks, *The Young Louis Armstrong on Records: A Critical Survey of the Early Recordings, 1923-1928* (Lanham, MD: Scarecrow Press, 2002), 357.

the still unreleased Hot Five recording, but he could have learned it from Dodds himself, who was present at the "Snag It" session to replace Albert Nicholas on "Someday Sweetheart."[12]

The blue notes missing from Dodds's solo become the focus of Armstrong's vocal solo (Example 6.6). Disregarding the apparent melody, he establishes his solo's boundaries as the perfect fifth from the dominant F down to the tonic B♭ in the first phrase. Measures 1-7 of his first chorus (counting the pick-up bar) explore the expressive possibilities of the blue third (D♭), and bars 8-12, the expressive possibilities of the blue fifth (F♭). A restricted range and the downward motion from the dominant to the tonic typify the classic blues melody, which blues singers of Armstrong's era imbued with immediately-resolved blue notes in predictable locations. Armstrong's soulful delivery, however, is characterized by agonizingly prolonged resolutions, and his heartfelt moans (mm. 3-4 and 8) rival those of any of the blues queens he frequently accompanied.

Example 6.6. Armstrong's Vocal Solo in "Lonesome Blues"

12Walter Allen and Brian Rust, *"King" Oliver*, rev. Laurie Wright (Chigwell, Essex: Storyville, 1987), 66.

"Sweet Little Papa"*

Table 6.4. Structural Outline of "Sweet Little Papa" [F Major]

SECTION	INSTRUMENTATION	BARS
Introduction	Trombone / Ensemble	2 / 2
Verse	Trombone Solo / Trombone Break / Ensemble	12 / 2 / 2
Interlude	Cornet / Ensemble / Clarinet / Ensemble	2 / 2 / 2 / 2
Chorus 1	Ensemble / Clarinet Break / Ensemble	8 / 4 / 4
Chorus 2	Piano Solo / Ensemble Break / Piano Solo	8 / 4 / 4
Chorus 3	Trombone Solo / Tromb. Break / Tromb. Solo	8 / 4 / 4
Chorus 4	Cornet Solo / Cornet Break / Cornet Solo	8 / 4 / 4
Chorus 5	Ensemble / Banjo Break / Ensemble	8 / 4 / 4
Chorus 6	Ensemble / Cornet Break / Ensemble	8 / 4 / 4
Tag	Cornet / Ensemble	1 / 1

The antiquated style of "Kid" Ory's "Sweet Little Papa," a trombone feature with ragtime overtones like "Muskrat Ramble" and "Ory's Creole Trombone," suits his aggressive and unnuanced manner of playing. The opening trombone call and ensemble response around which the verse and interlude are built (Example 6.7, mm. 1-4, on the following page) present the F major / minor conflict of the piece, one that is not fully resolved in favor of F major until Armstrong's break in the tag (Example 6.8, on the next page). Armstrong prolongs Ory's flirtation with the relative minor during his break in the interlude (mm. 21-22), but Dodds sticks resolutely to F major during his (mm. 24-26), which he begins too soon and ends too late. The ensemble break in the piano solo (Example 10.2) continues the Hot Five's experiments with arranged enhancements that emerged in "I'm Gonna Gitcha" (Example 5.3) and reappeared in later pieces.

The three ensemble choruses are highlights of the piece, of which the first is typical (Example 6.9 on page 109). But after two contrapuntal phrases of four measures, the second and third phrases feature a repeated eighth-note figure in the trombone followed by four bars of stop-time break, and this chorus concludes with four contrapuntal bars recalling the first phrase. The counterpoint falters (mm. 3 and 6) when the clarinet plays in octaves with either the trombone or cornet, and the clarinet and cornet

Example 6.7. Ensemble Introduction, Verse, and Interlude of "Sweet Little Papa"

Example 6.8. Armstrong's Tag in "Sweet Little Papa"

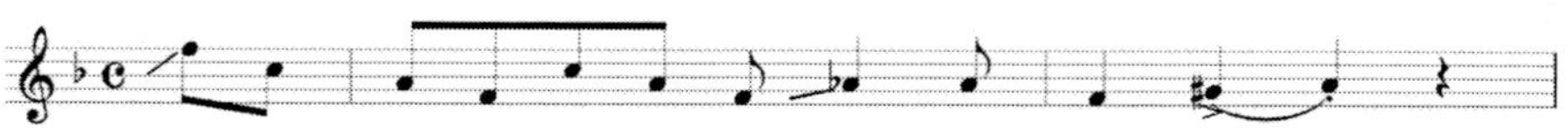

are slightly out of sync (m. 4). Dodds's "suicidal break"[13] (mm. 9-12) and Ory's and Armstrong's stop-time breaks[14] border on the spectacular, throwing into even greater relief their inconsequential trombone and cornet solos, which, in Ory's case (Example 6.10 on page 110), equals a

[13]André Hodeir, *Jazz, Its Evolution and Essence*, 60.

[14]Armstrong borrows his "Sweet Little Papa" break from his stop-time chorus in "Cornet Chop Suey" (see Example 4.8).

glorified ensemble part, and, in Armstrong's case (Example 6.11, also on page 110), offers a mildly embellished melody. St. Cyr's "perfectly useless" break[15] in the second chorus measures up neither technically nor emotionally to those by the other instrumentalists but remains, of course, "absolutely necessary" to maintain the a - a′ - b - a′′ form adopted for each chorus. Yet, "Sweet Little Papa" represents a stylistic milestone for Armstrong. The showy aspects of his performances that formerly stood out in sharp contrast to the rest of his playing—rips, embellishing shakes, flutter-tonguing, etc.—have now become integrated into his overall style.[16]

Example 6.9. First Ensemble Chorus of "Sweet Little Papa"

[15]André Hodeir, *Jazz, Its Evolution and Essence*, 61.

[16]Gunther Schuller, *Early Jazz*, 103.

Example 6.10. Ory's Solo in "Sweet Little Papa"

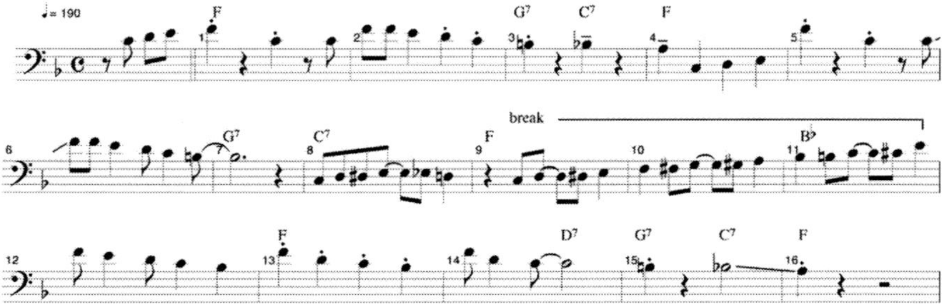

Example 6.11. Armstrong's Solo in "Sweet Little Papa"

Sunset Café Stomp

Over the summer of 1926 Armstrong continued his grueling schedule of doubling at the Vendome and the Sunset Café. Maintaining the facade of a happy couple despite their mutual marital indiscretions, Louis and Lil managed a two-week respite in mid-August at their Idlewild race resort lakefront property in Michigan. Armstrong relaxed with swimming and horseback-riding, activities his wife despised.[1]

With Dickerson's band at the Sunset Armstrong got the chance to hone his entertainment skills. "Big Butter and Egg Man" from the sixth Hot Five recording session on 6 November 1926, for example, was written by floor show producer Percy Venable as a routine for Armstrong and Mae Alix, a Chicago entertainer famous for her running splits across the dance floor while picking up dollar bills spread along the way.[2] Earl Hines, at the time Dickerson's pianist and Armstrong's closest friend, described Louis's debut as a variety entertainer:

> Louis had never had an opportunity to be out on the floor, and when he went out for the first time to sing with Mae Alix he was frightened, and he wasn't sure of his lyrics. Also, although she didn't know it, he really liked Mae, and that probably made him a bit nervous. A number called "Big Butter and Egg Man" had been written for them. . . . Now Mae was a very good-looking girl, and she really had a lot on the ball. . . . She knew Louis was timid and she just took advantage of him. On opening night, when Louis went out there, he forgot the lyrics and everything else. He was just looking at Mae. . . . He didn't know whether to sit down, stand up, or what, but Mae got a kick out of it and had fun with him, and the whole house cracked up. He got accustomed to it finally, but when she used to put her arms around him and look at him and sing "I need a big butter-and-egg man," he would stand there and almost melt, and everybody in the band would get up and shout, "Hold it, Louis! Hold it."[3]

[1] *Chicago Defender* (28 August 1926), 6; and Louis Armstrong, *Swing That Music* (New York: Longmans, Green, 1936; reprinted New York: Da Capo Press, 1993), 83-84.

[2] Louis Armstrong, *Louis Armstrong: In His Own Words*, ed. Thomas Brothers (New York: Oxford University Press, 1999), 55. A photograph of Alix appears in the *Chicago Defender* (5 May 1928), 7.

[3] Stanley Dance, *The World of Earl Hines* (New York: Scribner's, 1977; reprinted New York: Da Capo Press, 1983), 49.

In addition to singing and mugging, Louis, having done "his little dance" on tour with Oliver,[4] added the Charleston to Sunset performances:

> Percy Venable, the producer of the show, staged a finale with four of us band boys closing the show doing the Charleston. . . . There was Earl Hines, as tall as he is; [drummer] Tubby Hall, as fat as he was; [saxophonist] little Joe Walker, as short as he is; and myself, as fat as I was at the time. We would stretch out across that floor doing the Charleston as fast as the music would play it. Boy, oh boy, you talk about four cats picking them up and laying them down—that was us.[5]

The Sunset Café, a white-owned black and tan run by Joe Glaser, Armstrong's future long-term manager, was the most popular after-hours club on the Stroll frequented by whites.[6] Controlled by gangsters like all Chicago cabarets during Prohibition, it was a site of frequent violence. Police raids were so common, according to Earl Hines, that he would "run and get a seat" to avoid standing in the wagon on the way to the police station.[7] The club, nonetheless, attracted the top black vaudeville personalities and alternated floor shows with dancing. A 1926 publicity photograph shows a cavernous structure with approximately one-hundred tables and a large dance floor at the far end in front of a low bandstand.[8]

In August 1926 the *Defender* identified venues for twenty-nine local ensembles (see Illustration 7.1). Dave Peyton, its columnist on the jazz scene ("The Musical Bunch"), is listed as one of Armstrong's "rivals." His criticism of the cornetist and his Stompers may not have been unbiased.[9]

[4]Louis Armstrong, *In His Own Words*, 163.

[5]Nat Shapiro and Nat Hentoff, *Hear Me Talkin' To Ya: The Story of Jazz as Told by the Men Who Made It* (New York: Rinehart, 1955; reprinted New York: Dover Publications, 1966), 111.

[6]William Howland Kenney, *Chicago Jazz: A Cultural History, 1904-1930* (New York: Oxford University Press, 1993), 21.

[7]Earl Hines, quoted in Mike Pinfold, *Louis Armstrong: His Life and Times* (New York: Universe Books, 1987), 47. See also James Lincoln Collier, *Louis Armstrong: An American Genius* (New York: Oxford University Press, 1983), 151-53; and Stanley Dance, *The World of Earl Hines*, 46-47, 58-62.

[8]Stanley Dance, *The World of Earl Hines*, 44.

[9]See Chapter 8, 133-34 and 137. For more on Peyton and his views as a jazz critic, see Lawrence Schenbeck, "Music, Gender, and 'Uplift' in the *Chicago Defender*, 1927-1937," *The Musical Quarterly* 81/3 (Fall 1997), 348-49; John Lax, "Chicago's Black Jazz Musicians in the Twenties: Portrait of an Era," *Journal of Jazz Studies* 1/2 (June 1974), 113-17; and Thomas J. Hennessey, "The Black Chicago Establishment 1919-1930," *Journal of Jazz Studies* 2/1 (December 1974), 16-20.

Chicago Orchestras and Where They Play

Erskine Tate's orchestra—Vendome theater; 15 men; movie house.

Sammy Stewart's orchestra—Metropolitan theater; 12 men; movie house

George Smith's orchestra — Grand theater; 5 pieces; variety house.

Jimmy Bell's orchestra—Twentieth Century theater; seven men; movie house.

Walter Dyett's orchestra—Pickford theater; four men; movie house.

Clarence Jones' orchestra — Owl theater; seven men; movie house.

Carroll Dickerson's orchestra — Sunset cafe; 12 men; cabaret.

Joe Oliver's orchestra—Plantation cafe; 10 men; cabaret.

Charles Cooke's orchestra—Harmon's Dreamland dance hall; 12 men.

Charles Elgar's orchestra—Harmon's Arcadia dance hall; 12 men.

Wynne's orchestra — Virgil Williams' Dreamland; eight men; cabaret.

Brown's orchestra—D o w n t o w n club; eight men; cabaret.

Brown's orchestra — Blue Heron cafe; eight men; cabaret.

Roulett's orchestra — Jeffrey tavern; 10 men; cabaret.

Swift's orchestra — Beverly gardens; 10 men; roadhouse.

Goodwin's orchestra—Midway gardens; 10 men; dance hall.

Lovie Austin's orchestra—Monogram theater; two players.

Dave Peyton's orchestra — Opens Grand theater Sept. 6; seven men.

Lottie Hightower's o r c h e s t r a—Dance work.

Doc Watson's orchestra — Dance work.

Society Syncopators—Dance work.

The Metronones—Dance work.

Louie Armstrong's "Hot Five"—Recording.

Russell's Six—Recording.

Richard Jones' Three—Recording.

James F. Wade's orchestra—Club Alabam', New York; 10 men; cabaret.

Art Simms' orchestra—Wisconsin Roof; 10 men; dancing.

Robinson's orchestra — Kenwood Village; seven men; cabaret.

Stomp King and His Assassinators —Roadhouse; three men.

Illustration 7.1.
1926 Roster of Chicago Ensembles and Performance Venues

From *Chicago Defender* (7 August 1926), 7.

"Jazz Lips"*

Table 7.1. Structural Outline of "Jazz Lips" [F Major]

Section	Instrumentation	Bars
Introduction	Ensemble / Trombone Break	1 / 1
	Ensemble / Trombone Break	1 / 1
	Ensemble	4
Verse	Ensemble	16
Chorus 1	Ensemble Alternating with Trombone Breaks as in Introduction (4 Times)	32
Chorus 2-3	Ensemble (Last Halves)	16 / 16
Chorus 4	Series of Breaks with Ensemble	32
Chorus 5	Ensemble / Cornet Break	16 / 2
	Ensemble	8
	Breaks for Clarinet, Banjo, Trombone, Piano	2 / 2 / 2 / 2
Tag	Cornet / Ensemble	3 / 1

In many respects Lil's "Jazz Lips," also recorded at the sixth session, amounts to a recycled "Sweet Little Papa": the recurring trombone motive in "Jazz Lips" (Example 7.1, m. 2) mimics its opening lick (Example 6.7, m. 1), the cornet lead in the verse of "Jazz Lips" (Example 7.2) corresponds to a portion of its first chorus lead (Example 6.9, mm. 1-3), the keys of the two pieces are the same, their tempos and chord changes are similar, and their complex forms feature frequent breaks. "Jazz Lips," however, pushes these characteristics to the extreme—from a fast tempo to a frantic tempo, from a highly-arranged form to an overly-arranged form, and from breaks occupying a quarter of its length to breaks occupying a third of its length.

Unfortunately for the listener, the palpable excitement generated by the frenzied tempo, intricate arrangement, surfeit of breaks, and near-virtuosic playing may be offset by anxiety over the players' successful navigation of the piece. One such spot occurs in the partial third chorus (Example 7.3). Armstrong fluffs notes (mm. 11-12), and Ory seems to be lost until bar 9. After a tentative entrance (m. 5), he plays something in bar 6, although it is difficult to hear what. Armstrong's fingers get tangled in the second chorus (mm. 18-19), but earlier in the section he adds half-valve to his timbral palatte (first used in his solo on the verse of "You're Next") to accompany flutter-tonguing (introduced in verse of "Come Back Sweet Papa"). Nevertheless, given the numerous possibilities for mistakes of all kinds, the overall performance level of "Jazz Lips" is admirably high while its ending on a diminished triad (heard as a rootless tonic seventh) would become a jazz cliché.

Example 7.1. Bars 1-4 of the Introduction to "Jazz Lips"

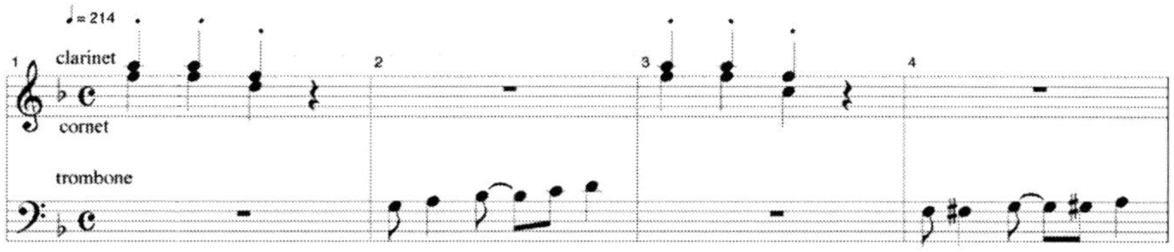

Example 7.2. Bars 1-4 of Armstrong's Lead in the Verse of "Jazz Lips"

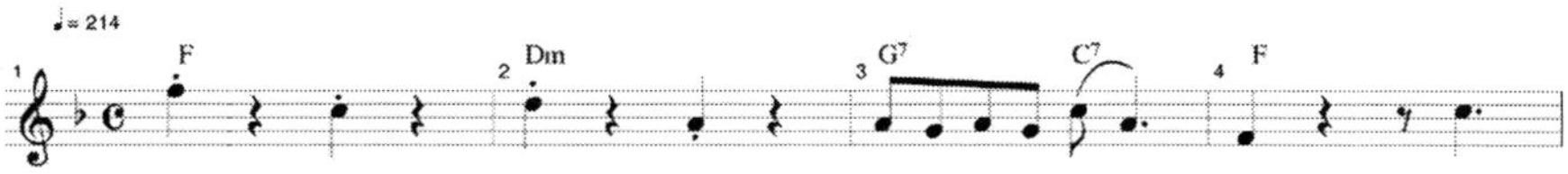

Example 7.3. Partial Third Chorus of "Jazz Lips"

"Skid-Dat-De-Dat"*

Table 7.2. Structural Outline of "Skid-Dat-De-Dat" [C Major]

SECTION	INSTRUMENTATION	BARS
Introduction	Cornet	2
Chorus 1	Ensemble / Cornet Break	4 / 2
	Ensemble / Trombone Break	8 / 2
	Ensemble / Clarinet Break	4 / 2
Chorus 2	Ensemble / Piano Break	4 / 2
	Ensemble / Clarinet Break	8 / 2
	Ensemble / Scat Break	4 / 2
Chorus 3	Clarinet Solo / Scat Break	4 / 2
	Trombone Solo / Clarinet Solo / Vocal Solo	4 / 4 / 2
	Clarinet Solo / Scat Break	4 / 2
Chorus 4	Ensemble / Trombone Break	4 / 2
	Ensemble / Cornet Break	8 / 2
	Ensemble / Scat Break-Tag	4 / 2

Although Lil conceived "Skid-Dat-De-Dat" to capitalize on the scatting success of "Heebie Jeebies,"[10] the piece should be perceived as unique in the quintet's repertory. Its peculiarities begin with an introductory, tonally ambivalent cornet solo that Gunther Schuller singled out as being far ahead of its time.[11] Strangely, the introduction does not sound that tonally ambivalent, and even less so in retrospect as the piece progresses. The reason for its perceived stability could be that Armstrong's introduction distills "Skid-Dat-De-Dat" to its melodic and harmonic essence. The "kernel," (G) - B♭ - A - G, provides the melodic framework for the piece, and the tonic (C) and subdominant (F) as triads and seventh chords (with and without blue notes) provide the harmonic framework (Example 7.4).[12]

Plagal harmonic relationships characterize the tune's main theme—a four-bar progression of C - Dm7 - Fm - C. Although obscured by the voice-leading of the melodic instruments, the Dm7 chord behaves like a subdominant with an added sixth rather than as a supertonic harmony.

[10]Louis Armstrong, *In His Own Words*, 133.

[11]Gunther Schuller, *Early Jazz: Its Roots and Musical Development* (New York: Oxford University Press, 1968), 106.

[12]Schuller's transcription has a repeated B♭ rather than an A dotted-quarter. The final F in parentheses indicates that it is implied rather than sounded on the recording.

This reassessment reduces the progression to I - IV (embellished with a major sixth and minor third) - I (Example 7.5). Seventh-chord versions of these harmonies (F7 and C7) extend the main theme (mm. 13-16, 35-38, 57-60, and 79-82). (See Example 7.6 on the following page).

Example 7.4. Harmonic and Melodic Implications of Armstrong's Introduction to "Skid-Dat-De-Dat"

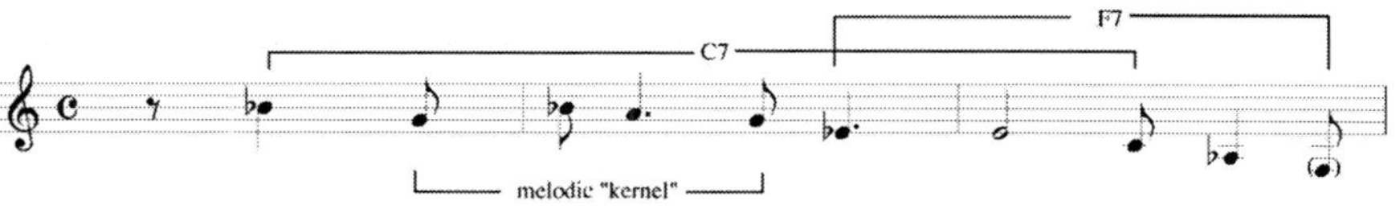

Example 7.5. Harmonic and Voice-Leading Reduction of the Theme of "Skid-Dat-De-Dat"

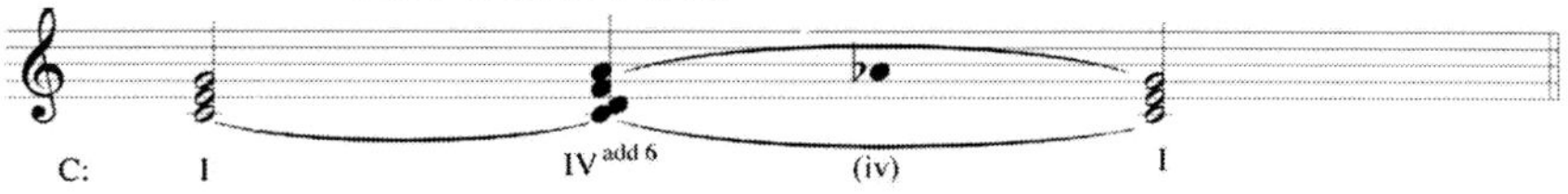

Throughout "Skid-Dat-De-Dat," Armstrong's introduction acts as his personal *leitmotiv*, neither borrowed from nor referenced by any of the other players. Louis recalls it in his first two vocal breaks (mm. 45-46 and 51-52) and in his vocal tag, which is adjusted to end on tonic. Otherwise, the kernel permeates his cornet leads in its original form (mm. 14-16, 37-38, and 81) or transposed up a fourth (mm. 7, 12-13, 34-35, and 71). One other appearance—against F minor harmony (m. 77)—presents a rare example of a missed chord change.

Schuller's invidious comparisons between the performances of the leader and his sidemen in "Skid-Dat-De-Dat" are not without validity.[13] Ory, in particular, stubbornly plays the same break over and over (mm. 17-18, 67-68, and 73-74), even incorporating it into his solo (mm. 53-56), which is further marred by wrong chord changes and the premature entrance by Dodds. The clarinetist's breaks and solos with their blue thirds and occasional bursts of technique may be more inventive than Ory's, but Lil's break (mm. 29-30)—rhythmically square, free of blue notes, and emphasizing the only dominant (G) harmonies of the piece—seems the most out of place.

The form of "Skid-Dat-De-Dat," though, may be its most original feature. Armstrong's motivically-related breaks and leads provide one

[13]Gunther Schuller, *Early Jazz*, 105.

Example 7.6. Line Score of "Skid-Dat-De-Dat"

stratum of coherence, but the opening chorale-like theme (mm. 3-6) acts as the structural glue binding all parts into an architechtonic whole. Each statement of the theme (A) and its four-bar extension (A′) concludes with a break in tonic harmony—with partial exception of the piano (m. 30). These original and extended thematic statements with their punctuating breaks are symmetrically organized into four twenty-two-bar "choruses" of A - break, A′ - break, A - break in groupings of 6 + 10 + 6 bars.[14]

"Skid-Dat-De-Dat" is the Hot Five's most structured work. As argued above, the introduction, which returns to end the piece, embodies its quintessence—the source of its melodic and harmonic content, which, in turn, is absolutely minimal. In the hands of mediocre musicians, interest dependent on a single constantly repeated theme supported by only two alternating harmonies would be arduous to maintain. Armstrong and the Hot Five perform the minor miracle of balancing musical expectation and fulfillment, however, by contrasting the formidable unities of melody, harmony, and form with imaginative varieties of rhythm, timbre, and texture.

[14]For a different interpretation of the form, see Edward Brooks, *The Young Louis Armstrong on Records: A Critical Survey of the Early Recordings, 1923-1928* (Lanham, MD: Scarecrow Press, 2002), 342-43. Joshua Berrett perceives echoes of the four-note theme that opens the finale of Mozart's "Jupiter" Symphony in the recurring four-bar units of "Skid-Dat-De-Dat"; see his *Louis Armstrong & Paul Whiteman: Two Kings of Jazz* (New Haven: Yale University Press, 2004), 73.

"Big Butter and Egg Man"*

Table 7.3. Structural Outline of "Big Butter and Egg Man" [G Major]

SECTION	INSTRUMENTATION	BARS
Chorus 1	Ensemble	32
Chorus 2	Vocal Solo (Alix)	32
Chorus 3	Vocal Solo (Louis)	32
Interlude	Piano	4
Chorus 4	Cornet Solo	32
Chorus 5 (Last Half)	Vocal Solo (Alix) / Ensemble	8 / 8

Armstrong's solo on "Big Butter and Egg Man" has long been hailed as among his best. Trumpeter Francis "Muggsy" Spanier, who later reproduced the solo note-for-note on a recording with his Ragtime Band, was among its earliest admirers:

> Another of the thrills in my life was when Louis asked (or allowed me, I should say) to sit in and play. Well, just no one in the world can play it ["Big Butter and Egg Man"] like Louis, and no one in the world can improve on the way he plays it, so I'm frank to say that as nearly as possible (because I heard him play it so much and listened so intently) I've always tried to do those famous breaks as Louis did them.[15]

André Hodeir lavished the solo with critical praise thirty years later:

> In this record, Armstrong manages to transfigure completely a theme whose vulgarity might well have overwhelmed him; and yet his chorus is only a paraphrase. The theme is not forgotten for a moment; it can always be found there, just as it was originally conceived by its little-known composer, Venable. Taking off melodically from the principal note of the first phrase, the soloist begins with a triple call that disguises, behind its apparent symmetry, subtle differences in rhythm and expressive intensity. This entry by itself is a masterpiece; it is impossible to imagine

[15]Francis "Muggsy" Spanier, "Louis My Idol and Inspiration," *Down Beat* 17/14 (14 July 1950), 4. Spanier plays Louis's solo on his 1939 recording of "Big Butter and Egg Man." Trumpeter Joseph "Wingy" Manone recreates Mae Alix's and Louis's vocals (but not Armstrong's cornet solo) on his 1930 recording of the number with Barbecue Joe and His Hot Dogs.

anything more sober and balanced [Example 7.7, mm. 1-7]. During the next eight bars [mm. 8-15], the paraphrase spreads out, becoming freer and livelier. Armstrong continues to cling to the essential notes of the theme, but he leaves more of its contour to the imagination. At times he gives it an inner animation by means of intelligent syncopation repetitions, as in the case of the first note of the bridge [m. 17]. From measures 20 to 23, the melody bends in a chromatic descent that converges toward the theme while at the same time giving a felicitous interpretation of the underlying harmonic progression. This brings us to the culminating point of the work. Striding over the traditional pause of measures 24-25, Armstrong connects the bridge to the final section by using a short, admirably inventive phrase. Its rhythmic construction of dotted eighths and sixteenths forms a contrast with the more static context in which it is placed, and in both conception and execution it is a miracle of swing. During this brief moment, Louis seems to have foreseen what modern conceptions of rhythm would be like. In phrasing, accentuation, and the way the short note is increasingly curtailed and finally it is merely suggested (m. 25), how far removed all this is from New Orleans rhythm!

This astonishing chorus is a perfect example of the phenomenon of "transformation without sacrifice of fidelity" in which subsequent jazz has abounded. Even more important, [excluding piano solos] it is perhaps the first example of a typically individual esthetic conception to be found in the history of recorded jazz.[16]

For Schuller, who provides a transcription with his commentary, the solo is a summation of Armstrong's capacity at this stage of his career and "displays his intuitive grasp of musical logic and continuity, coupled with an imaginative sense of variation."[17] Like Hodeir, he singles out the opening "triple call" for special recognition—"no composer, not even a Mozart or a Schubert, composed anything more natural and simply inspired"—and cites the "astonishing swing" of bar 24 as the high point

[16]André Hodeir, *Jazz, Its Evolution and Essence*, trans. David Noakes (New York: Grove Press, 1956; reprinted New York: Da Capo Press, 1975), 56-57.

[17]Gunther Schuller, *Early Jazz*, 103-05. Because his transcription is cast in F major rather than G, the names of notes and harmonies have been adjusted accordingly in the quotation of Schuller's analysis.

Example 7.7. Comparison of Armstrong's Lead, Alix's Solo, and Armstrong's Solo in "Big Butter and Egg Man"

of the solo. He calls attention to

> the repeated use of the melodic-rhythmic component [of an eighth note followed by a dotted quarter] . . . in measures seven, nine, fifteen, and nineteen and its rhythmic variant in measure 10. What is interesting is that in each instance the phrase is completed in a different manner. Diversity is combined with identity and repetition.
>
> The bridge [mm. 17-24] is certainly the imaginative climax of the solo. First there are repeated *d*'s (measure sixteen), making use initially of the alternate-fingering effect available to brass players, then elongating this into quarter-note triplets. The chord progression shifts to C [m. 19], but in measure twenty Louis returns unexpectedly to the *d* with which be started the bridge, now the ninth of the chord, initiating a superbly syncopated descending chromatic line.[18]

A recent study by Brian Harker generally supports Hodeir's and Schuller's analyses of Armstrong's solo but in even greater depth and finer detail.[19] Of particular interest is Harker's identification of the descending pitches, B - A - G - E - D, derived from the fourth phrase of the melody (mm. 13-16), as a "kernel" or unifying device. The kernel in retrograde (minus A) forms the anacrusis to each of the "triple calls," while their "answer" (mm. 6-7) and the following two four-bar phrases (mm. 8-11 and 12-15) present increasingly complete versions of the original kernel, though adding an F♯ to balance the previously missing A.[20] For Harker, proof that the kernel "truly governs" the first half of the solo is its final and most concise appearance in bar 25 at the return of A (mm. 1-8). He concludes his insightful analysis with the following observation:

[18] *Ibid.*

[19] Brian Harker, "'Telling A Story': Louis Armstrong and Coherence in Early Jazz," *Current Musicology* 63 (1999), 66-76. Harker, like Schuller, considers the piece to be in F. Requisite changes to G are made for the discussion of his study.

[20] Basically unaffected, Harker's argument for a governing kernel would have been strengthened by using an accurate version of the melody, which, in the absence of the copyright deposit, must be based on Armstrong's lead to the first chorus and Mae Alix's vocal. Both contain an F♯ in bar 14, which is missing in Harker's transcription. The kernel would thus be a descending major hexachord rather than a descending pentatonic scale, thereby eliminating the need for additions.

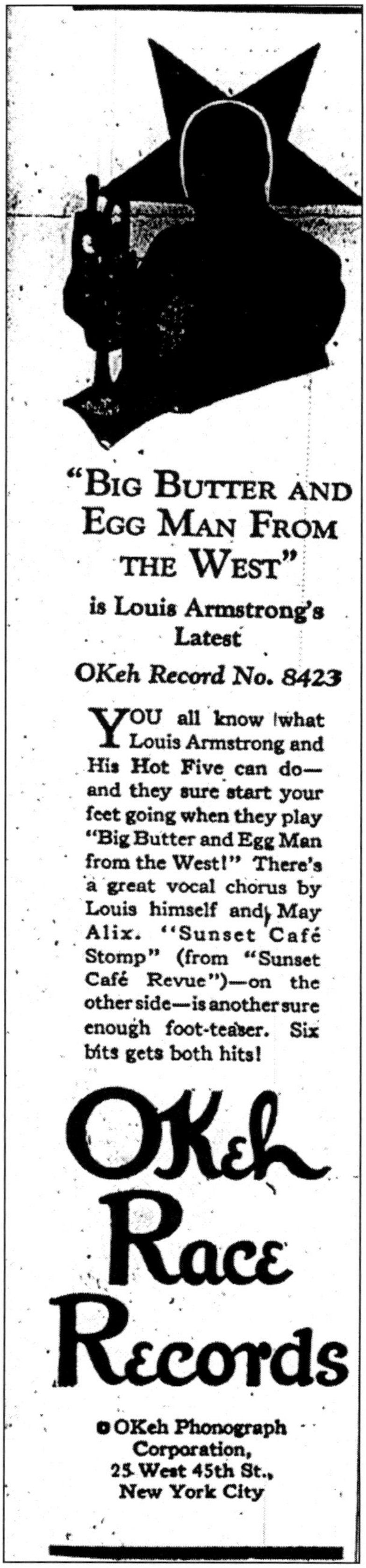

Illustration 7.2. OKeh Ad for "Big Butter and Egg Man from the West"

From *Chicago Defender* (8 January 1927), 7.

> Armstrong's approximately reverse approach to his material—choosing a melodic fragment from the end of a section, beginning with retrograde forms, and saving the most transparent paraphrase for the middle of the solo—counters traditional assumptions that jazz variations move from the familiar to the abstract.[21]

While Armstrong's "Big Butter and Egg Man" solo may be a model of originality, it should not be overlooked that several of its principal ideas, rather than springing from mid-air, emanate from his first chorus lead (Example 7.7). Besides bars 15 and 32 being exact repetitions of each other, bars 4-5 of the lead supply the model for the solo's "triple call." The ghosted-note passage in bar 24, so admired by Hodeir and Schuller, is heralded in the lead (m. 31), and its shape is foreshadowed in Mae Alix's solo (m. 24). Even in the portions of the solo most clearly derived from the melody certain decorative rhythmic and melodic aspects from the lead appear (as in mm. 8-11, 13-14, and 22). This cross-fertilization of musical ideas suggests that Armstrong's concept of coherence extended beyond his solos to the works as a whole—that to understand his solos fully, his leads and the solos of other players (as in "Gut Bucket Blues") need to be taken into account.

[21] Brian Harker, "'Telling a Story,'" 68.

"Sunset Café Stomp"

Table 7.4. Structural Outline of "Sunset Café Stomp" [B♭ Major]

Section	Instrumentation	Bars
Introduction	Piano / Clarinet	6 / 2
Chorus 1	Ensemble	34
Verse	Cornet Solo	20
Chorus 2	Vocal Solo (Alix)	34
Chorus 3	Ensemble / Clarinet Break	6 / 2
	Ensemble / Trombone Break	6 / 2
	Ensemble	18
Chorus 4 (Last 10 Bars)	Cornet / Ensemble	4 / 6
Tag	Cornet / Ensemble	2 / 2

A second Venable composition, "Sunset Café Stomp," concludes the Hot Five's sixth recording episode. Like "Georgia Grind" and "Heebie Jeebies," it celebrates a dance and, like "Big Butter and Egg Man," it was written for floor shows at the Sunset Café. Armstrong's solo on the twenty-bar verse seems to follow the melody as does Mae Alix's thirty-four-bar vocal chorus (Example 7.8). At first hearing, the introduction appears to have nothing in common with the piece, but examination discloses the

Example 7.8. Alix's Solo in "Sunset Café Stomp"

piano portion to be based on the first two bars of the melody and the clarinet break to introduce its most prominent blue note, D♭ (Example 7.9). The introductory gestures, moreover, incorporate a chromatic version of Ory's trombone motive from "Jazz Lips."

Example 7.9. Introduction to "Sunset Café Stomp"

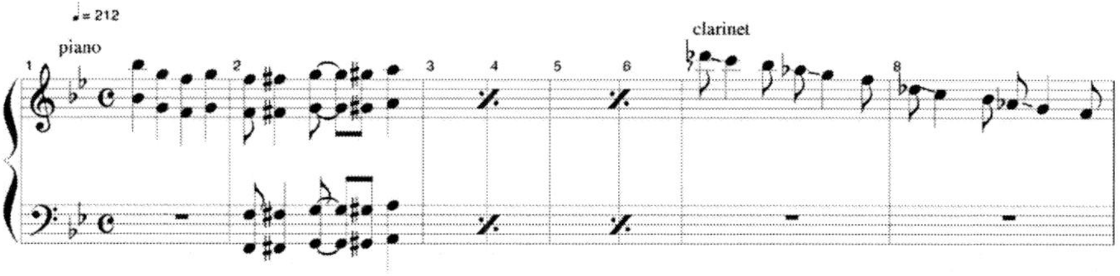

Dodds's otherwise admirable ensemble playing lapses in the first chorus, where he misses or ignores the Charleston rhythms (mm. 8-9) and neglects to provide the customary clarinet fill (m. 28). Ory recycled his hemiola break in the final chorus, one of his best, from the recording of Morton's "Black Bottom Stomp" two months earlier (Example 7.10).[22] The arranged stop-time-like ending of "Sunset Café Stomp," like arranged breaks in other numbers, exemplifies attempts by the players to bring their music up to date.

Example 7.10. Ory's Third-Chorus Break in "Sunset Café Stomp"

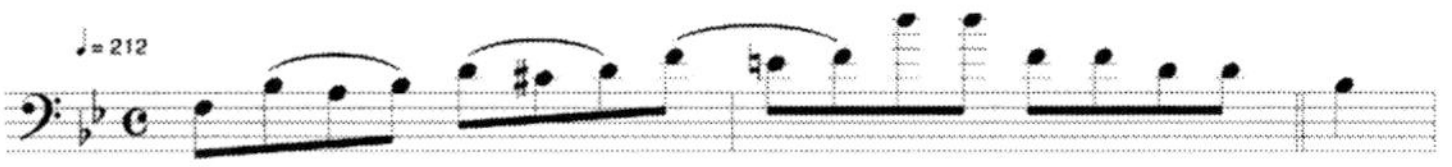

Two more compositions by Venable, additional floor show vehicles for Armstrong at the Sunset, and another by Paul Barbarin were waxed during the final Hot Five studio visit of the year on 27 November 1926. With the exception of Venable's novelty number, "Irish Black Bottom," which survives in the repertories of revival and trad bands, the session counts among the Original Hot Five's less memorable. "You Made Me Love You," the other Venable tune, qualifies as the most obscure recording by the ensemble, and OKeh rejected Barbarin's "Leave Mine Alone." Henry "Hy" Clark's substitution for Ory, absent for unknown reasons, contributes to the session's mediocrity. Clark was probably recruited by Richard M. Jones, who later hired him for a session with his Jazz Wizards.[23]

[22]Ory's "Black Bottom Stomp" break outlines a B♭ seventh chord rather than a B♭ triad.

[23]Christopher Hillman and Roy Middleton, *Richard M. Jones: Forgotten Man of Jazz* (Tavistock, England: Cygnet Publications, 1997), 48. On Clark's presence at the Hot Five session, see "Afterthoughts," *Storyville* 48 (August-September 1973), 240.

"You Made Me Love You"*

Table 7.5. Structural Outline of "You Made Me Love You" [C Major]

SECTION	INSTRUMENTATION	BARS
Introduction	Cornet / Ensemble	1 / 1
Chorus 1	Ensemble	32
Chorus 2	Trombone Solo / Clarinet Break	14 / 2
	Clarinet Solo / Vocal Break (Louis)	14 / 2
Chorus 3	Vocal Solo (Louis)	32
Interlude	Piano	8
Chorus 4	Cornet Solo / Cornet Break	14 / 2
	Ensemble	16

The maudlin lyrics of "You Made Me Love You" suggest a romantic ballad rather than the spirited stomp into which the Hot Five attempt to transform it. Armstrong's raspy vocal contradicts the song's tender message (Example 7.11), and his ensemble lead lacks its usual melodic, rhythmic, and timbral subtlety. Save for the trademark rip (m. 31), he avoids dipping into his "bag" of idiomatic cornetisms and adopts—more than in any of his Hot Five leads heretofore—a harsh, clipped, almost staccato articulation from beginning to end.

Uninteresting though his lead may be in most respects, Armstrong maintains a modicum of variety by avoiding literal repetition upon each return of the opening phrase (mm. 5-8 and 17-20).[24] The same holds true for his vocal solo but with fewer pitches and within a more restricted range. Conversely, Clark's solo, plagued by faulty intonation, thrives on repetition and obstinate adherence to the melody, while Dodds's solo, despite the stock figures (mm. 15-16, 25, and 30) exhibits comparatively more invention and creativity.

[24]Armstrong's paraphrases that stay close to the melody embody what Lawrence Gushee calls an "ethic of variation" learned from Joe Oliver, in which literal repetition is avoided. The slightly varied and nuanced lines may be analytically uninteresting but "deeply satisfying to hear"; see Lawrence Gushee, "The Improvisation of Louis Armstrong," *In the Course of Performance: Studies in the World of Musical Improvisation*, ed. Bruno Nettl (Chicago: University of Chicago Press, 1998), 292. See also Example 4.12.

Example 7.11. Comparison of Armstrong's First-Chorus Lead, Clark's Solo, Dodds's Solo, and Armstrong's Vocal Solo in "You Made Me Love You"

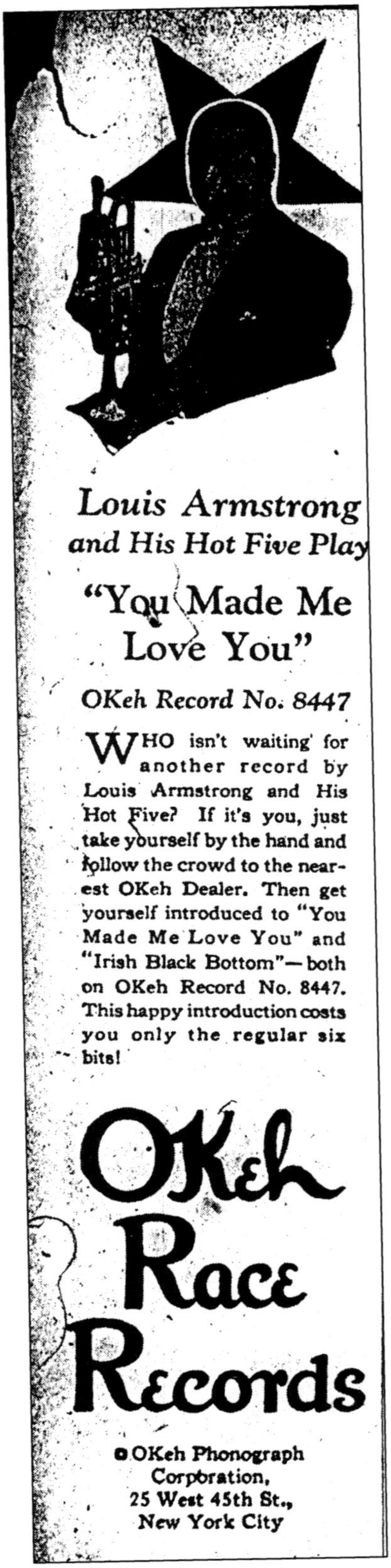

Illustration 7.3.
OKeh Ad for
"You Made Me
Love You"

From *Chicago Defender*
(2 April, 1927), 9.

"Irish Black Bottom"

Table 7.6. Structural Outline of "Irish Black Bottom" [F Major]

SECTION	INSTRUMENTATION	BARS
Introduction	Ensemble	8
Chorus 1	Ensemble	32
Interlude	Piano	6
Verse	Vocal Solo (Louis)	16
Chorus 2	Vocal Solo (Louis)	32
Chorus 3	Piano Solo / Trombone Solo / Clarinet Solo	4 / 4 / 4
	Ensemble / Cornet Solo	2 / 2
	Ensemble	16
Coda	Ensemble	4

"Irish Black Bottom" establishes its ethnic credentials in the initial ensemble lead by means of Scotch snap rhythms and a vague melodic reference to "Wearing of the Green," while pentatonicism implied by an avoidance of the fourth scale degree (B♭) prolongs the Irish folk song conceit into the chorus (Example 7.12). The "Black Bottom" of the title refers to a dance that rivaled the Charleston in popularity during the mid-twenties. Familiar to the southern black community since early in the century, it crossed over to the general public by virtue of Ann Pennington's

Example 7.12. Armstrong's Lead in the Introduction and First Chorus of "Irish Black Bottom"

performance of the "Black Bottom" by DeSylva, Brown, and Henderson in George White's *Scandals of 1926*.[25] But there is no hint of the DeSylva, Brown, and Henderson tune in "Irish Black Bottom," which features Armstrong speech-singing the following lyrics:

Verse

All you heard for years in Ireland
Was the wearin' of the green;
But the biggest change that's come in Ireland
I have ever seen
All the laddies and cooies ["colleens"?]
Laid aside their Irish reels;
And I was born in Ireland,
So imagine how I feels.

Chorus

Now Ireland's gone Black Bottom crazy.
See them dance, you oughta see 'em dance.
Folks supposed to be related
Even dance, I mean they dance.
They play that strain;
Works right on their brain.
Now it's called Black Bottom,
A new rhythm drivin' the folks insane.
I hand you no blarney
When I say that song really goes.
And they put it over
With a wow—I mean now!
All over Ireland
You can see the people dancin' it
'Cause Ireland's gone Black Bottom crazy now.

[25]Marshall Stearns and Jean Stearns, *Jazz Dance: The Story of American Vernacular Dance* (New York: Macmillan, 1968; reprinted New York: Da Capo Press, 1994), 110-11. *Scandals* opened in New York City's Apollo Theater on 14 June 1926 and ran until 18 June 1927; see Richard C. Norton, *A Chronology of American Musical Theater*, 3 vols. (New York: Oxford University Press, 2002), II, 448. Photographs of Pennington illustrating steps to the Black Bottom appear in Virginia Swain, "The Dance That Set America Wiggling," *McClure's* 58/4 (April 1927), 42-43, 120-21. In the same article, Perry Bradford, composer of "The Original Black Bottom Dance" in 1919, claimed that the Black Bottom was first danced on Broadway by Ethel Ridley in the 1923 black revue *Dinah*. For a video of the Black Bottom dance, see Carol Téten, *Dancetime!*, Vol. 2 (Kentfield, CA: Dancetime Publications, 1998).

CHAPTER 8

Modulation

After being sidelined by a "severe cold" during the first part of December, Louis Armstrong returned to his old jobs at the Vendome and Sunset.[1] But the relative stability of his life was over, for the new year would prove to be the most eventful of his early career. Although he may not have been aware of them, social changes initiated by urban reformers set in motion more than a year before would lead to the eventual closing of South Side cabarets and the passing of Chicago's fabled Jazz Age by the end of the decade.[2] In actions symptomatic of these changes, the police raided the Sunset and other South Side black and tans over the 1926 Christmas and 1927 New Year's holidays. Sunset manager Joe Glaser was arrested and fined for allowing black and white patrons to mix and indulge in "indecent exhibitions of dancing."[3]

Probably during the cornetist's absence or shortly after his return to work, Glaser fired Dickerson for his alleged heavy drinking and turned the Sunset orchestra over to his star attraction.[4] With Armstrong as front-man and Earl Hines as music director, the band—reborn as Louis Armstrong's Stompers—received a blistering review laced with unsolicited "advice" for the new leader by black establishment music critic and rival band leader of the previous generation, Dave Peyton:

> Louis Armstrong, the Race's hottest jazz cornetist, has his own orchestra of 12 players doing their stuff nightly in one of Chicago's night life resorts. Louis knows how to play the cornet and he plays it well, but he should let orchestras alone. It takes leaders of experience and technical knowledge to handle musicians

[1] *Chicago Defender* (4 December 1926), 7, and (25 December 1926), 6.

[2] William Howland Kenney, *Chicago Jazz: A Cultural History, 1904-1930* (New York: Oxford University Press, 1993), 148.

[3] *Variety* (19 January 1927), 47. Glaser was later charged with "mistreating a 14-year-old school girl"; see *Variety* (2 March 1927), 47, and *Variety* (23 March 1927), 49. For more on this incident and Glaser's other troubles with the law, see James. L. Dickerson, *Just for a Thrill: Lil Hardin, First Lady of Jazz* (New York: Cooper Square Press, 2002), 109-11.

[4] Stanley Dance, *The World of Earl Hines* (New York: Scribner's, 1977; reprinted New York: Da Capo Press, 1983), 47. In early January Dickerson and his "new orchestra" were playing at Chicago's White City Ballroom three nights a week as announced in the *Chicago Defender* (8 January 1927), 6. Max Jones and John Chilton, *Louis: The Louis Armstrong Story, 1900-1971* (Boston: Little, Brown, 1971; reprinted New York: Da Capo Press, 1988), 117-18, cite Chicago trombonist Preston Jackson's claim that Dickerson's firing was spurred by complaints of the band leader's unsolicited attention to Bebe Daniels, a movie-star patron of the Sunset. See also Frank Driggs and Harris Lewine, *Black Beauty, White Heat: A Pictorial History of Classic Jazz, 1920-1950* (New York: William Morrow, 1982; reprinted New York: Da Capo Press, 1995), 65.

nowadays. He must deal fair at all times and tell the truth regardless of who it hits. This orchestra of Louis's is way out of gear. It is noisy, corrupt, contemptible, and displeasing to the ear. You have to put your ear muffs on to hear yourself talk in the place. Louis will learn in time to come that noise isn't music. He should hire a capable violin director with experience who knows expression and orchestral conduct, and with the material he has in his line-up, the band could be whipped into efficient shape. I am criticizing this organization without malice or jealousy, with the ardent hope that they will take heed and remedy the many defects that now predominate the orchestra.[5]

Armstrong's recording activity, of which the Hot Fives represented only a portion, continued unabated. In addition to twenty-four Hot Five titles since arriving in the Windy City, he had participated in thirty-seven more, mostly under the names of blues artists like Bertha "Chippie" Hill, Blanche Calloway, Hociel Thomas, and Beulah "Sippie" Wallace. He occasionally violated his exclusive contract with OKeh by recording with rival companies.[6] On such dates Armstrong "disguised" his presence, although the attempted duplicity—transparent to modern ears—likewise fooled none of his contemporaries. Sometime after cutting "Wild Man Blues" with Johnny Dodds's Black Bottom Stompers for Brunswick in late April 1927, Armstrong received a call from E. A. Fearn:

In those days, I mean, we didn't take recording that serious, I mean, we thought it just like another gig, say, for instance, we playin' at the Country Club tonight and Johnny Dodds might have the Pickwick Club in New Orleans. So he say well, "Come on man. I'm goin' to play this job. You play this with me and just disguise yourself, you know, as far as your playin' and your tone. . . ." That's what he did on that recording. So when I say, "Well, Johnny, I don't think I oughta do this here," but [Johnny said] "I'll give you so much [money]." [Armstrong said] "Oh, let's see, maybe I can." I went in there, man, and when the record

[5]Dave Peyton, "The Musical Bunch," *Chicago Defender* (19 March 1927), 6. A rare photograph of Armstrong's Stompers at the Sunset is found in *Down Beat* 10/24 (15 December 1943), 28.

[6]Armstrong's relationship with OKeh was confirmed in a letter from Tommy Rockwell to E. A. Fearn on 7 January 1927: "It is our understanding that Armstrong himself will not make records for any company other than our own organization, or, as a part of any other musical unit." The letter, held in the Fearn Collection of the Armstrong Archives at Queens College in New York City, is reproduced in the booklet accompanying Sony's *Complete Hot Five and Hot Seven Recordings*, 30.

> came out, Mr. Fearn—he's a very nice fella [with] a big sense of humor, you know—he called me up that morning he bought this record. He say, "Satch, come on down. I got a nice tune I want ya to hear." "Be right down, boss." [After listening Armstrong said] "You know I didn't do that."[7]

Shortly before the Black Bottom Stompers' recording date, Peyton had announced the publication of two books devoted to Armstrong's music: *50 Hot Choruses for Cornet* and *125 Jazz Breaks for Cornet*. Even allowing for advertising hyperbole, the anonymous foreword to *50 Hot Choruses* testifies to Armstrong's already established fame and influence:

> Throughout the world the name of Louis Armstrong is known to thousands of musicians. It is a byword with the interpretation of jazz and commands at all times a place of honor. During the past few years jazz music has come into international vogue. Armstrong was among the pioneer proponents that brought it into popularity and has been a big factor in keeping it to the front. His influence is felt everywhere. Hundreds of jazz cornetists . . . have adopted the Armstrong style of playing. Many of the greatest hot men we have today . . . will tell you they conceived many of their tricks and ideas from the Armstrong style of playing. His ability is enthusiastically endorsed by all the great and near great.[8]

According to the *Defender*, the appearance of these two publications represented an unprecedented achievement for an African-American musician, especially one working in the popular realm.[9]

Armstrong severed his connection with the Vendome Theater in mid-April 1927.[10] He did not explain his reasons for leaving Erskine Tate's celebrated orchestra after sixteen months other than his having grown

[7]Bill Rand, interview (ca. 1953) with Louis Armstrong for WERE Radio (Cleveland), Casette 26 (New York: Louis Armstrong Archives, Queens College).

[8]Louis Armstrong, *50 Hot Choruses for Cornet* (Chicago: Melrose Bros., 1927). The choruses, recorded with pianist Elmer Schoebel on Edison cylinders in the studio and in Louis's home before being transcribed by Schoebel, were based on popular tunes of the day to fit into orchestrations published by Melrose and included none of the Hot Five repertory. The cylinders have since been presumed lost or destroyed; see George Hoefer, "Will the Louis Sides on Cylinder Ever Turn Up?," *Down Beat* 17/14 (14 July 1950), 11, and "Celebrated Mecca Flats to Go Way of Vendome," *Down Beat* 17/16 (11 August 1950), 11.

[9]Dave Peyton, "The Musical Bunch," *Chicago Defender* (16 April 1927), 6.

[10]*Chicago Defender* (9 April 1927), 6.

weary of the doubling grind and preferring his own band at the Sunset, which included close friends, notably Earl Hines, Darnell Howard, and Fred "Tubby" Hall.[11] Actually, like the cabarets, the days of the theater orchestras were numbered. In little more than a year, the first talkies would arrive in Chicago, and orchestras in all the major houses would be replaced by organs or canned music.[12]

In early May 1927 Louis added Peter Briggs, tuba player from his Sunset band, and drummer Warren "Baby" Dodds, younger brother of Johnny Dodds, to the Hot Five to make in the space of a single week an extraordinary set of recordings known as the "Hot Sevens." Dodds's seven-member Black Bottom Stompers, with whom Armstrong had recorded two weeks before, may have furnished the inspiration for an expanded Hot Five; three of the eleven Hot Sevens were Stompers' tunes.

The same month he left the Vendome, Louis learned that his mother had been ill for several months in New Orleans. He sent Lil to accompany her to Chicago for treatment, but she died in his home in mid-July. The local announcement of her death and funeral read as follows:

> Mrs. Mary Armstrong, mother of Louis Armstrong, well known musician and recording artist, who died here last week, was buried with appropriate services from Kersey, McGowan & Morsell's undertaking parlors Friday. She had been a resident of this city only two months, coming here from New Orleans, La., upon the invitation of her son, who wished her to share his home with him. Rev. Prentice A. Bryson, pastor of Carter Temple C. M. E. church, of which Louis and his wife are members, conducted the funeral services. The many floral designs expressed the heartfelt sympathy of the city's music bunch for Louis in his bereavement.[13]

Regardless of Mayann's failures as a parent, Louis mourned her passing:

> I tell you I felt bad to see her go—she had always done so much

[11]Louis Armstrong, *Swing That Music* (New York: Longmans, Green, 1936; reprinted New York: Da Capo Press, 1993), 85; and Louis Armstrong, *Louis Armstrong: In His Own Words*, ed. Thomas Brothers (New York: Oxford University Press, 1999), 99.

[12]*Chicago Defender* (7 July 1928), 7; (4 August 1928), 6; (18 August 1928), 6; (8 September 1928), 6; and (6 October 1928), 7. To save money, major Chicago theaters began cutting back on orchestras already in early 1927 according to the *Chicago Defender* (8 January 1927), 6.

[13]"Loses Mother," *Chicago Defender*, City Edition (16 July 1927), 8.

> for me and loved me so and I was beginning to be able to give her what she needed and planning to see she had a nice comfortable old age; after the undertaker closed her coffin, I let out *plenty* of tears—and I just couldn't stop crying.[14]

Towards the end of July 1927 Armstrong's Stompers broke Chicago's color line by beginning a two-week "extra" engagement at the Black Hawk Grill in the Loop. The residency was intended to last longer but, when the entertainment failed to please and when the management demanded that Armstrong cut the group from twelve players to six, he compromised by shortening his residency.[15] Without naming him directly, *Defender* columnist Peyton again excoriated Armstrong, this time for failing to take advantage of this racial "opportunity."

> Just recently we had an orchestra playing in a swell Loop café and they had to flop on the job by not making time. They would come on the job five to fifteen minutes late. Then, too, their service was bad. They played too loud and nearly blew the roof off the building, and they also went into this aristocratic place singing a lot of rotten blue songs. All of these things go to make it hard for us. It takes responsible experienced leaders to handle these propositions and the Musicians Union should immediately enact a law to bar non-recognized leaders and contractors from securing these jobs.[16]

When the Original Hot Five reassembled in September and December 1927 for their final recordings, the group's function as a showcase for Armstrong's talents had become increasingly evident. In the first twenty-four Original Hot Fives, Armstrong normally soloed once per piece, either vocally or instrumentally, but in four instances —"My Heart," "Come Back Sweet Papa," "Jazz Lips," and "Skid-Dat-De-Dat"—not at all. Clearly the cornet feature, "Cornet Chop Suey," as well as his vocal and instrumental solos in "Big Butter and Egg Man" and "You Made Me Love You," were

[14]Louis Armstrong, *Swing That Music*, 85-86; and Louis Armstrong, *In His Own Words*, 90.

[15]*Chicago Defender* (30 July 1927), 6. Because the *Defender*'s notice identifies the residency as an "extra engagement," this may not mean that the Sunset was closed as James Lincoln Collier surmised in *Louis Armstrong: An American Genius* (New York: Oxford University Press, 1983), 163; see Chapter 9, note 2.

[16]Dave Peyton, "The Musical Bunch," *Chicago Defender* (6 August 1927), 6.

exceptions to this practice. In four of the eleven Hot Sevens, however, Armstrong contributed multiple instrumental solos, instrumental and vocal solos, or multiple instrumental and vocal solos. The tendency to dominate the musical proceedings continued in the final nine Hot Fives, in which Armstrong sings and plays solos in three ("Put 'Em Down Blues," "The Last Time," and "Hotter Than That") and plays multiple trumpet solos in one ("Once in a While").

The ambiguity between Armstrong's styles of solo and lead in these final Hot Fives came to confuse even his own sidemen. In "Put 'Em Down Blues," for example, Dodds's and Ory's tentative entrances in the final sixteen bars of the chorus after Armstrong's solo and break imply that they were uncertain when Louis's solo ended and his lead began.[17] Further attention-grabbing devices are his ever more virtuosic breaks, often climaxing on rips to a high C ("Ory's Creole Trombone" and "The Last Time"), and his routinely ascending into the high register for the out-chorus ("Struttin' with Some Barbecue").[18]

[17]On this passage, see also Brian Harker, "Louis Armstrong and the Clarinet," *American Music* 21/2 (Summer 2003), 151.

[18]Many of these observations are also noted in Brian Harker, *The Early Musical Development of Louis Armstrong, 1901-1928* (Ph.D. dissertation, Columbia University, 1997), 281-86.

"Put 'Em Down Blues"*

Table 8.1. Structural Outline of "Put 'Em Down Blues" [G Major]

SECTION	INSTRUMENTATION	BARS
Introduction	Trombone / Clarinet, Trumpet / Banjo	1.5 / 2 / 4
Chorus 1	Ensemble	16
	Ensemble / Trombone Break / Clarinet Break	12 / 3 / 1
	Ensemble / Clar. Break / Ensemble / Clar. Break	8 / 4 / 2 / 2
Extension	Clarinet	2
Chorus 2	Vocal Solo (Louis)	16
	Vocal Solo / Vocal Break (Louis)	12 / 4
	Vocal Solo (Louis)	16
Interlude	Piano	8
Chorus 3	Trumpet Solo	16
	Trumpet Solo / Trumpet Break	12 / 4
	Ensemble / Trpt. Break / Ensemble / Trpt. Break	8 / 4 / 2 / 2
Tag	Trumpet	2

How Armstrong came to record "Put 'Em Down Blues" by Eloise Bennett at the eighth Hot Five session on 2 September 1927 is not known. The title may have been suggested by Fearn, whose publishing company owned the tune, although its copyright deposit was not submitted until five months after the recording (see Appendix 1).[19] Armstrong may have first met Bennett, an actress, vaudeville star, and native Chicagoan, when she appeared at the Dreamland during his first week back from New York City.[20] She recorded two sides for Paramount in 1926 and two more for the short-lived Black Patti label in 1927.[21] A line drawing of her as a petite figure in a dancing pose appears in Black Patti's inaugural advertisement in the *Chicago Defender* of 21 May 1927 (see Illustration 8.1 on the next page). In 1928 Bennett was lauded in the Negro press as the solitary

[19]Except for a different introduction based on the first four bars of the vocal chorus, the deposit, in an unknown hand, is a rough transcription of the recording that includes the trombone and clarinet breaks but not the lyrics. In addition to several notational mistakes, the first chorus contains two superfluous measures (mm. 23-24).

[20]*Chicago Defender* (31 October 1925), 6. The Dreamland ad includes a head shot of Bennett as does the ad for her appearance in DeKoven Thompson's *Melody Land* at the Avenue Theater the previous week. See Illustration 2.1.

[21]David Evans, liner notes to *Female Blues Singers,* Vol. 1, *1924-32* (Document Records DOCD-5505, 1997). According to Evans, "Effervescent Daddy" for Paramount was Bennett's own composition.

Illustration 8.1. Line Drawing of Eloise Bennett from Black Patti Ad

From *Chicago Defender* (21 May 1927), 6.

black member of the Broadway show, *Lovely Lady*, in which she scored a "big hit" with her performance of "At the Barbecue."[22]

Conceived as a popular song rather than a blues and built around a forty-eight-bar chorus divided into three sixteen-bar sections (A - B - A′), "Put 'Em Down Blues" is formally unique among Hot Five recordings. Ory's opening break begun in mid-measure for a seven-and-one-half-bar introduction, Dodds's two-measure extension of his second break for a fifty-bar first chorus, the lack of breaks in the second portion of the vocal chorus, and the eight-bar piano interlude add to the tune's structural oddities. The fifty-bar first chorus is offset, however, by the final chorus in which Armstrong extends his final break with a two-bar solo tag. Yet, the better instrumental balance provided by electrical recording, confident playing, lack of technical mistakes, bright timbre of the trumpet, and consistent "light ensemble swing" combine to produce a more musically

[22]*Chicago Defender* (21 January 1928), 7. A modestly successful show in its day that opened to mixed reviews in *Variety* (11 January 1928), 51, and *Billboard* (7 January 1928), 11, *Lovely Lady* ran for 164 performances between 29 December 1927 and 19 May 1928. *Variety*'s reviewer ignored Bennett's contribution, but Gordon Leland from *Billboard* patronizingly noted that she "put over the 'At the Barbecue' number in the best manner of her race (colored)." Bennett reprised her rendition of "At the Barbecue" on Broadway four years later in *Yeah Man*, an "All-Negro Revue of Song, Dance, and Laughter," which closed after two performances; see Richard C. Norton, *A Chronology of American Musical Theater*, 3 vols. (New York: Oxford University Press, 2002), II, 523, 670. See also Bennett's brief biography in Laurie Wright, "Pieces of the Jigsaw Puzzle," *Storyville* (1998-99), 165-66.

satisfying and less dated-sounding performance than many earlier Hot Fives.[23]

As one of the few items in this study exhibiting both instrumental and vocal solos by Armstrong for which the original melody is known, a comparison of these with a portion of his first chorus lead is worth a look (Example 8.1). Armstrong's three versions of the melody move from the quasi-literal to the largely abstract—from his now familiar lead-solo "thesis" through a minimalist vocal solo "antitheses" to a trumpet solo "synthesis," thereby providing further evidence of Armstrong's holistic approach to individual performances.

Example 8.1. Comparison of the Copyrighted Melody with Armstrong's Ensemble Lead, Vocal Solo, and Trumpet Solo in "Put 'Em Down Blues"

[23]The phrase "light ensemble swing" is the characterization of Gunther Schuller in *Early Jazz: Its Roots and Musical Development* (New York: Oxford University Press, 1968), 109-10. To my ears, "Put 'Em Down Blues" is the first recording on which Armstrong unequivocally plays the trumpet rather than the cornet (see Chapter 3, note 32).

Example 8.1 Continued.

Appropriating the A♯ - B neighboring motive of the melody (m. 5) as an anacrusis, Armstrong's lead duplicates the melody exactly for only one bar before lapsing into paraphrase. His most significant deviations from the original tune involve adjustments to its regular four-bar phrasing by the addition of extended pick-ups (mm. 1 and 9), segmentation (mm. 1-2 and 3-4), or compression (mm. 5-7 and 13-15). At the repeat of bar 1 (m. 9), Armstrong's full measure of pick-up (m. 8), intervening rests and anacrusis-like figure (m. 10) effectively produce a five-bar phrase divided into 2 + 3.[24]

Armstrong's vocal solo adopts the first note of the melody or the fifth of the tonic triad (D) for the beginning of most phrases where motion is often tangential (m. 1) or contrary (mm. 3-4, 9-10, and 11-12) to their original direction. Besides adherence to harmonic changes, the lead and vocal have little in common. Vocal phrasing, however, generally follows

[24]Armstrong's phrasing here bears similarities to that in his "Mandy, Make Up Your Mind" solo; see Gunther Schuller, *Early Jazz*, 92-93.

that of the lead except for bars 9-12, which are broken into two-bar segments. Here, it may be noted, phrasing takes precedence over the lyrics whose meaning is mangled as a consequence.

Combining the A♯ - B motive from his lead with the contrary phrase direction from his vocal, Armstrong's trumpet solo otherwise bears little resemblance to either but proceeds logically from both. The opening bars portray his synthesizing techniques in microcosm. Taking as raw ingredients the lead's half-step motive, the lead's approach to the tonic by a third, and the vocal's quarter-quarter-half rhythm (an Armstrong trademark), Louis displaces the phrase rhythmically and inverts his approach to the tonic to create an entirely new melodic gesture. The trumpet solo's phrasing corresponds roughly with the lead and vocal until the last half of the excerpt, where bars 9-12 match up with the original tune and bars 13-16 are divided into two-bar segments.

As the solo continues, it increasingly asserts its own identity and internal coherence. Phrase two (mm. 3-4) applies the downward motion of a fifth from the vocal to the pitches of the E-minor triad from the lead, and phrase three (mm. 5-8) begins like the lead and ends like the vocal. But the three phrases are more closely related to each than to either the lead or vocal. Each begins with a variation of the A♯ - B motive and ends on a successively lower note of the inverted E-minor arpeggio—G (m. 1), E (m. 4), and B (m. 7)—with the third phrase completing the octave to low B and supplying the intervening pitches, A, G, F♯, D, and C. After beginning bars 9-16 with a retrograde of the lead's opening pitches (m. 1), though, Armstrong cuts his ties to his lead and vocal by improvising a new melody with an expanded register (m. 8), new implied harmonies (mm. 11 and 15), cadences on the third rather than the fifth of the chord (mm. 12 and 16), and dissonant melodic intervals of the major seventh and tritone (mm. 11 and 16).

A peculiarity of the melody's first sixteen bars is its melodic emphasis on the relative minor or submediant triad (E - G - B), which is resolved unequivocally to the home key in the second sixteen bars. The melody, lead, and vocal perpetuate this ambiguity of key by avoiding the direct progression of leading tone to tonic (F♯ - G) as part of a cadence anywhere in this section, making the arrival on the tonic G (m. 17) less compelling than it might be. In his trumpet solo Armstrong prepares the transition from implied minor to relative major (mm. 9-16) by arpeggiating a descending G-major triad from the third beat of bar 8 through the notes falling on the beat in bar 9 and by starting the last two phrases on pitches of the G-major triad. The half cadences on the leading tone (mm. 12 and 16) beg the question of the rightful tonic while the A♯ - B motive at the beginning (m. 9) and the end (m. 15) neatly link this section with the first eight bars.

"Put 'Em Down Blues" ends with what Brooks calls an "out of key" coda.[25] The tonal instability actually begins in the final two measures of Armstrong's break in which an F♮ and E♭ over G harmony implies a deflection to the minor subdominant (C). The re-established F♯'s shortly thereafter confirm the tonic G through the penultimate measure while the E♭ and B in the final measure suggest a cadence in parallel minor on a picardy third (Example 8.2).

Example 8.2. Armstrong's Final Break and Solo Tag in "Put 'Em Down Blues"

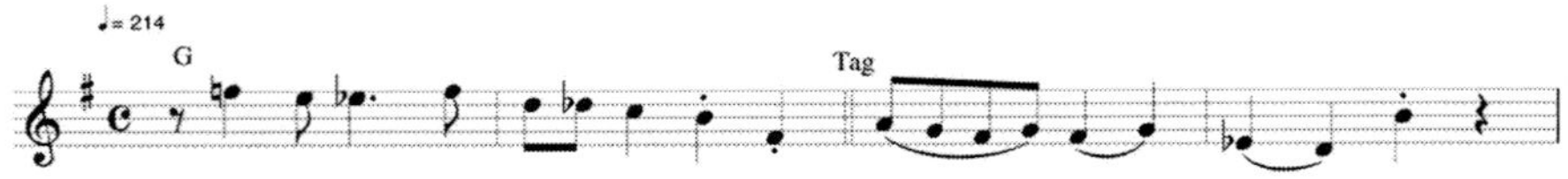

[25]Edward Brooks, *The Young Louis Armstrong on Records: A Critical Survey of the Early Recordings, 1923-1928* (Lanham, MD: Scarecrow Press, 2002), 404.

"Ory's Creole Trombone"

Table 8.2. Structural Outline of "Ory's Creole Trombone"

SECTION	INSTRUMENTATION	BARS	KEY
Introduction	Trombone / Ensemble	3 / 2	F Maj
Chorus A	Trombone Alternating with Ensemble	16	F Maj
Chorus B	Ensemble / Trombone Break / Ensemble	12 / 2 / 2	F Maj
Chorus B	Ensemble / Trombone Break / Ensemble	12 / 2 / 2	F Maj
Chorus A	Trumpet Alternating with Ensemble	16	F Maj
Chorus C	Ensemble	16	B♭ Maj
Interlude 1	Trumpet, Trombone, Clarinet Alternating with Trombone	2 / 2 / 2 / 6	B♭ Maj
Chorus C	Ensemble	16	B♭ Maj
Interlude 2	Trumpet Alternating with Clarinet	2 / 2 / 2 / 2 / 4	B♭ Maj
Chorus C	Trumpet Solo / Trumpet Break	14 / 2	B♭ Maj
Chorus C	Ensemble	16	B♭ Maj

"Kid" Ory, absent from Hot Seven sessions while touring with "King" Oliver in New York, returned to Chicago in June to join Clarence Lee's band at the Plantation.[26] "Ory's Creole Trombone," originally rejected by OKeh, was not issued until rediscovered in the Columbia vaults by George Avakian in the early 1940s.[27] Ory had already recorded the piece with his Sunshine Orchestra in the early twenties in Los Angeles[28] but did not get around to copyrighting the tune until three months after its delayed release (see Appendix 1). Armstrong, however, in a 1951 interview for *Esquire*, remembered it as a featured number in the Ory band's repertoire in New Orleans [ca. 1915]:

> "Ory's Creole Trombone" is one tune that always did fascinate me. . . . I remember when I was a kid in short pants (years ago in New Orleans, when Kid Ory and his band used to play every Sunday night at the St. Katherine's Hall), I used to sell newspapers

[26]*Chicago Defender* (11 June 1927), 7.

[27]Joe Klee, "George Avakian—In the Right Place at the Right Time," *Mississippi Rag* (September 1997), 1.

[28]See a complete transcription in Florian Hüger, "'Ory's Creole Trombone': Transkription und Analyse der ersten Schallplattenaufnahme einer schwarzen New Orleans Jazzband," *Jazzforschung* 23 (1991), 9-115; see also Chapter 2, note 39.

and save up enough money to pay my admission, which wasn't much. . . . And I would just listen to them play this particular tune. . . . Mutt Carey was playing cornet in the band at the time . . . Johnny Dodds, who was really in his prime, played clarinet. . . . And when those guys would play the tune "Ory's Creole Trombone," everybody would dance . . . they had a rhythm on this tune wherein, after several choruses, they would get 'way down, real soft, real soft, and Kid Ory would make those slide tones on his trombone, and the more choruses they played, the softer they would get. . . . And they would get so soft until you could hear the feet of the dancers, "just shuffling." . . . My, my, they sure used to knock me out on "Ory's Creole Trombone."[29]

The ragtime origins of "Creole Trombone" are reflected in its form: three sixteen-bar strains in the order of A - B - A - C, with a modulation to the subdominant on the final strain. In trad band circles the tune is sometime called the "Carbolic Rag," supposedly after Clarence Wiley's "Car-Barlick-Acid Rag-Time" (published in 1903). The two-bar ensemble passages in the first strain (mm. 3-4, 7-8, and 11-12 of the copyright deposit) indeed correspond somewhat with the first six bars of "Car-Barlick's" opening strain's treble part, but with not much else, including the form. The direct relationship, if ever one existed, remains remote (Example 8.3).[30] The roots of "Creole Trombone," more than likely, are to be found in "trombone smears," such as Withrow's "Trombonium" and Fillmore's "Lassus Trombone," played throughout the country by concert, circus, and vaudeville bands around the turn of the century.[31]

Example 8.3. Bars 1-6 of the First-Strain Treble Part of "Car-Barlick-Acid Rag-Time"

Basically the same as Ory's Sunshine Orchestra recording, the Hot Five version of "Creole Trombone" modernizes its earlier rendition by varying the repeat of chorus A, varying the repeat of the interlude, and

[29]Louis Armstrong, *In His Own Words*, 133-34.

[30]The example, taken from *Ragtime Rarities*, ed. Trebor Jay Tichenor (New York: Dover Publications, 1975), 282, is transposed from the original key of A♭ major for ease of comparison.

[31]Rudi Blesh and Harriet Janis, *They All Played Ragtime* (New York: Oak Publications, 1971), 151.

replacing the third ensemble C chorus with a solo. A small but aurally significant detail from the 1922 recording that would have been wise to include in 1927, however, is the change of harmony on the final trombone break in bar 12 of the A chorus (Example 8.4). The F-dim and G7 chords provide a greater sense of finality to the cadence of this section by setting up the circle-of-fifths progression: D diminished seven (implied) - G7 - C7 - F. But Armstrong and Dodds swing more than Thomas "Papa Mutt" Carey and Oliver "Dink" Johnson of the Sunshine band, and the composer animates his ensemble part in the C chorus with an ebullient passage previously heard as a break in "Sunset Café Stomp" (Example 7.10). In the second C chorus Ory, unfortunately, undershoots the high B♭ by a step, which, when combined with his technical errors in the first interlude, certainly influenced the decision to forego the recording's immediate release.

Example 8.4. Final First-Chorus Trombone Breaks in the 1921/1922 and 1927 Recordings of "Ory's Creole Trombone"

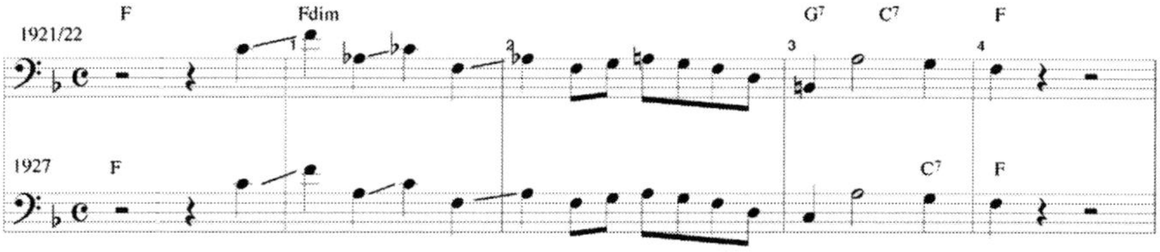

Blame for the rejection cannot be placed at Ory's feet alone, for Armstrong himself contributes an unusually high number of fluffed notes, particularly in his solo (Example 8.5 on the following page). In an otherwise nicely constructed harmonic paraphrase, Armstrong avoids the redundancies of the copyrighted melody of which the second eight bars are a repeat of the first. Armstrong's second eight bars begin with spiky arpeggios ending with step-wise motion that echo those in the final two bars of his first eight. He expands the register of his first eight measures by a step in both directions and embellishes the C7 harmony (m. 12) with the solo's only E♮, which, in turn, displaces his only reference to the melody by two beats. Unfortunately, Armstrong exceeds the limits of his own technique with a daring but out-of-control break (mm. 15-16) that probably sealed the number's banishment to the vault for the next fourteen years.[32]

[32]Armstrong's break, according to Humphrey Lyttelton in *The Best of Jazz: Basin Street to Harlem, 1917-1930* (New York: Taplinger, 1978), 130, came from a "rush of imaginative zeal" and is technically unplayable on the trumpet.

Example 8.5. Comparison of the Copyrighted Melody with Armstrong's Solo in "Ory's Creole Trombone"

"The Last Time"

Table 8.3. Structural Outline of "The Last Time" [F Major]

SECTION	INSTRUMENTATION	BARS
Introduction	Clarinet / Clarinet, Trumpet, Trombone	3 / 1
Chorus 1	Ensemble	18
Verse	Ensemble	16
Chorus 2	Clarinet Solo / Clarinet Break / Clarinet Break	8 / 4 / 6
Verse (1st Half)	Piano Solo	8
Chorus 3	Vocal Solo (Louis) / Vocal Break / Vocal Solo	8 / 4 / 6
Chorus 4	Vocal Solo (Louis) / Vocal Break / Vocal Solo	8 / 4 / 6
Chorus 5	Trombone Solo / Tromb. Break / Tromb. Solo	8 / 4 / 6
Chorus 6	Ensemble / Trumpet Break / Ensemble	8 / 4 / 6

The "divine" Sara Martin recorded "The Last Time" in New York almost eighteen months before the Hot Five, making it the group's only legitimate "cover."[33] (In Illustration 8.2 a *Chicago Defender* advertisement for her original rendition is provided.) How Armstrong came to record Martin's song at the ninth Hot Five session on 6 September 1927 has not been documented.[34] Although he is not known to have worked with Martin, Armstrong certainly knew the exclusive and well-established OKeh artist who starred along with the Hot Five at the Race Record Artists Night in June of the previous year. Unlike the Hot Five's "Last Time," initially rejected until rediscovered by George Avakian (see "Ory's Creole Trombone"), Martin's came out less than a month after being waxed.[35]

Comparison of Martin's recording of the song with that of the Hot Five shows an evolution from what must have been Lil's original conception to something radically different. Recounting the story of a good love gone bad, which may have reflected the relationship of Lil and Louis at the time,

[33]Brian Rust, *Jazz and Ragtime Records, 1897-1942,* 2 vols. (Denver: Mainspring Press, 2002), II, 1099. On Martin, see Daphne Duval Harrison, *Black Pearls: Blues Queens of the 1920s (*New Brunswick, NJ: Rutgers University Press, 1988), 234-36. The epithet, "divine," comes from an advertisement of the Race Record Artists Night in the *Chicago Defender* (12 June 1926), special supplement.

[34]Record label copy in the Sony Archives names Sara Martin and Billy H. Ewing as composers for "The Last Time," but a copyright deposit for "The Last Time Blues" (E674699) secured by Lil Hardin on 14 October 1927 may be for the same composition; see David Chevan, *Written Music in Early Jazz* (Ph.D. dissertation, City University of New York, 1997), 507. Until Lil's missing deposit is located, the issue of possible plagiarism must remain unresolved.

[35]*TMW* 22/4 (15 April 1926), 135.

Illustration 8.2.
OKeh Ad for
Sara Martin's
"The Last Time"

From *Chicago Defender* (8 May 1926), 6.

Martin sings a twenty-bar verse followed by a thirty-two-bar chorus that concludes with an eight-bar coda (Example 8.6).

The form is a patch-work of repeated sections with anti-climatic extensions. A repeated eight-bar section (A - A′) ending with an extension of two repeated bars (mm. 17-18 and 19-20) comprise the twenty-bar verse, and the two sixteen-bar sections of the chorus begin with the same eight bars (mm. 21-28 and 37-44), but each ends with eight contrasting bars (B - C - B′ - D). The final four bars of the coda repeat the final four bars of the chorus (mm. 49-52). The phrase "[it's the] last time," usually set to the same music, acts as a unifying device in the chorus and coda, appearing a total of eight times. The piano frames the vocal solo with a four-bar introduction and a four-bar conclusion based on the last four bars of the coda. The Hot Five recording completely reworks the form and much of the music.

Example 8.6. Martin's Vocal Solo in Her Recording of "The Last Time"

A perky clarinet arpeggio beginning on tonic harmony and ending abruptly on an ensemble third-inversion dominant-seventh serves as a rather incongruous introduction to a sentimental ballad (Example 8.7). Incongruity is perpetuated by the relatively fast tempo for a redesigned chorus, whose music corresponds with only the first twelve bars of the second half of Martin's chorus (mm. 37-48). The melody to the verse in two balanced eight-bar phrases is entirely new, while Armstrong's two vocal choruses retain most of Martin's lyrics but with alterations befitting the perspective of an insensitive male (Example 8.8). In short, the Hot Five version of "The Last Time" remedies the structural problems of Martin's version but fails to capture the song's original pathos and melodrama.

Example 8.7. Introduction to the Hot Five's "The Last Time"

Example 8.8. Armstrong's Vocal Solo in "The Last Time"

The apparent reasons for OKeh's rejection of "The Last Time" are less apparent than with "Ory's Creole Trombone." The most obvious technical mistakes—the rhythm instruments' failure to observe the four-bar break in Armstrong's trumpet solo and his fluffed notes in the thirteenth bar—seem relatively minor. On the other hand, Ory, Dodds, and Lil play respectable if undistinguished solos, the ensemble work is good, and Armstrong's final break (ending on a ripped-up-to high C) sounds positively exuberant.

In September *Chicago Defender* critic Dave Peyton wrote a more favorable review of Armstrong's Stompers than several months earlier: "Armstrong and his Sunset Orchestra have tamed down. They are playing softer and sweeter and are hitting the bulls [*sic*] eye these days. In the combination are 13 players. Earl Hines directs the bunch."[1] This notice, however, marked the end of Armstrong's stay at the Sunset, which closed shortly thereafter.[2] In October he and his ensemble were to be found playing three nights a week in a "local night life café" and participated as one of fifteen bands in a Halloween party given by the Musicians Local 208 at the Coliseum Annex.[3]

After leaving the Sunset, Louis and his two best friends—drummer Arthur "Zutty" Singleton and pianist Earl Hines—formalized a "little corporation" and vowed never to accept jobs separately.[4] Taking out a year's lease on Warwick Hall at 543 East 47th Street, the trio hoped to make money sponsoring their own dances (see Illustration 9.1). Their new club opened, unfortunately, about the same time as the much grander Savoy Ballroom two blocks away. In spite of struggling through the end of the year, their venture was doomed from the start.[5] The friends tried

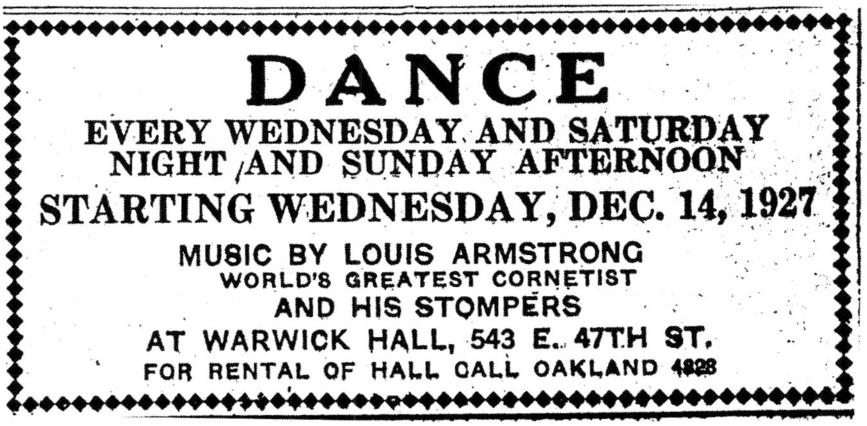

Illustration 9.1. Ad for Dances at Warwick Hall by Armstrong's Stompers

From *Chicago Defender* (10 December 1927), 6.

[1]Dave Peyton, "The Musical Bunch," *Chicago Defender*, City Edition (17 September 1927), 9.

[2]According to the *Defender* (19 May 1928), 6, and (2 June 1928), 6, the Sunset opened under new management on 26 May 1928 after having been closed for six months.

[3]*Chicago Defender* (29 October 1927), 9.

[4]Stanley Dance, *The World of Earl Hines* (New York: Scribner's, 1977; reprinted New York: Da Capo Press, 1983), 54. Hines nursed a long-standing grudge against Armstrong and Singleton for joining Dickerson at the Savoy while he was on a trip to New York.

[5]*Chicago Defender*, City Edition (10 December 1927), 6.

again at a West Side dance hall but were soon vanquished by rough crowds and rampant violence.[6] In the meantime Armstrong had begun doubling at the Metropolitan Theater, where he became the "feature man" for Clarence Jones. In his column for the *Defender*, Peyton gushed over the band's opening night on 12 September:

> The medley started off with the introduction of "Madame Butterfly," merging into a violin solo by Wright Smith, whose great command of the instrument was evident by his masterful control. Then the trombonist, Mr. [William] Franklin sang the chorus of the butterfly song with his sweet lyric tenor voice which broke up the overture for two minutes. Well, now comes the big punch and Louis Armstrong delivered the knockout wallop with that famous jazz version of his on the butterfly song. After this rendition the applause was deafening for at least five minutes. Flowers by the basket were showered on the new music makers at the Metropolitan theater.[7]

Armstrong tendered his notice to the contractor at the Metropolitan in early December, just three months later.[8]

[6]Louis Armstrong, *Louis Armstrong: In His Own Words*, ed. Thomas Brothers (New York: Oxford University Press, 1999), 99-100.

[7]Dave Peyton, "The Musical Bunch," *Chicago Defender* (17 September 1927), 6. Joshua Berrett, in "Louis Armstrong and Opera," *The Musical Quarterly* 76/2 (1992), 216-41, overlooks this reference to Puccini's *Madame Butterfly*. Editor's Note: It is possible, however, that the song in question, while inspired by that opera, was not an excerpt from Puccini's score. A song titled "Poor Butterfly," with words by John L. Golden and music by Raymond Hubbell (New York: T. D. Harms, 1916), enjoyed considerable popularity during the 1920s.

[8]*Chicago Defender* (3 December 1927), 7.

"Struttin' with Some Barbecue"*

Table 9.1. Structural Outline of "Struttin' with Some Barbecue" [A♭ Major]

Section	Instrumentation	Bars
Verse	Ensemble	12
Chorus 1	Ensemble / Banjo	30 / 2
Chorus 2	Clarinet Solo / Clarinet Break	14 / 2
	Stop-Time Trombone Solo / Trombone Break	14 / 2
Chorus 3	Stop-Time Trumpet Solo / Trumpet Break	14 / 2
	Stop-Time Trumpet Solo / Clar., Trpt., Tromb.	14 / 4
Chorus 4	Ensemble / Banjo Break	14 / 2
	Ensemble / Clarinet, Trumpet, Trombone	8 / 10

When "Struttin' with Some Barbecue" was published under Louis's name, Lil filed suit, claiming the piece as a collaboration from the early days. She was, in fact, awarded the copyright that was submitted six months after the recording in 1927,[9] and yet, years later in a 1951 interview for *Esquire*, he still took credit for its creation:

> This tune was derived and thought of when Zutty Singleton and I were playing at the Savoy Ballroom on the South Side of Chicago. . . . And after the dance was over every night, Zutty and I would drive out to 48th and State Street. . . . There was an old man there who made some of the most delicious barbecue that anyone would love to smack their chops on (their lips). . . . One night, while Zutty and I were manipulating those "Chime Bones" (barbecue), a thought came into my head. . . . I said to Zutty—"Say Zoot, as I sit here eating these fine-tasting ribs, it dawned on me that I should write a tune and call it 'Struttin with Some Barbecue'." . . . Zutty said, "Dush, that's a real good idea." . . . So then and there, "Struttin' with Some Barbecue" was born.[10]

[9]Max Jones's 1967 *Melody Maker* interview with Lil is reprinted in Joshua Berrett, ed., *The Louis Armstrong Companion: Eight Decades of Commentary* (New York: Schirmer Books, 1999), 44. See also Laurence Bergreen, *Louis Armstrong: An Extravagant Life* (New York: Broadway Books, 1997), 378.

[10]This is a colorful but problematic story because Armstrong did not begin playing at the Savoy until April 1928. The title probably refers to a "man's swaggering gait as he shows off the lady friend on his arm" according to Robert O'Meally, "An Appreciation of Armstrong's Hot Five and Seven Recordings," liner notes for Sony's *Complete Hot Five and Seven Recordings*, 66—an interpretation supported by the *Chicago Defender* ad (see Illustration 9.2).

Illustration 9.2.
OKeh Ad for "Struttin' with Some Barbecue"

From *Chicago Defender* (26 May 1928), 2.

No matter its pedigree, "Struttin' with Some Barbecue," from the tenth session on 9 December 1927, survives as the most enduring number from the Hot Five repertory after "Muskrat Ramble." (See the newspaper announcement of its release as Illustration 9.2 on the facing page.)

The outlining of the tonic major seventh chord is the most striking and progressive feature of the melody represented by Armstrong's first-chorus lead (mm. 0-1, 4-5, and 16-17). (See Example 9.1 on the following pages). The prominence of this feature, the composition's unequivocal two-beat rhythm, Armstrong's "daring break" (mm. 15-16), his "modern" handling of the changes in his solo (mm. 25-28), the arranged nature of the stop-time accompaniment to Ory's and Armstrong's solos, the stop-time break after Armstrong's solo, the harmonic changes themselves, and even the piece's "cornball" ending all point away from New Orleans toward a newer Chicago jazz tradition.[11]

Outside of references to the melody (mm. 1 and 6-7), Dodds's clarinet solo is a harmonic improvisation largely comprised of stock phrases and mannerisms from earlier low-register solos. The figure in bar 6 and its variation in bar 12, for example, are motives heard in "Wolverine Blues" recorded with "Jelly Roll" Morton the previous June. Other gestures (mm. 7.5-8 and 13-14.5) resemble those over the same harmony in "My Heart" (see Example 3.3, mm. 13-14 and m. 8, respectively). Dodds's penchant for repeating melodic figures on different beats as in "My Heart" (Example 3.3), in "Yes! I'm in the Barrel (Example 3.8), and in "Who'sit" (Example 5.7, mm. 19-20) reappears here (mm. 2 and 3-4).[12]

The stop-time accompaniment energizes Ory's solo by throwing its melodic simplicity into sharp relief. Like his earlier Hot Five solos, Ory here constructs improvisations around triads, often with blue thirds, relying on smears and syncopation for variety. His "Struttin'" solo is likewise centered around the tonic triad, A♭ - C♭/(C) - E♭, with the sixth scale degree (F) either substituting for the fifth (E♭) or embellishing it as an incomplete neighbor (mm. 17-22 and m. 31). His preoccupation with the blue third might have blinded him to the changes four measures before his break,

[11]Frank Tirro, *Jazz: A History*, 2nd ed. (New York: W. W. Norton, 1993), 174, 192-93; and David Baker, "Two Classic Louis Armstrong Solos," *Down Beat* 38/16 (16 September 1971), 1030. The major seventh and the stop-time chorus are primary arguments for Lil's composition of the tune; see Joshua Berrett, *Louis Armstrong & Paul Whiteman: Two Kings of Jazz* (New Haven: Yale University Press, 2004), 72.

[12]Two figures from mm. 2 and 15 from Dodds's "Struttin'" solo also surface, respectively, in m. 7 and mm. 5-6 of his recording of "Brown Bottom Bess" cut with the Chicago Footwarmers in July 1928; see Schuller's transcription in *Early Jazz: Its Roots and Musical Development* (New York: Oxford University Press, 1968), 202.

making for some rather harsh dissonances when C♭ sounds successively as the lowered root (m. 27), the lowered fifth (m. 28), the lowered second (m. 29), and the lowered sixth (m. 30).

Armstrong's solo, his first non-stop-time solo based on arpeggios,[13] begins with the F - A♭ - F of Ory's break and incorporates, in the first phrase, the twin functions of the blue third presented separately by the

Example 9.1. Comparison of Armstrong's First-Chorus Lead with Dodds's Solo, Ory's Solo, and Armstrong's Solo in "Struttin' with Some Barbecue"

[13]Brian Harker, "'Telling A Story': Louis Armstrong and Coherence in Early Jazz," *Current Musicology* 63 (1999), 65.

Example 9.1 Continued.

clarinet and trombone—as a lower neighbor (B♮) of the mediant (C) from Dodds's solo (mm. 6 and 12) and as the lowered mediant itself (C♭) from Ory's (mm. 19 and 31). Sidestepping overt references, he expands the range, melodic complexity, and length of each phrase from his lead. Phrases one and two (mm. 1-4 and 5-8) of the lead and solo, for example, share melodic shapes and approaches to cadences. But, while the lead moves from high G to the fifth below in both phrases, the solo's range extends from high A♭ to a major thirteenth below in the first phrase and from high C to two octaves below in the second. He resists alluding to the most distinctive aspect of the melody, the G major seventh, and instead concentrates on developing the chordal third (C). Phrase three (mm. 9-12) embellishes F—the lead's most prominent pitch—with a swoop from high F to an octave below and back again. The first half of the solo's fourth phrase (mm. 13-14) prolongs the lead's F with a descending octave, and the second half's bravura break (mm. 15-16) embellishes in triplets the lead's descending D♭ octave.

In the second half of the solo Armstrong diverges from the lead more drastically but without abandoning critical affinities. In phrase five (mm. 17-20) he duplicates the lead's rhythm two beats later while incorporating a variation of Ory's solo (m. 19). The first half of phrase six (mm. 21-22) has several pitches and a rip in common with the lead but also clarifies the A♭7 harmony with a G♭ (a detail overlooked by Dodds and Ory); the second half (mm. 23-34) elaborates the lead's bar 23. Hemiola rhythms in phrase seven (mm. 25-28), the most radical departure from the lead, bring the solo to its climax, after which, as if in compensation, he concludes by quoting the melody.

"Internal variation" and a goal-directed approach to voice-leading provide coherence and a sense of inevitability to Armstrong's "Struttin'" solo.[14] Variations of two pitch cells characterized initially (m. 1) by a returning third figure ("a") and a downward leap followed by a half-step return ("b") comprise the solo's basic building blocks. Furthermore, the resolution by half-step in "b" sets up voice-leading expectations that are invariably fulfilled. Occasionally expectations are satisfied even more forcefully by voice-leading from above as well as from below, as in bars 9-11 in which the A♭'s move down to G in the middle of bar 10 and then to F at the beginning of bar 11. Simultaneously a preliminary resolution to F by E♮ at the onset of bar 10 in E♭7 harmony is reinforced by a more decisive motion from middle D♭ to E♭ on the second beat of bar 10 and then to a second E♮ - F, but now cadencing in F minor harmony. Similar voice-leading procedures govern the shape of Armstrong's break (mm. 15-16): E♮ - F, C - D♭, A♮ - (C) - B♭, (F) - A♭ - G, E♭♭ - D♭, and B♮ - C.

After Armstrong's third chorus solo, the clarinet and trombone join him for an arranged stop-time break that lengthens the chorus by two bars. That the players exhibit no hesitation in performing this anomaly indicates that it was planned. Furthermore, a longer version of the ensemble break idea ends the next chorus and the piece, again after thirty-four bars. The arranged ending harkens back to "Sunset Café Stomp"; the arranged break recalls "I'm Gonna Gitcha" and "Sweet Little Papa." The "Struttin" break demonstrates the continuing interest of Hot Five members in such up-to-date novelties, which resurface in the sustained breaks of "Once in a While" and in the riffs of "I'm Not Rough."

[14]Richard Domek, "Musical Organization and Trademarks in the Maturing Solos of Louis Armstrong," *Jazz Research Papers* (Manhattan, KS: NAJE, 1996), 34-35, 42, 44.

“Got No Blues”*

Table 9.2. Structural Outline of “Got No Blues” [E♭ Major]

SECTION	INSTRUMENTATION	BARS	KEY
Introduction	Banjo	4	E♭ Maj
Chorus 1	Ensemble / Trumpet Break	14 / 2	E♭ Maj
Chorus 2	Ensemble / Banjo Break	14 / 2	E♭ Maj
Modulation	Banjo	6	E♭ / F
Chorus 3	Stop-Time Trumpet Solo / Trumpet Break	14 / 2	F Maj
Chorus 4	Stop-Time Trumpet Solo / Trumpet Break	14 / 2	F Maj
Modulation	Trumpet	2	F / E♭
Chorus 5	Clarinet Solo / Clarinet Break	14 / 2	E♭ Maj
Chorus 6	Trombone Solo / Trombone Break	14 / 2	E♭ Maj
Chorus 7	Ensemble / Clarinet, Trumpet, Trombone	14 / 2	E♭ Maj

The “Struttin’” session also yielded “Got No Blues,” another tune by Lil and “one of those quickies that was made up right there at the studio.”[15] Like its companion piece, it possesses progressive features of dynamic variation in the last chorus, an arranged ending, and pairing of keys more remotely related than major and relative minor. Armstrong and Dodds play satisfactory solos, but Ory’s is marred by faulty intonation and fluffs.

The relationship of copyright deposits for “Got No Blues,” “I’m Not Rough,” and “Hotter Than That” to their respective recordings presents something of a puzzle. All three, claimed by Lil, were filed on the same day six months later but almost certainly are not in her hand. Because nothing precludes their use as lead sheets in the studio, it is assumed for the purposes of this study that they were so employed—that their role was prescriptive and that differences between them and the recordings resulted from decisions or choices made by the performers (see Appendix 1).

The introduction and modulation allow St. Cyr the most solo space since “Oriental Strut” (Example 9.2 on the next page). Beginning with a melodic sequence that reaffirms the tonic (m. 3 from the lead sheet), his introduction ends on a blue third—an element subsequently adopted as a motive by Armstrong (Example 9.4, lead, mm. 8 and 16; Example 9.5, m. 4) as well as by Dodds (Example 9.6, m. 16). St. Cyr’s skillfully wrought modulation opens with an arpeggiation of the tonic triad and, like the

[15]Louis Armstrong, *In His Own Words*, 135.

introduction, continues with a descending melodic sequence (Example 9.3). But unlike the introduction, the sequence descends by whole step through the blue third to E♭ (m. 4), where begins a circle-of-fifths

Example 9.2. St. Cyr's Introduction to "Got No Blues"

Example 9.3. St. Cyr's Modulation in "Got No Blues"

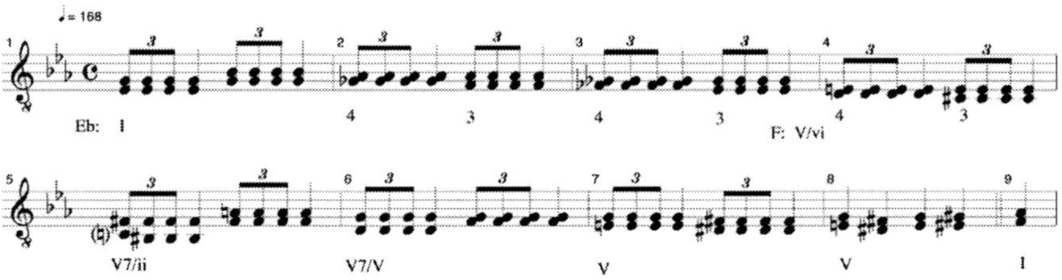

Example 9.4. Comparison of the Copyrighted Melody with Armstrong's

Example 9.4 Continued.

progression concluding on the dominant of F (m. 7) before resolving to the tonic in the initial measure of Armstrong's trumpet solo.

In spite of his growing tendency to create harmonically-based solos like those in "Oriental Strut" and "Muskrat Ramble" at the third session in February, Armstrong never completely abandoned melodic paraphrase during the Original Hot Fives. His solo here is a "paraphrase once removed" in effect—a paraphrase of the lead that itself paraphrases the original tune (Example 9.4). Schuller noted the motivic use of triplets in the breaks,[16] but more compelling unifying factors are the arpeggiated variations on the opening repeated A's, which become ever more elaborate (mm. 3 and 9), and the accompanying anacrusis G♯ - A, which also appears separately (mm. 4-5). Before an interruption by Armstrong's double-time break, the repeated-note figure resurfaces intact on tonic (m. 11), dominant (m. 13), and submediant (m. 14).

In the second chorus Armstrong explores alternatives to the repeated A's (mm. 17, 19, and 25) and invokes the related pitch cell G♯ - A (mm. 21 and 29-30). The two choruses reconnect by means of repeated F's (m. 27), after which the repeated-note motive disappears until the solo's final bar in

[16]Gunther Schuller, *Early Jazz*, 110. The motivic relationship exists between the break in Armstrong's first chorus lead (Example 9.4, m. 16) and the break at the end of his solo (Example 9.5, m. 4).

preparation for Dodds's entrance (Example 9.5, m. 4). As in the previous examples, Dodds and Armstrong exploit the ambivalent character of the blue third as a lower neighbor to the mediant or as the lowered mediant itself. In bar 8 of Armstrong's lead this dichotomous function arises in immediate succession—a motivic microcosm of his approach to the melody.

Dodds's solo (Example 9.6), reviled as "faltering and corny,"[17] stands as a fairly typical attempt—a highly arpeggiated harmonic variation with a single allusion to the melody (m. 12). Dodds shuns any references to the melody's most conspicuous attribute—repeated pitches (mm. 1, 3, 9, and 13). His apparent indifference to their structural importance suggests a preoccupation with harmony identified previously in "I'm Gonna Gitcha." Contradicting the title, he flavors the endeavor with blues inflections, most prominently the blue seventh (D♭), along with lipped pitches and a proclivity for the relative minor over tonic major harmony. The pitch cells, F♯ - G and D♭ - C, impose motivic structure, and the reshuffled pitches from the first two bars (plus pickup) that end his solo frame it neatly.

Example 9.5. Armstrong's Modulation-Break in "Got No Blues"

Example 9.6. Comparison of the Copyrighted Melody with Dodds's Solo in "Got No Blues"

[17]D. Leon Wolff, "Bix Half-baked, Johnny Dodds Corny, Tesch Out of Tune," *Down Beat* 8/11 (1 June 1941), 8. Wolff was hardly an impartial critic.

"Once in a While"*

Table 9.3. Structural Outline of "Once in a While" [C Major]

SECTION	INSTRUMENTATION	BARS
Introduction	Ensemble / Trumpet	2 / 2
Verse 1	Ensemble	16
Chorus 1	Ensemble / Banjo Break	14 / 2
	Ensemble / Trumpet Break	14 / 2
Verse 2	Trumpet Solo	16
Chorus 2	Ensemble / Clarinet, Trumpet, Trombone Break	30 / 2
Chorus 3	Clarinet Solo / Clarinet Break	14 / 2
	Clarinet Solo / Clar., Trpt., Tromb. Break	14 / 2
Chorus 4	Stop-Time Trumpet Solo / Trumpet Break	14 / 2
	Trumpet Solo	16
Tag	Trumpet / Ensemble	2

William H. Butler, the composer of "Once in a While," may be the "William" or "Billy Butler" listed as a saxophonist / violinist in Charles "Doc" Cooke's band for its recording at the Columbia studios in Chicago on 11 and 15 June 1927.[18] If so, Johnny St. Cyr, also a member of Cooke's band, could have provided the Hot Five connection for this particular tune.

"Once in a While," a popular song cut at the eleventh Hot Five session on 10 December 1927, sports a distinctive hemiola or secondary rag pattern in the chorus (the bracketed pitches in Example 9.7 on the next page). The stop-time accompaniment to Armstrong's solo on the chorus (Example 9.8 on page 167) and the ensemble breaks, both at the end of his solo on the verse and at the end of the clarinet solo (Example 9.7, mm. 31-32), constitute the tune's most prominent arranged features.[19] Both Dodds and Armstrong turn in fine solos incorporating astounding breaks.

[18]Brian Rust, *Jazz and Ragtime Records, 1897-1942*, 2 vols. (Denver: Mainspring Press, 2002), I, 371. Other possible candidates, if not the same individual, are Billy Butler, a band leader active in Harlem around 1925; see Demas Dean, "Travellin' Man," *Storyville* 72 (August-September 1977), 210; Billy Butler, the singing drummer who moved from Detroit to Chicago in late 1927; see the *Chicago Defender* (6 August 1927), 6 and (25 February 1928), 6; and William H. "Billy" Butler, the orchestra director for the *Blackbirds of 1934* while on tour in England; see Howard Rye, "Visiting Firemen 9: The Blackbirds and Their Orchestras," *Storyville* 112 (April-May 1984), 138, 143, and *Storyville* 114 (August-September 1984), 216-17.

[19]Gunther Schuller, *Early Jazz*, 113-14, calls the stop-time pattern based on the secondary rag at the beginning of the chorus an augmented Charleston rhythm.

Example 9.7. Comparison of Armstrong's First-Chorus Lead with Dodds's Solo in "Once in a While"

Interestingly, in this solo as in "Got No Blues," Dodds overlooks or ignores the melody's obvious characteristic—the secondary rag rhythm—as well as refrains from any reference to the melody itself (represented by Armstrong's lead). Except for the break, the solo is built on an embellished C pentatonic scale (C - D - E - G - A - C), with the bulk of the structure resting on the pitches of its upper tetrachord (E - G - A - C).

Dodds nicely balances unity and variety among his solo's eight four-bar phrases (Example 9.7). The first phrase (mm. 1-4) both introduces the germinal tetrachord and prolongs E, the second phrase (mm. 5-8) prolongs A by means of its lower neighbor, and the third and fourth phrases (mm. 9-12 and 13-16) expand the range to the C - C octave and beyond while adding the heretofore missing D. After an unprecedented (for Dodds) break that features a glissando over the space of a fourth and the duration of a whole note, the clarinetist begins the second half of his solo with an inversion of his opening leap. The fifth phrase (mm. 17-20) explores the lower fifth of the scale, C - G, and the sixth phrase (mm. 21-24), like the second, prolongs A. Dodds signals the beginning of the seventh phrase (mm. 25-28) in bar 24 with the same G - A - C trichord with which he introduced the third phrase (m. 8). The remainder of the solo (mm. 29-32), a final prolongation of E, recalls the E - G - A trichord from the first phrase but filled in chromatically.

Armstrong solos twice—once on the verse and once on the chorus. Of the two, his solo on the verse paraphrases his previous lead on the verse, but the solo on the chorus (Example 9.8) derives from the harmony alone. Although Schuller discerns discomfort by Armstrong with the stop-time accompaniment (not to mention Ory's famous goof in bar 19), and

Example 9.8. Armstrong's Stop-Time Solo and Tag in "Once in a While"

Brooks imagines that the trumpeter's musical ideas sometimes outstrip his technique, the solo is nonetheless tightly-constructed and memorable.[20]

The first eight measures embody "Bix" Beiderbecke's by-now-familiar "correlated chorus" (see my commentary on "Yes! I'm in the Barrel" and "Cornet Chop Suey"). The descending line (mm. 3-4) complements, for example, the saw-tooth pattern (mm. 1-2) as do the chromaticism and wide leaps (mm. 7-8) and the two-note oscillations (mm. 5-6). Bars 1-4 and 5-8 relate to one another similarly, with the arpeggiation (mm. 1-2) corresponding to the returning leaps (mm. 5-6) and with the step-wise motion (mm. 3-4) corresponding to the chromatic motion (mm. 7-8). Binding these measures still more tightly, a further division into a 6 + 2 grouping can be made on the basis of the arching line, E - G - G♯ - A - A♭ - G - E, which ascends to A (mm. 1-6) and returns to E (mm. 7-8).

The next nine bars (mm. 9-17) divide differently into a grouping of 4 + 2 + 3 by means of successive repeated-note cadences on a descending tonic arpeggio, E - C - G (mm. 12, 14, and 17). Exhibiting some phrasing sleight-of-hand, Armstrong elides the end of his nearly out-of-control break and the beginning of the next phrase (signaled by the return of the stop-time), thus seeming to start the second half of the chorus "one bar late" (m. 18).[21]

The final fifteen bars of the chorus begin by recapping material from the first eight bars with yet another partitioning of phrases. The three-bar phrase (mm. 18-20), whose last two bars echo bars 3-4, allows the regular pattern to be reestablished in bar 21, itself a repeat of bar 5, but now the beginning of a four-bar phrase (mm. 21-24). Armstrong seems to run out of ideas in the final eight bars of the chorus (mm. 25-32), in which 2 + 2 phrasing reappears for the first four bars (mm. 25-28) but then dissolves into repetitions that mark time until the rather abrupt ending.

[20]Gunther Schuller, *Early Jazz*, 113; and Edward Brooks, *The Young Louis Armstrong on Records: A Critical Survey of the Early Recordings, 1923-1928* (Lanham, MD: Scarecrow Press, 2002), 414.

[21]Joshua Berrett, "Louis Armstrong and Opera," 234-35, traces this break to one by Armstrong in "Changeable Daddy Of Mine," recorded by Margaret Johnson with Clarence Williams's Blue Five on 25 November 1924. A more likely precursor, however, is Armstrong's "Struttin' with Some Barbecue" break (Example 9.1, mm. 15-16), of which the "Once in a While" break is largely an inversion.

"I'm Not Rough"*

Table 9.4. Structural Outline of "I'm Not Rough" [A♭ Major]

SECTION	INSTRUMENTATION	BARS
Introduction	Piano	4
Chorus 1	Ensemble	12
Chorus 2	Ensemble / Clarinet Break / Ensemble	6 / 2 / 4
Chorus 3	Ensemble	12
Chorus 4	Guitar Solo	12
Chorus 5	Vocal (Louis) and Guitar Duet	12
Chorus 6	Clarinet / Ensemble (Double-Time) / Ensemble	4 / 4 / 4
Tag	Ensemble	2

The final three Hot Five recordings are notable because of the addition of New Orleans guitarist Lonnie [Alonzo] Johnson, whose participation transformed the quintet into a "Hot Six."[22] As a youngster Louis had known and admired the older Johnson, now an exclusive recording artist for OKeh, and he undoubtedly talked E. A. Fearn into hiring him to sit in.[23] Johnson, also an accomplished violinist, rivals Armstrong as a soloist. Besides his Hot Five appearances, his facile single-string technique is best displayed on OKeh recordings such as "Playing with the Strings" from 1928 and "Guitar Blues" from 1929.

Copyrighted by Lil (see Appendix 1), "I'm Not Rough" re-creates a blues Louis remembered from New Orleans:

> I can see King Joe Oliver, right this minute, blowing his cornet, and playing this tune in the advertising wagons on Sundays. . . . He was with Kid Ory's band at the time. . . . And they played an arrangement to "I'm Not Rough" which we tried to remember the idea when we recorded it.[24]

[22]It was probably remnants of Armstrong's Stompers who were struggling to find work around this time rather than an expanded Hot Five who were praised in the *Chicago Defender* (31 December 1927), 7: "Louis and his Hot Six really play dance music."

[23]Louis Armstrong, *In His Own Words*, 136.

[24]*Ibid.* According to William Russell, interview (27 March 1957) with Paul Barbarin (New Orleans: Hogan Jazz Archive, Tulane University), circa February 1919 Oliver's talking cornet in "I'm Not Rough" won him the title of "King" at the Royal Gardens during his first appearance in Chicago.

Unlike earlier Hot Five blues, "I'm Not Rough" is dominated by ensemble work rather than by the soloists and contains an unusual amount of timbral, melodic, and rhythmic variety—mostly supplied by Johnson. After a rather plodding piano introduction, the guitarist, who leaves the "comping" duties to St. Cyr, introduces what Schuller aptly calls a "zither-like" figure that animates the performance.[25] This tremolo in augmentation —repeated pitches in eighth-note triplets—becomes the central idea in Johnson's solo (Example 9.10); his contrapuntal accompaniment enhances Armstrong's vocal solo (Example 9.11).

The differing approaches and melodic shapes of the first eight bars of Armstrong's solo-like leads complement each other (Example 9.9). Except for anticipating the first two notes of the original tune by two beats, his first chorus paraphrases the melody.[26] In the second chorus, missing from the copyrighted lead sheet, he explores the individual pitches of the tonic triad at the duration of a half note. Taking low E♭ for his departure, he leisurely ascends to its upper octave where he remains before detouring to the blue seventh as in his first chorus before finally dropping to the tonic at the clarinet break. In the third chorus (included on the deposit; see Example 9.11), Armstrong again explores the individual pitches of tonic harmony as in the second chorus but now over the duration of several bars apiece by means of neighboring embellishments.[27] To a varying extent, all leads retain the last four bars of the first chorus from the copyright deposit.

Increasing the level of diversity, the second chorus provides the only break of the piece while the third chorus features a mini call-and-response between the ensemble and guitar (Example 9.9, m. 1)—an event predicted in the first chorus between the trumpet and trombone (m. 1) and repeated in the final chorus between the clarinet and trombone. Finally, the four measures of double-time in the concluding chorus and the six repetitions of a "brutal riff" thereafter to the end of the piece are unparalleled in Original Hot Five recorded literature.[28]

[25]Gunther Schuller, *Early Jazz*, 112.

[26]For a discussion of the origin and ubiquity of the figure in measure 5 of the melody, see Gunther Schuller, *Early Jazz*, 163 (note 40).

[27]Although Armstrong does not often quote himself or resort to stock figures, bar 10 of the third chorus lead is taken from bar 19 of his "Struttin' with Some Barbecue" solo (Example 9.1).

[28]James Lincoln Collier, *Louis Armstrong: An American Genuis* (New York: Oxford University Press, 1983), 185. "Once in a While" also ends with uncharacteristic repetitions. Opinions differ on the effectiveness of double-time in "I'm Not Rough." Gunther Schuller, *Early Jazz*, 112-13, considers Ory's arhythmic glissando at the beginning of the section an "astonishing moment" whose contrast with the change in tempo "is one of those fortunate accidents of intuition that can happen in inspired ensemble improvisation." Edward Brooks, *The Young Louis Armstrong on Records*, 416, finds the device incongruous and "meaningless from a musical standpoint," and John Chilton, in liner notes to

Example 9.9. Comparison of the Copyrighted Melody with Armstrong's First-, Second-, and Third-Chorus Leads in "I'm Not Rough"

Example 9.10. Lonnie Johnson's Solo in "I'm Not Rough"

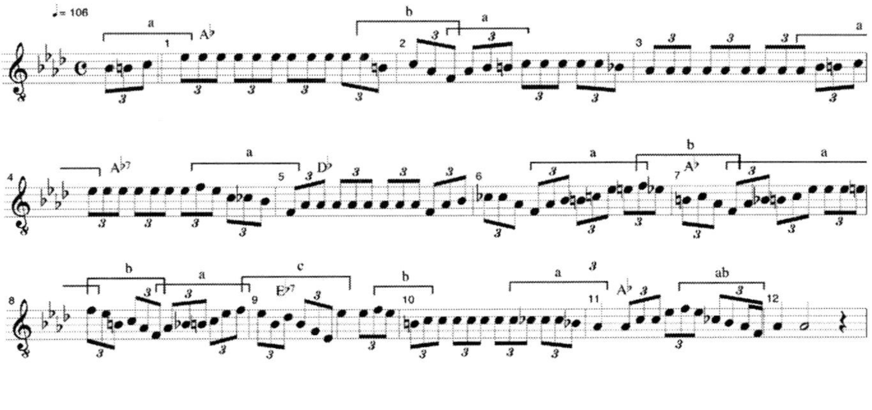

Armstrong's Hot Five and Hot Seven, Vol. III (CBS Records CK44422, 1989), thinks that "the performance never quite recovers from [the] abrupt change of mood."

Example 9.11. Comparison of the Copyrighted Melody with Armstrong's and Johnson's Vocal and Guitar Duet in "I'm Not Rough"

The tone system of Johnson's intriguing solo (Example 9.10 on the previous page) is based on the F minor permutation of the A♭ pentatonic scale with chromatic passing tones between scale degrees three-four and five-six: F - A♭ - B♭ - (B♮ / C♭) - C - E♭ - (E♮) - F. Johnson constructs his solo on reiterated pitches of the tonic triad (A♭ - C – E♭) connected by an "a" version of this scale featuring a chromatic triplet, B♭ - B♮ - C, and a "b" version featuring a descending diminished fourth, E♭ - B♮. His varied and unpredictable connections between the reiterations produce a steady increase in melodic tension until its resolution at "c."[29] Other than the approaches to E♭ at the beginning of the solo and in bar 4, all other reiterated pitches are preceded and/or left by different versions of "a" and "b." As the solo unfolds, the reiterations decrease while the scalar connections increase until bars 6-8 where the latter supercedes the former.

[29]Johnson's style seemed to confuse his accompanist St. Cyr, who moved to the E♭7 a bar early in bar 3, to the subdominant (D♭) a beat too soon in bar 4, and to the dominant (E♭) five beats too soon in bar 7.

At "c" the solo climaxes with its only fully arpeggiated seventh chord, its only rhythmic relief in the stream of triplets, and its "missing" subdominant (D♭) and leading tone (G) to complete the A♭ major scale. After a final reiteration of C, the most "neglected" pitch of the tonic triad heretofore, the solo concludes with a descending scale combining features of "a" and "b."

Armstrong sings the lyrics from the copyrighted lead sheet to a melody approximating the second of the two blues choruses from the deposit (Example 9.11). In contrast with his trumpet leads, Armstrong's vocal line paraphrases the first eight bars of the melody but parts company with it on the last four bars. Johnson's guitar part, heterophonic for the first four bars and contrapuntal for the remainder, rarely matches up rhythmically with the soloist except at cadences. Within phrases he favors three-to-two relationships—triplets against Armstrong's duplets or the reverse. Because of the guitar's independence, the chorus is more of a duet between equals than an accompanied solo. The counterpoint stumbles only briefly on parallel octaves (mm. 3-4).

"Hotter Than That"*

Table 9.5. Structural Outline of "Hotter Than That" [E♭ Major]

SECTION	INSTRUMENTATION	BARS
Introduction	Ensemble	8
Chorus 1	Trumpet Solo / Trumpet Break	14 / 2
	Trumpet Solo / Clarinet Break	14 / 2
Chorus 2	Clarinet Solo / Clarinet Break	14 / 2
	Clarinet Solo / Scat Break	14 / 2
Chorus 3	Scat Solo / Scat Break (Louis)	14 / 2
	Scat Solo / Scat Break (Louis)	14 / 2
Interlude	Ad libitum Vocal / Guitar Alternation	2 / 2 / 2 / 2
	Ad libitum Vocal / Guitar Alternation	2 / 2 / 2 / 2
Transition	Piano	4
Chorus 4	Trombone Solo / Trumpet Break	14 / 2
	Ensemble / Trpt. Break / Ensemble / Guitar Break	8 / 4 / 2 / 2
Coda	Trumpet / Guitar	2 / 2

"Hotter Than That," a tune recorded at the twelfth Hot Five session on 13 December 1927 and copyrighted by Lil but claimed by Armstrong in a 1951 interview,[30] has become canonized as the Hot Five masterpiece in particular and the paradigm of hot jazz practice in general. (See the announcement of its release by OKeh in Illustration 9.3 on page 176.) Conventional in most respects, the piece nevertheless contains several progressive features: an out-chorus accompanied by a trumpet riff on beats one and four, a swing era cliché;[31] a series of dotted quarters in quadruple time, later another jazz cliché;[32] and a final cadence on an unresolved diminished triad, C - E♭ - G♭. This "diminished submediant," also the harmony of Armstrong's and Johnson's antiphonal exchanges in the Interlude (Table 9.5), is less anomalous if viewed as a tonic with a blue

[30]Louis Armstrong, *In His Own Words*, 136.

[31]Frank Tirro, *Jazz: A History*, 178. Armstrong's trumpet riff—twelve consecutive written high C's—actually occurs on beats one and the second half of three.

[32]James Lincoln Collier, *Louis Armstrong*, 188, and "Armstrong, Louis," *The New Grove Dictionary of American Music*, ed. H. Wiley Hitchcock and Stanley Sadie, 4 vols. (New York: Macmillan, 1986), I, 69. The string of dotted quarters, grouped in pairs by long-short articulation, amounts to duplets in triple meter or implied polymeter (Example 9.13, m. 17ff.).

third above and a minor third below, which explains its functional relationship to the prevailing key.[33]

The interesting formal scheme embraces an introduction based on the last eight bars of the thirty-two-bar chorus, no verse, a first chorus solo instead of an ensemble, a thirty-bar third chorus segueing into an off-tempo ad libitum interlude in place of a concluding break, an *a tempo* transition, a segmented out-chorus, and a call-and-response coda. Despite the formal variety, symmetries of sonority and texture supply structural logic. After the ensemble introduction, the instrumentation reduces to soloists with rhythm accompaniment and finally to two soloists without accompaniment (Interlude) before expanding again to soloists with rhythm accompaniment and a concluding ensemble. The predictable pattern of breaks early in the piece leads to a section of continuous breaks (in the Interlude), whose harmony and texture are recalled at the end.[34]

Table 9.6. Harmonic Changes in the Chorus of "Hotter Than That"

BARS	CHANGES
1-8	I / I / I / I / I / I / V7 / V7
9-16	V7 / V7 / V7 / V7 / V7 / V7 / I (Break) / I
17-24	I / I / I / I / V7 - IV / V7 - IV / IV / IV
25-32	IV / vii - V / I / V7- ii / V7 - V / V7 / I (Break) / I

The trio strain of "Tiger Rag," an old New Orleans flag-waver, serves as the harmonic model for "Hotter Than That." A staple in the repertoire of early Crescent City bands, "Tiger Rag" would have been familiar to Hot Five members, with the possible exception of Lil. Armstrong's own knowledge of the tune is dramatically confirmed by a report of a truly memorable evening at the Sunset, where, according to trumpeter Wild Bill Davison, Louis exchanged "one-hundred and twenty-five" choruses of "Tiger Rag" with King Oliver: "People went insane—they threw their clothes on the floor—it was the most exciting thing I ever heard in my life."[35] The simple changes and slow harmonic rhythm must have also contributed to the relaxed confidence projected by the players at the

[33]On use of the submediant as a harmonic pitch above tonic changes in major keys, see commentary on "Georgia Grind," "Got No Blues," and "I'm Not Rough" in this study.

[34]Gunther Schuller, *Early Jazz*, 111-12.

[35]Bill Davison, quoted in James Lincoln Collier, *Louis Armstrong*, 162.

Illustration 9.3.
OKeh Ad for
"Hotter Than That"

From *Chicago Defender* (25 February 1928), 2.

recording of "Hotter Than That," even at the blistering tempo of 220 per quarter note.

In his analysis of "Hotter Than That," William Austin identifies the figure in bars 4-5 as the principal motive in Armstrong's solos and leads.[36] This motive, however, seems rather a variation of the opening gesture "a"—an anacrusis in eighth notes followed by three quarter notes starting on the downbeat. The opening gesture's consequent "b," a further transformation of "a," extends the eighth-note anacrusis, thereby shifting the entry of the quarters to mid-measure (Example 9.12). Bars 6-7 complete the set of correlated phrases that are punctuated by a cadential figure beginning on an eighth-note triplet "c." Because these motives dominate Armstrong's contributions to "Hotter Than That" and his playing or singing occupies more than two-thirds of its duration, much of the melodic material of the piece can be said to stem from the introduction (or his interpretation of the introduction from the copyrighted lead sheet). And, inasmuch as motives "a" and "b" can be regarded as variations of each other, the source of Armstrong's contributions can be further reduced to the opening two bars—a most striking example of his organic approach to improvisation.

Example 9.12. Melodic Motives of Armstrong's Introductory Lead in "Hotter Than That"

Example 9.13 (on the next page) identifies the most conspicuous motivic relationships between Armstrong's introductory lead and his trumpet and vocal solos. In general, Armstrong "develops" the motives from the introduction in his trumpet solo by means of extension and embellishment—a consequence of his switch from two-bar phrasing in the

[36]William Austin, *Music in the 20th Century* (New York: W. W. Norton, 1966), 280-83. Because of the accent on beat three of bar 5, Austin also hears bars 4-6 as two measures of 3 / 2 meter rather than three measures of 4 / 4.

former to four-bar phrasing in the latter. Tension rises (mm. 13-17) when, after the apparent reestablishment of two-bar phrasing (mm. 13-14), one expects the customary break. Instead, Armstrong rips into a high B♭, announcing a break that functions as an anacrusis rather than as a cadence and whose momentum propels the phrase four measures into the second half of the solo.[37] Armstrong reverts to two-bar phrasing towards the end of his solo, which he closes with the motives with which it began.

Example 9.13. Comparison of Copyrighted Melody with Trumpet, Clarinet, and Scat Vocal Solos in "Hotter Than That"

[37]Gunther Schuller, *Early Jazz*, 110, notes that the break in bars 15-16 "is the first instance, in my recollection, of a trumpet break that is not a phrase ending, but a connection to the next improvised segment." For an alternate interpretation of Armstrong's phrasing at this location, see James Lincoln Collier, *Louis Armstrong*, 188.

Example 9.13 Continued.

Aspects of the "correlated chorus" add further to the first half of the trumpet solo's coherence. Descending over the range of a twelfth (F - B♭), phrase one (mm. 1-4) is answered a step higher by the comparable shape and range (G - C) of phrase two (mm. 5-8), which ends with a partial rising return. Acting as a kind of interlude, phrase three (mm. 9-12) descends and ascends within the C - C octave outlined by the second phrase's partial return before phrase four recollects the shapes of phrases one and two in two-bar subphrases (mm. 13-14 and 15-16). The shortening phrase lengths (4 + 4 + 4 + 2 + 2) impose a feeling of acceleration heightened by the step-wise ascent of the phrases' opening pitches that culminate on the dominant (B♭) at the solo's formal and musical climax.

In place of unifying motives derived from the melody by Armstrong, Dodds creates his own—a trichord consisting of a lower chromatic neighbor to the tonic third followed by a leap down to the tonic (F♯ - G - E♭) or up to the fifth (F♯ - G - B♭). He resorts to this pitch cell in whole or in part no less than seven times as well as one of its transpositions (C♯ - D - F) and a quasi inversion (D♭ - C - B♭) at least three times apiece. As in earlier Hot Five solos, Dodds toys with the enharmonicism of the raised second (F♯) and lowered (blue) third (G♭) by introducing the former early in the solo in "preparation" for the latter, which he reserves for climactic spots like breaks or cadences. Bars 25-26, incidentally, correspond to a lick from the same location in Dodds's "You Made Me Love You" solo (Example 7.11).

Armstrong saves the biggest surprises for his scat solo, in which he fragments the motives from the introduction.[38] The phrasing of the first half parallels that of his trumpet solo, including the approach to the second half—but with a twist. Bars 12-15 suggest a repeat of his earlier solo until the appearance of the "b" motive (m. 16). The momentum of the break this time propels the phrase far deeper into the second half of the solo with a chain of dotted quarters in both rhythmic and melodic counterpoint to Johnson's guitar. Armstrong's linear thinking clashes with the harmony in bars 21-22, where he scats a B♮ against the prevailing tonic seventh (V7 / IV). Its eventual resolution to C (m. 23) in conjunction with the descending G - F - E♭ from above makes the dissonance "work."[39] Bars 28-29 again suggest a cadence similar to that of the trumpet solo, but, in place of a concluding break, Armstrong launches into a rhythmically free antiphonal interlude with the guitar on the "diminished submediant."

[38]Bars 1-2 predict Ory's solo, which in turn became the basis for the 1936 hit "Goody Goody."

[39]James Dapogny, "Performance Notes," *Hotter Than That as Recorded by Louis Armstrong and His Hot Five*, transcr. Randy Sandke (Washington, DC: Smithsonian Institution, National Museum of American History, 2000).

"Savoy Blues"*

Table 9.7. Structural Outline of "Savoy Blues" [A♭ Major]

SECTION	INSTRUMENTATION	BARS
Verse 1	Trumpet Solo	16
Chorus 1	Ensemble / Clarinet, Trumpet, Trombone	10 / 2
Interlude 1	Guitar-Banjo	4
Chorus 2	Guitar-Banjo Solo	12
Interlude 2	Guitar-Banjo	4
Chorus 3	Trumpet Solo	12
Chorus 4	Trumpet Solo	12
Chorus 5	Trombone Solo / Trombone Break	10 / 2
Chorus 6	Ensemble / Clarinet, Trumpet, Trombone	10 / 2
Chorus 7	Ensemble / Trumpet Break	10 / 2
Tag	Guitar-Banjo	1

Ory's "Savoy Blues" makes a fitting conclusion to a study of Hot Five achievements. In spite of James Lincoln Collier's designation of it as a "classic New Orleans number,"[40] the piece leaves the Crescent City as far behind as Armstrong has by now left his band mates. In retrospect, at least, it seems a propitious time for Ory, Dodds, St. Cyr, and Lil Armstrong —their styles frozen in time—to be replaced by "Chicago" personnel more compatible with Armstrong's advanced musical ideas.[41]

The tune, which Ory said he wrote two days before the recording,[42] takes its title from Chicago's elegant new ballroom that had opened on Thanksgiving Eve (see Illustration 9.4 for an announcement of its grand opening). Ory had played there with Clarence Black, whose band alternated with Charles Elgar's from opposite ends of its enormous dance floor.[43] The copyright deposit of "Savoy Blues," an unusually complete transcription of the recording not likely in the composer's hand (see

[40]James Lincoln Collier, *Louis Armstrong*, 185.

[41]The personnel change is discussed at length in Brian Harker, *The Early Musical Development of Louis Armstrong, 1901-1928* (Ph.D. dissertation, Columbia University, 1997), 338-45.

[42]Edward "Kid" Ory and Lester Koenig, "The Hot Five Sessions," *The Record Changer* (July-August 1950), 17.

[43]Ory probably joined Black after "William Oray" is listed on page 7 of the 19 November 1927 issue of the *Defender* as the trombonist of a Dave Peyton outfit at Club Bagdad [sic] and before Albert Wynn is listed in his place on page 6 of the 31 December 1927 *Defender*. For a photograph of Ory with Black, see Marili Ertegun, "Just Playing the Music I Love," *Down Beat* 18/16 (10 August 1951), 16. On Black's as a "one-tune" band, see Louis Armstrong, *In His Own Words*, 100-01.

Appendix 1), appears to be the lead sheet for a potential big-band chart, doubtlessly prepared for the Carroll Dickerson Band (featuring Armstrong), which replaced Elgar's on 11 April 1928.[44] This arrangement may have been the one used during a novel performance delivered by the combined forces of Dickerson, Black, and Erskine Tate on 28 April and instigated by I. J. Faggin, the owner of the establishment.

> A note was handed to the house orchestras [Dickerson's and Black's] by Mr Fagin [*sic*], asking them to join in and play "Savoy Blues" with the guest orchestra [Tate's]. This was wonderful. Three bands, consisting of 37 players, rocked the beautiful ballroom with their scintillating music. It was Louis Armstrong, a member of Carroll Dickerson's Orchestra, whom this writer has

Illustration 9.4. Ad for the Grand Opening of the Savoy Ballroom

From *Chicago Defender* (5 November 1927), 10.

[44] *Chicago Defender* (14 April 1928), 7. The copyright deposit was secured on 9 April 1928. In February Armstrong returned to the Metropolitan Theater and the Clarence Jones Band, which was now directed by Carroll Dickerson according to the *Chicago Defender* (4 February 1928), 6; (18 February 1928), 6-7; and (25 February 1928), 6.

termed the "Jazz Master," who saved the hour. As the boys would say, Louie poured plenty of oil and it soaked in too. The crowd gathered around him and wildly cheered for more and more.[45]

The form of "Savoy" is unusual for a Hot Five blues. Rather than opening and closing ensemble choruses framing a series of solos with few, if any, breaks, the relatively complex structure begins with a sixteen-bar solo verse, inserts interludes between the first two choruses, employs mostly arranged instead of improvised ensemble passages, and includes group as well as solo breaks.

Assigned no solos or breaks, Dodds plays a wholly supportive and unassertive role in the proceedings. He and Ory enter so tentatively on the final improvised chorus as to suggest a forgotten or broken "routine." Johnson's simple but elegant solo contrasts in character and execution with Ory's, which is distinguished only by the long glissando break at the end.[46] But Armstrong's two solo choruses shine as the crown jewel of "Savoy Blues"—introspective, reflective, and innovative.

As a measure of Armstrong's development, it is instructive to contrast his solo in "Savoy Blues" with his first solo preserved on record, two successive choruses in "Chimes Blues" with "King" Oliver's Creole Jazz Band in 1923 (Example 9.14 on the next page). Notwithstanding the faster tempo of the earlier one, the two seem to share a similar restrained and subdued nature. With a shared ethos, however, any likeness ends. Built on a single primary idea, a one-bar arpeggiated figure whose repetitions are adapted to the harmonic changes, the "Chimes" solo is assuredly not improvised.[47] Its riff-like construction, in fact, strains its very classification as a solo by its resembling, instead, a glorified accompaniment. And, unlike any Armstrong back-to-back choruses recorded before 1927, both are virtually identical. Nevertheless, several features of the solo herald future Armstrong trademarks: melodic traits of a rip to a high note on a weak beat (m. 12), of the leap to the raised supertonic (mm. 8 and 11), and of the ascending chromatic triplet followed by a descending arpeggio

[45] *Chicago Defender* (5 May 1928), 6.

[46] See Winthrop Sargeant's analysis of portions of Johnson's solo in *Jazz, Hot and Hybrid* (1938), 2nd ed. (New York: E. P. Dutton, 1946; reprinted New York: Da Capo Press, 1975), 93, 101.

[47] "Chimes Blues," recorded in 1927 for Armstrong's *50 Hot Choruses for Cornet* (Chicago: Melrose Bros., 1927), is essentially the same as the first chorus of his 1923 solo. For the solo's "clarinet-like" construction, see Brian Harker, "Louis Armstrong and the Clarinet," *American Music* 21/2 (summer 2003), 143-44.

in the second chorus (mm. 9-10); the relatively advanced harmonies of a passing diminished chord and an implied dominant thirteenth (mm. 6 and 10, respectively); and the metric displacement (mm. 8-9) of the second chorus.[48]

Example 9.14. Armstrong's Solo in "Chimes Blues"

By 1927 the restraint and simplicity of Armstrong's "Chimes Blues" solo, for one writer, had matured into the "quiet tenderness, shading into outright sadness" of his "Savoy Blues" solo.[49] For a different commentator, Armstrong is "sparkling" in "Savoy,"[50] and for another, his playing is characterized by "a certain detachment."[51] Yet another writer finds that the solo's "impassioned phrases"[52] with their "sinuous, subtle, ravishing lines"[53] exude melancholy, while still another hears it as a threnody for

[48]See also the commentary on "Chimes Blues" in Gunther Schuller, *Early Jazz*, 83; James Lincoln Collier, *Louis Armstrong*, 104-05; Brian Harker, "Louis Armstrong and the Clarinet," 143-44; and Edward Brooks, *The Young Louis Armstrong on Records*, 13-16.

[49]James Lincoln Collier, *Louis Armstrong*, 186-87.

[50]Gunther Schuller, *Early Jazz*, 113.

[51]Edward Brooks, *The Young Louis Armstrong on Records*, 420.

[52]Max Jones and John Chilton, *Louis: The Louis Armstrong Story, 1900-1971* (Boston: Little, Brown, 1971; reprinted New York: Da Capo Press, 1988), 263.

[53]Hugues Panassié, *Louis Armstrong* (New York: Charles Scribner, 1972), 80.

racial injustice, suffering, and inequality.[54] Despite these divergent interpretations, most critics agree that the "Savoy" solo is extraordinary and one of Armstrong's best (Example 9.15).

Example 9.15. Armstrong's Solo in "Savoy Blues"

Reasons for such disagreement on the affect of "Savoy Blues" are difficult to specify, but they are probably associated with the relatively relaxed tempo that allows Louis to "stretch out" melodically, swooping and gliding from phrase to phrase in undulating streams of eighth notes and eighth-note triplets. Similarly fluid is Armstrong's rubato-like rhythm enhanced further by his transfer from eighth notes to triplets within most phrases, the implied accelerando impelling the music ever forward.

Beyond their dramatic differences, the antecedent / consequent phrasing of the two solo choruses complements one another even though such relationships are measured by different criteria. First-chorus phrases (mm. 1-8) are formed of a descending arpeggio (mm. 1 and 5) answered by an ascent to a repeated pitch (G in m. 2, D in mm. 6-7); second-chorus phrases in the same portion of the piece are rough sequences of each other. Both choruses embellish prolonged neighbor relationships but on different pitches—D and E in the first and G and A in the second—and for different durations. Both choruses compensate for the absence of traditional fills by employing phrase extensions and expanded pick-ups (mm. 3-4, 7-8, and 11-12), with the extensions and expansions of the

[54]Charles L. Black, Jr., "My World with Louis Armstrong," *Yale Review* 69/1 (Autumn 1979), 150-51.

second chorus being more elaborate, harmonically adventurous, or technically challenging than the first. In short, as its melodic, harmonic, and rhythmic amplification, the second chorus plays consequent to the first chorus's antecedent (Example 9.16).

Example 9.16. Melodic Reduction of Armstrong's Solo in "Savoy Blues"

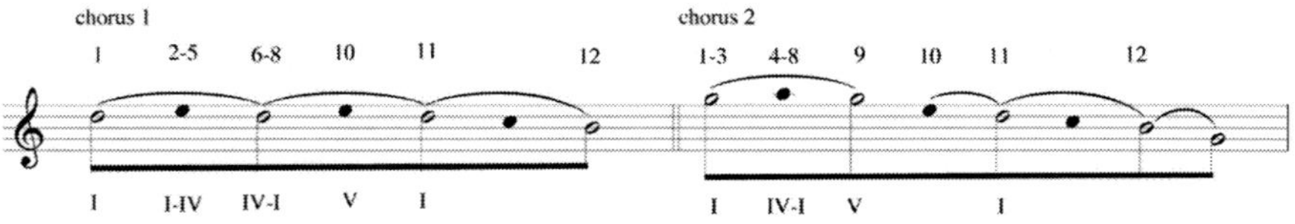

Armstrong's most innovative accomplishments in relation to his Hot Five colleagues lie in his treatment of harmony. Harker notices, for example, that permutations of a passing figure from earlier blues solos, C - D♯ - E - B, becomes, in "Savoy Blues," fully integrated into the trumpeter's musical language (mm. 5 of both choruses; mm. 9 and 11-12 of the second chorus). His predilection for major sevenths in "Struttin' with Some Barbecue" extends to interest in expanded harmonies as well: A as a thirteenth in both choruses (m. 6); E and G as ninths and elevenths in both choruses (m. 9).[55]

What makes these expanded harmonies aurally digestible is that Armstrong serves them up with liberal doses of compelling voice-leading. "Thirteenths," often understood as extensions of the triad to the lower third (*e.g.*, E in m. 11 of both choruses; A in m. 6 of both choruses; and B in m. 10 of the second chorus), also function in "Savoy" as the upper neighbor of the chordal fifth (E in mm. 1 and 3 of the second chorus; A in mm. 2 and 5 of the second chorus). Major sevenths occur as independent harmonies (CM7 in mm. 2 and 10 of the first chorus; GM7 in m. 8 in the second chorus), but ninths and elevenths are more often resolved by step (A to B through an octave-displaced A♯ in mm. 3-4 of the first chorus; A to G in mm. 4-5 of the second chorus and m. 8 in both choruses; C - B in mm. 11-12 of both choruses).

The CM7 against D7 harmony in both choruses (m. 9) emerges as the solo's most striking harmonic juxtaposition. Armstrong demonstrates here that skillful voice-leading trumps blind conformity to the changes. Preparing the move to the dominant with a lengthy anacrusis establishing upper and lower lines (m. 8), he continues the polyphonic melody (m. 9) to converge on the tonic triad (m. 10). This attention to line makes

[55]Brian Harker, *The Early Musical Development of Louis Armstrong*, 245-46.

inevitable the resolution of these passages despite temporary dissonance and prepares for the satisfying return of G harmony (m. 11) (Example 9.17).

Example 9.17. Melodic Reduction of Bars 8-10 of Armstrong's Solo in "Savoy Blues"

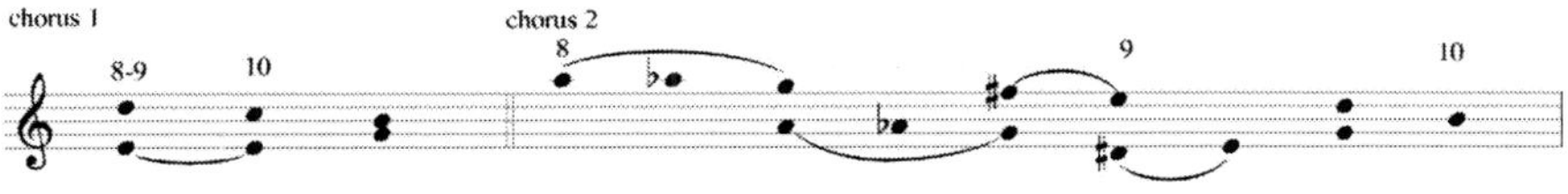

The astonishing passage in bar 8 of the second chorus (see Example 9.15 on page 185) epitomizes the difference between Armstrong and his colleagues, for whom such a lick would be largely unthinkable, if not unplayable. Other than him, one of the few capable of conceiving and executing anything comparable was Earl Hines: his counterpart on piano around whom he forms a new Hot Five in 1928 and with whom he artistically culminates and concludes the entire Hot Five story with "Weather Bird" in 1928.[56]

[56]Gunther Schuller, *Early Jazz*, 124-27; and Jeffrey Taylor, "Louis Armstrong, Earl Hines, and 'Weather Bird,'" *The Musical Quarterly* 83 (Spring 1998), 1-40.

CHAPTER 10

Reflections

Armstrong's Hot Five was a product as well as a representative of its time. Created for commercial reasons—the exploitation of a newly recognized niche market—and sustained on the strength of its recordings alone, the group endured for an unprecedented three years through an augmentation (the Hot Seven) and in spite of a complete transformation (the Chicago Hot Five). But beyond the success of "Heebie Jeebies" and a handful of others,[1] most Original Hot Five recordings are today obscure or entirely forgotten. The appreciation of these evergreen historical treasures by jazz connoisseurs, jazz scholars, and jazz students represents, of course, a conspicuous exception.

The group played a mixture of popular songs, blues, and rags. On the basis of formal considerations, twenty-four of its recorded thirty-three-piece repertory fall into the first category, five into the second, and two into the third, with the remaining two best assigned to a separate hybrid or novelty category. Several numbers, however, contain traits of more than one formal type, *e.g.*, popular songs with a distinct second chorus ("Oriental Strut"), with a separate blues chorus ("Yes! I'm in the Barrel" and "Big Fat Ma and Skinny Pa"), or with ragtime overtones ("Sweet Little Papa").

Popular songs typically exhibit a sixteen-bar verse and a thirty-two-bar chorus, although five of the Hot Fives lack verses and one boasts two. Verses are played only once, usually placed for variety between repeats of the chorus, the vehicle for solos. Because all phrasing is organized in multiples of two or four bars, verses consist of two eight-bar phrases or periods in the pattern of a - a′ or a - b, and choruses consist of four phrases or periods, most often in the pattern of a - b - a′ - c. Eighteen- and thirty-four-bar choruses end with a ten-bar phrase of which the final two bars produce an extended or double cadence. The thirty-bar chorus of "I'm Gonna Gitcha" results from a shortened second phrase of six bars that ends with a two-bar ensemble break. Breaks typically occur in the final two bars of an eight-bar phrase or a sixteen-bar section. None of the Hot Fives are cast in what has come to be known as the standard popular song form: a - a′ - b - a″.

[1]According to Joel Whitburn, *Pop Memories 1890-1954* (Menomonee Falls, WI: Record Research, 1986), 32, "Muskrat Ramble" hit the equivalent of number eight on the pop charts in July 1926, "Big Butter and Egg Man" hit thirteen in April 1927, "Hotter Than That" hit ten in May 1928, and "Struttin' with Some Barbecue" hit fourteen in July 1928.

Hot Five blues adhere to the traditional blues harmonic progression and represent formally the most conservative pieces in the group's repertory: they contain few breaks, are usually constructed of a series of solos between opening and closing ensemble choruses, and probably required little or no rehearsal before cutting the master. Critics are split over the effectiveness of the double-time section in "I'm Not Rough," the most structurally complex blues the Hot Five recorded.

Of the four remaining pieces, "Ory's Creole Trombone" qualifies as a genuine instrumental rag by virtue of its multi-thematic structure, sixteen-bar choruses, and modulation to the subdominant at the third chorus. "Muskrat Ramble" shares these ragtime characteristics except for the modulation, while the idiosyncratic construction of "Skid-Dat-De-Dat" and "King of the Zulus" defies a specific formal classification.

Despite having little time for practice and lacking the luxury of a regular gig where they could hone and polish repertoire before recording, the members of the quintet, nevertheless, paid no small attention to details of performance. Their earliest pieces display evidence of arrangement, awareness of current musical trends, and concern for balancing musical unity and variety. Given their superb musicianship and familiarity with each other's style, what might need rehearsal by lesser players could be handled by a few words or brief demonstration in the studio. Indeed the arpeggiated introduction, stop-time, and 8 - 4 - 4 segmentation of the second half of the final chorus in "My Heart" might be so accomplished, and the same might be assumed for the ensemble riff in the final chorus of "Gut Bucket Blues." But the introductory passage of "Yes! I'm in the Barrel" must have required more time to work out, particularly because it deviates from the lead sheet (see Appendix 1).

In roughly two-thirds of the Hot Five recordings the introductions are short—the apparent point, more often than not, to define the key, to set the character, or to grab the listener's attention rather than to introduce the melody. Sometimes this approach produced incongruous results as in Lil's bombastic beginning of "You're Next" (Example 4.11) or Johnny Dodds's arpeggiated introduction to "The Last Time" (Example 8.7).

The Hot Five believed in ending with a bang. Armstrong's inevitable move into the high register, the front line's increased contrapuntal activity, and a change in the pattern of breaks and ensembles combined to make the typical out-chorus climactic as well as exhilarating. About half of the Hot Fives have two- or four-bar tags built frequently around dazzling cornet breaks. Several of these have ingenious and subtle relationships to the piece: the ascending perfect fourths at the end of "Come Back Sweet Papa" are integral to the melodic structure, the chromaticisms ending "Oriental Strut" come from the trombone part at the beginning of the verse, and the chromatic cornet descent concluding "Sunset Café Stomp" sounds over the tune's Charleston rhythms (Example 10.1). Among the most novel endings are the relatively quiet cadences on diminished harmonies in "Jazz Lips" and "Hotter Than That," but otherwise drastic changes of dynamics are not exploited for purposes of musical variety.

Example 10.1. Tag of "Sunset Café Stomp"

The inclusion of arranged elements in Hot Five renditions probably can be ascribed to Lil. She recalled with pride how "Perdido Street Blues" was entirely written out for its July 1926 recording,[2] and it is tantalizing to imagine that she might have done the same for other performances under consideration in this study.[3] Ensemble breaks, like the one in Lil's "I'm Gonna Gitcha" (Example 5.3), needed some advance preparation, as did the beautiful chorale break in her "Sweet Little Papa" solo that boasts an implied German augmented sixth chord (Example 10.2). Lil's arranging prowess culminates with "Jazz Lips" and "Skid-Dat-De-Dat," in which breaks replace solos, and with "Got No Blues," in which modulations and transitions are navigated to a foreign key (the dominant of the home key's dominant) and back.[4]

Example 10.2. Ensemble Break of "Sweet Little Papa"

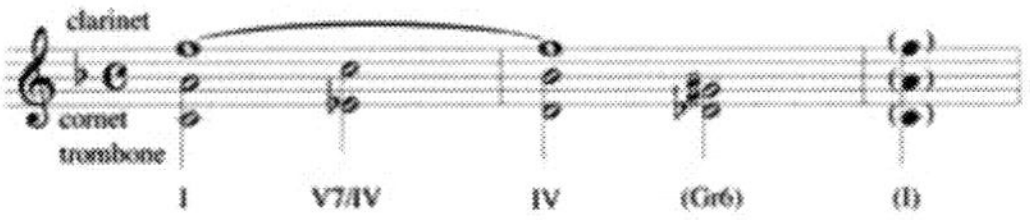

Almost all the Hot Fives are more or less equally distributed among the concert keys of C, F, B♭, E♭, and A♭ major; two, however, are cast in G major, and one, in its relative minor. This distribution is mildly counter-intuitive because it obliged Armstrong to play in sharp keys on half of the

[2]See Chapter 2, note 24.

[3]Louis Armstrong, *Louis Armstrong: In His Own Words*, ed. Thomas Brothers (New York: Oxford University Press, 1999), 132. Lil added instrumental parts to lead sheets composed by Louis.

[4]If "Got No Blues" was indeed a "quickie" made up at the studio as Armstrong claimed, increased respect must be accorded Hot Five musicianship.

recordings. While written high C (concert B♭) is a formidable but playable pitch on the cornet, high B, on which Armstrong ends "Cornet Chop Suey" and which appears repeatedly in several other solos, high C♯ in his "King of the Zulus" solo, and high D in his "Struttin' with Some Barbecue" solo are disproportionately more difficult to play, for reasons of embouchure and control, than their proximity to high C suggests.

Variety of dynamics, key, and tempo lacking in the Hot Five sides is compensated for by variety of texture, instrumentation, and form. In these respects every recording is unique and unformulaic. Armstrong dominates the solo space, especially in the later Hot Fives, with instrumental solos on eighteen numbers and vocal solos on thirteen—sometimes one of each in the same tune. Dodds solos on twenty-one (twice on saxophone); Ory, on fourteen; Lil, on nine; and St. Cyr, on two. Sitting in on guitar, Johnson solos on two numbers, and Clark, substituting for Ory, solos on one. In addition, Armstrong is featured in a slide-whistle duet with Dodds and a vocal-guitar duet with Johnson.

While the Hot Five recordings are musically engaging and executed well, my study confirms that without Armstrong they would be of little interest today. But the study further confirms that the brightness of the Armstrong sun has succeeded in blinding listeners to the abilities and achievements of his colleagues. Dodds at his best is Armstrong's equal as a soloist. In another publication I argue for such equality in the Hot Seven's "Wild Man Blues,"[5] while among the Hot Fives, Dodds's solos in "My Heart," "Yes! I'm in the Barrel," "Who'sit," "Once in a While," and "Hotter Than That" are harmonically-based and motivically-organized minor masterpieces—different from but not inferior to Armstrong's better efforts. A superb ensemble player with excellent technique, Dodds also contributes an impressive, if limited, selection of exciting breaks. The clarinetist, although he did not compose for the Hot Five, left behind at his death a "trunk of music" and one copyrighted piece written for his own groups.[6]

As a recent reviewer aptly put it, Ory's "rawness—at times even crudeness"—forms part of this music's charm.[7] Like Dodds, an extremely competent if not consummate ensemble player, Ory fulfills ably the

[5]Gene Anderson, "Blues for You, Johnny: Johnny Dodds and His 'Wild Man Blues' Recordings of 1927 and 1928," *Annual Review of Jazz Studies* 8 (1996), 56.

[6]Gene Anderson, "Johnny Dodds in New Orleans," *American Music* 8/4 (Winter 1990), 416.

[7]Randy Sandke, review of Edward Brooks, *The Young Louis Armstrong on Records: A Critical Survey of the Early Recordings, 1923-1928*, in *Annual Review of Jazz Studies* 12 (2004), 206.

multiple roles of quasi-bassist and quasi-drummer in addition to his duties as trombonist. More rhythmically than melodically inventive, Ory renders his best solo of this set in "King of the Zulus," for whose "primitive" style and limited harmonies it is perfectly suited. Bursting energy suffuses all of his solos and breaks, however, while his copyrighted "Muskrat Ramble" endures as the most famous of the Hot Fives, and his "Savoy Blues" stands among the best.

Both St. Cyr and Lil keep exemplary time. In only a few tunes does the tempo flag or vacillate; normally it remains reliably consistent for the duration of the performances. These two know the "routines" of the pieces best and hold the band together with a confident supply of rhythmic and harmonic glue that binds even the most fragmented numbers into coherent wholes. Both have a solid working knowledge of common-practice harmony, which St. Cyr demonstrates in his "Got No Blues" modulation and Lil displays in "Lonesome Blues" with her "out-of-key" (V7 / IV - IV - V) introduction.

Assuming that the Hot Five sessions were conducted in the same manner as the Hot Sevens, Louis ran rehearsals and called the shots in the studio but on technical matters deferred to Lil, who transcribed music "as fast as Louis played."[8] "Baby" Dodds, drummer in the May 1927 Hot Sevens, remembered the circumstances:

> While we rehearsed the music in the recording studio we were not paid but when the technician held his hand up to signal that a master was made, that was your money. Each musician got thirty dollars a side. . . . With Louis' outfit [Hot Seven] we used to have rehearsals and anything that we had in mind for any particular number we would work out then. He would tell each of us when to take a solo or when not to, and who would come in at different times. . . . We would stop and talk it out more than anything else. If there was any writing involved, Lil would write down what the musicians were supposed to do. Of course we all had our ideas to give the band, and we would work them out at rehearsal. Later we rehearsed the number again in the recording studio. Whenever a fellow wanted to change something he

[8]Nat Shapiro and Nat Hentoff, *Hear Me Talkin' to Ya: The Story of Jazz as Told by the Men Who Made It* (New York: Rinehart, 1955; reprinted New York: Dover Publications, 1966), 102.

would ask Louis for his opinion and if it was agreeable it was in. But Louis allowed each of us to take a lot of responsibility for those records. If I would even ask him a question about playing he'd say "Ah go ahead, you know what to do." That made us responsible and gave us plenty of leeway to use our own ideas. The only thing that Louis demanded was that we worked to do our best on the records.[9]

Lil's role in the success of the Hot Five enterprise, nevertheless, has been undervalued and largely overlooked. Her classical training may have spawned the most progressive features of compositions like "Struttin' with Some Barbecue" and "Skid-Dat-De-Dat."[10] Extant copyright deposits testify to her compositional skills, and further research could confirm that she should be celebrated as one the Hot Five's unsung heroes rather than abused as one of its second-rate soloists.

Armstrong's brilliance, assumed at the beginning of this study, has been amply demonstrated by it and is thereby strongly reinforced. The Hot Five recordings chronicle a refinement of his creative powers into what Harker calls a unified solo style,[11] but they also show that the evolution of his harmonically-based style is more circuitous than Schuller's depiction of it.[12] Even if Armstrong did not escape the "hegemony of paraphrase" until after the Hot Fives as Gushee contends,[13] it might be more pertinent to question the primacy of harmonically-based improvisation over melodic variation as the capstone of Armstrong's singular accomplishments. As has been observed, Dodds normally disregarded the melody in his solos, and yet they are not universally acclaimed.

In addition to antecedent / consequent phrasing and the application of pitch-cells, kernels, germinal melodic / rhythmic motives, as well as other

[9]Warren "Baby" Dodds and Larry Gara, *The Baby Dodds Story, as Told to Larry Gara*, 2nd ed. (Baton Rouge: Louisiana State University Press, 1992), 72.

[10]Joshua Berrett, *Louis Armstrong & Paul Whiteman: Two Kings of Jazz* (New Haven: Yale University Press, 2004), 71-75.

[11]Brian Harker, "'Telling a Story': Louis Armstrong and Coherence in Early Jazz," *Current Musicology* 63 (1999), 58.

[12]Gunther Schuller, *Early Jazz: Its Roots and Musical Development* (New York: Oxford University Press, 1968), 103.

[13]Lawrence Gushee, "The Improvisation of Louis Armstrong," *In the Course of Performance: Studies in the World of Musical Improvisation*, ed. Bruno Nettl (Chicago: University of Chicago Press, 1998), 300-04.

unifying devices, Armstrong's harmonically-based solos exhibit compelling voice-leading, sometimes in conflict with underlying harmonic changes. This balance of the horizontal and vertical musical axes, evident to some extent in all his solos but most apparent in "Struttin' with Some Barbecue," is, in my opinion, what sets Armstrong apart from his contemporaries and is key to his greatness as a soloist. The ability to internalize the harmonic and melodic possibilities of a tune simultaneously when coupled with imaginative phrasing, mastery of rhythm, avoidance of stock figures, and the capacity to conceive the work as a whole completes Armstrong's awe-inspiring genius.

History has reduced the Hot Five's contemporary artistic rivals to one: the Red Hot Peppers of Ferdinand "Jelly Roll" Morton—specifically, the seventeen titles that band made for Victor between 15 September 1926 and 10 June 1927 in Chicago. Like the Hot Five, the Red Hot Peppers was exclusively a recording outfit composed almost entirely of New Orleans musicians, including, at times, Dodds, Ory, and St. Cyr from Armstrong's group. The Red Hot Peppers, too, have been said to epitomize the early New Orleans style of collective improvisation and, as such, represented jazz of the past as much as of the present or future.[14] Both bands, likewise, recorded a mixed repertoire of mostly original tunes in the form of blues, pop songs, stomps, and rags.

Size, instrumentation, and stability of personnel represent the most obvious distinctions between the Hot Five and the Red Hot Peppers. Beginning as a septet of cornet (George Mitchell), trombone ("Kid" Ory), clarinet (Omer Simeon), piano (Morton), banjo (St. Cyr), bass (John Lindsay), and drums (Andrew Hilaire), the Red Hot Peppers anticipated, except for a string bass instead of a tuba, the makeup of Armstrong's Hot Seven. After waxing eleven sides in 1926, Morton returned to the studio in 1927 with replacements on trombone (Gerald Reeves), clarinet (Johnny Dodds), and drums ("Baby" Dodds); with an added alto saxophone (Paul "Stump" Evans); with a guitar (Bud Scott) in place of the banjo; and with a tuba (Quinn Wilson) in place of the string bass. On 4 June 1927 this reincarnation of the Red Hot Peppers recorded Morton's "Wild Man Blues," which had already been recorded by the Hot Seven a little more than a month previously. A comparison of these events will serve to

[14]For the Hot Five, see Chapter 1, note 1. For the Red Hot Peppers, see Gunther Schuller, *Early Jazz*, 161.

illustrate basic differences between Armstrong and Morton as composers, performers, and leaders.[15]

The Hot Seven's "Wild Man" showcases Armstrong and Dodds, whose back-to-back solos on the thirty-two bar chorus are framed by a short introduction and tag ending. Both players follow the tune on the lead sheet submitted as the copyright deposit by Morton's publishers, the Melrose Brothers, parlaying its segmented construction into an alternating two-bar series of accompanied melody and solo breaks. Except for some preliminary hokum and a similarly brief introduction and ending, the Red Hot Peppers's version of "Wild Man" is formally much more intricate. Morton interpolates an alto saxophone solo on the twelve-bar non-blues verse between opening cornet and concluding piano and clarinet solos on the chorus. These latter solos elevate the implied breaks in the tune's construction to its predominant feature by assigning them to different instruments and changing their character (*e.g.*, double-time), thereby producing a variety of unexpected combinations of timbre and texture. Thus the structural simplicity, unity, and relative predictability of the Hot Seven performance is answered by one of complexity, contrast, and relative surprise by the Red Hot Peppers.[16] A reliance on timbre and texture as important formal devices in addition to rhythm, harmony, and melody distinguish Morton's ensembles from Armstrong's and others of the time.

A month or so after the Red Hot Peppers session, the Melrose Brothers published a stock arrangement of "Wild Man Blues," on which the names of "Jelly Roll" Morton and Louis Armstrong both appeared. Armstrong denied writing the tune, but the citation was no accident. Tiny Parham, the arranger, included a transcription of Louis's solo from the "Wild Man" recording by Johnny Dodds's Black Bottom Stompers made two weeks before the Hot Seven's. This incident exemplifies the reciprocal relationship of Armstrong and Morton to their craft: Louis as performer / composer and "Jelly Roll" as composer / performer, an observation borne out as well by the role each played in their respective groups and by the

[15]The following material for comparison is taken from my article, "Blues for You, Johnny," 39-51, which contains the relevant musical examples and formal diagrams.

[16]This synopsis only scratches the surface of Morton's mastery of form and orchestration, which has long been acknowledged; see Gunther Schuller, *Early Jazz*, 155-65, and Martin Williams, *The Jazz Tradition* (New York: Oxford University Press, 1970), 39-42, for additional examples and analyses. Morton's pursuit of timbral diversity also led him to add a clarinet trio on single choruses in "Sidewalk Blues" and "Dead Man Blues," a bass clarinet solo and two added violins in "Someday Sweetheart," vocal effects throughout "Hyena Stomp" and "Billy Goat Stomp," a reiterating gong in "Jungle Blues," and castanets during the cornet solo in "Original Jelly Roll Blues."

approach each adopted to studio sessions themselves. Louis's rehearsals, as has been noted, were minimalist and informal.[17] "Jelly," on the other hand, drilled his musicians meticulously until they satisfied his standards of musicianship and fulfilled his strongly held ideas about the piece. He fussed over details of orchestration—lavishing special attention on the beginnings, endings, and background accompaniments—but gave soloists free rein. Rather than using lead sheets or no music at all like the Hot Five, the Red Hot Peppers generally read stock arrangements that the Melrose Brothers later published.[18] "Baby" Dodds put it succinctly: "It was different from recording with Louis."[19] Morton's careful preparation paid off in superb cuts, enhanced further by Victor's electric recording process and the company's willingness to make multiple takes; Louis's and OKeh's musical and technical demands were less stringent.

Morton was a stylistic reactionary—an unrepentant chauvinist with regard to New Orleans music and an indefatigable champion of his own role in its creation. Omer Simeon noted that, "if the musicians couldn't play real New Orleans, he'd [Jelly] get somebody else."[20] Schuller's judgment may be accepted as definitive: Morton "represents the end of a line."[21]

> [His] hold-out . . . for the earlier ragtime-*cum*-blues admixture ran straight against the main current. . . . The fact remains that by the time Morton hit his peak in the Red Hot Peppers recordings, the kind of material he used and many of the ways in which he used it had become old-fashioned and no longer interested the young avant-gardists of the twenties.[22]

[17]See Chapter 10, note 9.

[18]Omer Simeon, "Mostly about Morton," *Selections from the Gutter: Jazz Portraits from* The Jazz Record, ed. Art Hodes and Chadwick Hansen (Los Angeles: University of California Press, 1977), 92-93.

[19]Warren "Baby" Dodds and Larry Gara, *The Baby Dodds Story*, 74.

[20]Omer Simeon, quoted without documentation in Alan Lomax, *Mister Jelly Roll: The Fortunes of Jelly Roll Morton, New Orleans Creole and "Inventor of Jazz"* (1949), 2nd ed. (Los Angeles: University of California Press, 1973; reprinted Los Angeles: University of California Press, 2001), 194.

[21]Gunther Schuller, *Early Jazz*, 150.

[22]*Ibid.*

Today one can "enjoy in retrospect the formal splendors of his work as a last great flowering of an already dying and superseded tradition."[23] Morton's preference for multi-themed compositions constitutes the main evidence for ragtime residue in his music,[24] with single-theme works like "Hyena Stomp" or "Jungle Blues" rare or deliberately elemental. Even so, his increasingly complex variations on the theme of "Hyena Stomp," for example, blur the distinction between a successive variation and a new theme, thereby retaining the multi-thematic effect.[25] As he demonstrated on the Library of Congress recordings, however, Morton was fully conversant with the characteristics differentiating ragtime from jazz and confidently and self-consciously made his stylistic choices.[26]

How influential was the Hot Five on jazz of its time? I find compelling Gushee's skeptical consideration of this question, of which the following is a summary.[27] Little solid evidence exists to support the sweeping claims made about the Hot Five by writers like Schuller[28] and Collier.[29] To evaluate their pronouncements two criteria might be proposed: imitation of repertory—or creation of jazz "standards"—and imitation of ensemble performance style. It is "striking that virtually none of the Hot Five and Hot Seven became 'standards,'"[30] in contrast to Morton's "Milenberg Joys" and "King Porter Stomp," and to a dozen or so tunes from the Original Dixieland Jazz Band's repertoire. Dissemination of Morton's music through publications and the technical excellence of the Victor recordings

[23]*Ibid.*, 151.

[24]James Dapogny, "Jelly Roll Morton and Ragtime," *Ragtime: Its History, Composers, and Music*, ed. John Hasse (New York: Schirmer Books, 1985), 265.

[25]See Martin Williams's informative, if flawed, analysis in *The Jazz Tradition*, 34-36. "Hyena Stomp" was "tricky" and "took quite a bit of rehearsing . . . to get just what Jelly wanted," according to "Baby" Dodds in *The Baby Dodds Story*, 74.

[26]Jelly Roll Morton, *The Library of Congress Recordings*, 4 vols., ed. James Dapagny (Cambridge, MA: Rounder Record Corporation 1091-1094, 1993).

[27]Lawrence Gushee, "The Improvisation of Louis Armstrong," 303-05.

[28]See Chapter 1, note 3.

[29]James Lincoln Collier, *Louis Armstrong: An American Genius* (New York: Oxford University Press, 1983), 169. According to Collier, the Hot Fives constitute "the most important set of recordings of twentieth century improvised music . . . recognized immediately by musicians, jazz fans, and a growing, if still small, larger public. All across the United States musicians were enthralled by what Armstrong was doing. . . ."

[30]Lawrence Gushee, "Modes of Reception / Influence: The Influence of Louis Armstrong," *Musica Oggi: Louis Armstrong verso il ventunesimo secolo* 21 (2001), 25. Only the Armstrong Orchestra's "Basin Street Blues" made Richard Crawford's list of jazz standards with twenty or more recordings; see his "Notes on Jazz Standards by Black Authors and Composers, 1899-1942," *New Perspectives on Music: Essays in Honor of Eileen Southern*, ed. Josephine Wright (Warren, MI: Harmonie Park Press, 1992), 247, 258.

increased the probability for its commercial success over Armstrong's relative lack of publications and OKeh's acoustically recorded sound. On the other hand, the idiosyncratic performance style of the Hot Five was difficult to emulate, let alone imitate successfully. Armstrong's influence, separate from that of the Hot Five and Hot Seven, accumulated gradually until by 1930-1931 "it's virtually a tidal-wave."[31] But, in the meantime, the Hot Five preached mainly to a small congregation of young Chicago musicians.

Judged by the popular music standards of its own day, the Original Hot Five was an extraordinary partnership of extraordinary players. All members understood their functions in the ensemble and fulfilled them admirably. Conversant with every aspect of their craft, they were "total musicians" capable of making sophisticated decisions that governed performances from their creation through their execution. But these professional entertainers were not self-consciously attempting to prove anything or to break new ground. According to Armstrong himself, the point was simply to make extra money and to play.[32]

Judged by the standards of formal aesthetics, the creations of the Original Hot Five fare less evenly but unexpectedly well overall. Close scrutiny of this body of music has been shown to enhance the group's reputation instead of reducing it, elevate admiration for its individual players instead of lowering it, uncover elegance instead of vulgarity, reveal strength instead of weakness, and disclose competence instead of incompetence. Most of all, this investigation finds Louis Armstrong, by any analytical measure, worthy of the universal adulation he experienced during his lifetime and the posthumous canonization to which he has already been elevated. He fully deserves the crown as "King of Jazz."[33]

[31]Lawrence Gushee, "The Improvisation of Louis Armstrong," 304.

[32]Louis Armstrong, *In His Own Words*, 135-36; and Max Jones and John Chilton, *Louis: The Louis Armstrong Story, 1900-1971* (Boston: Little, Brown, 1971; reprinted New York: Da Capo Press, 1988), 112.

[33]Dan Morgenstern, "Louis Armstrong and the Development and Diffusion of Jazz," *Louis Armstrong: A Cultural Legacy*, ed. Marc H. Miller (Seattle: University of Washington Press, 1994), 95. Editor's Note: The appropriation of this particular honorific by Paul Whiteman during the 1920s must be related to the use of the term "jazz" at that time and the widespread popularity of the Whiteman band.

Cited Sources and Suggested Readings

The following entries have been classified to distinguish between those studies that feature transcriptions and analysis and those that do not. The reader, in addition, should be alerted to the much more comprehensive compilation of Armstrong-related publications, organized by year since 1932, made available online by scholars associated with the Jazz-Institut in Darmstadt (http://www/jazzinstitut.de/Jazzindex/index-armstrong-index.htm) as well as the considerable holdings of various kinds, including Armstrong's personal collections, in the Louis Armstrong Archives at Queens College in New York City (see http://www.satchmo.net). The splendid documentary *Satchmo: Louis Armstrong* (Toby Byron, producer; *Masters of American Music* series, 1986) presents a generous amount of historic footage of Armstrong and his colleagues in complete performances as well as cameos of Armstrong taken from various commercial films. Please note, moreover, that the *Chicago Defender*, a newspaper rich in details for my study, was published in both a city and a national edition; the city edition carried local advertisements and occasionally local news items omitted from the national edition.

Titles Featuring Transcriptions and Analysis

Anderson, Charles. *Charles B. Anderson's Master Fake Book*. Rancho Palos Verdes, CA: Jim Jones / Yestertunes, 2001. Anderson's fake book contains lead sheets of twenty-three of the Original Hot Fives—eight not found elsewhere—with rough transcriptions of several Armstrong solos.

Anderson, Gene. "Blues for You, Johnny: Johnny Dodds and His 'Wild Man Blues' Recordings of 1927 and 1928," *Annual Review of Jazz Studies* 8 (1996), 39-62.

Armstrong, Louis. *Cornet Chop Suey as Recorded by Louis Armstrong and His Hot Five*, transcr. Randy Sandke, ed. David Baker. Washington, DC: Smithsonian Institution, National Museum of American History, 2000.

______. *50 Hot Choruses for Cornet*. Chicago: Melrose Bros., 1927.

______. *The Louis Armstrong Collection*, transcr. Forrest "Woody" Mankowski. Milwaukee: Hal Leonard, [n. d.]. Of the five Original Hot Five titles included, four transcriptions are identical to Castle's and the remaining one ("Muskrat Ramble") is taken from a later Armstrong performance.

______. *Louis Armstrong: Great Trumpet Solos*, transcr. Peter Ecklund. New York: Charles Colin, 1995. The collection, for B♭ trumpet, contains thirteen Original Hot Five solos, of which eight overlap with Castle. No leads are transcribed.

______. *Louis Satchmo Armstrong's Immortal Trumpet Solos*, transcr. Lee Castle [Castaldo]. New York: Leeds Music, 1947. The oldest but still the most reliable transcriptions of Armstrong solos and leads, this collection, in concert keys, includes thirteen of the Original Hot Fives, although "Irish Black Bottom" inexplicably is taken from a recording of the Yerba Buena Jazz Band. Castle, a late swing-era trumpeter and band leader of some repute, provides performance suggestions for each selection. This collection of transcriptions has gone through numerous editions by a variety of publishers.

______, and Lillian Hardin. *Hotter Than That as Recorded by Louis Armstrong and His Hot Five*, transcr. Randy Sanke. Washington, DC: Smithsonian Institution, National Museum of American History, 2000.

Austin, William. *Music in the 20th Century*. New York: W. W. Norton, 1966.

Baker, David. "Two Classic Louis Armstrong Solos," *Down Beat* 38 (16 September 1971), 1029-30.

Berrett, Joshua. "Louis Armstrong and Opera," *The Musical Quarterly* 76/2 (1992), 216-41.

Brooks, Edward. *Influence and Assimilation in Louis Armstrong's Cornet and Trumpet Work, 1923-1928*. Lewiston, NY: Edwin Mellon Press, 2000.

______. *The Young Louis Armstrong on Records: A Critical Survey of the Early Recordings, 1923-1928*. Lanham, MD: Scarecrow Press, 2002.

Brothers, Thomas. "Soul and Cycle in African-American Jazz," *The Musical Quarterly* 78/3 (Fall 1994), 479-509.

Caffey, H. David. "The Musical Style of Louis Armstrong, 1925-1929," *Journal of Jazz Studies* 3/1 (Fall 1975), 72-96.

Carlson, William Ralph. *A Procedure for Teaching Jazz Improvisation Based on an Analysis of the Performance Practice of Three Major Jazz Trumpet Players: Louis Armstrong, Dizzy Gillespie, and Miles Davis*. Ph.D. dissertation, Indiana University, 1981.

Collier, Geoffrey L., and James Lincoln Collier. "A Study of Timing in Two Louis Armstrong Solos," *Music Perception* 19/3 (Spring 2002), 463-83.

Collier, James Lincoln. "Armstrong, Louis," *The New Grove Dictionary of American Music*, 4 vols., ed. H. Wiley Hitchcock and Stanley Sadie. New York: Macmillan, 1986. I, 67-71.

______. "Armstrong, Louis," *The New Grove Dictionary of Jazz*, 2 vols., ed. Barry Kernfeld. London: Macmillan, 1988. I, 27-31.

______. *Louis Armstrong: An American Genius*. New York: Oxford University Press, 1983.

Dapogny, James. "Performance Notes" accompanying *Cornet Chop Suey as Recorded by Louis Armstrong and His Hot Five*, transcr. Randy Sandke. Washington, DC: Smithsonian Institution, National Museum of American History, 2000.

______. "Performance Notes" accompanying *Hotter Than That as Recorded by Louis Armstrong and His Hot Five*, transcr. Randy Sandke. Washington, DC: Smithsonian Institution, National Museum of American History, 2000.

Domek, Richard. "Musical Organization and Trademarks in the Maturing Solos of Louis Armstrong," *Jazz Research Papers*. Manhattan, KS: NAJE, 1996. 32-47.

Ecklund, Peter. "'Louis' Licks and Nineteenth-Century Cornet Etudes: The Roots of Melodic Improvisation as Seen in the Jazz Style of Louis Armstrong," *Historic Brass Society Journal* 13 (2001), 90-101.

Grigson, Lionel. *A Louis Armstrong Study Album*. London: Novello, 1992.

Gushee, Lawrence. "The Improvisation of Louis Armstrong," *In the Course of Performance: Studies in the World of Musical Improvisation*, ed. Bruno Nettl. Chicago: University of Chicago Press, 1998. 291-334.

Harker, Brian C. *The Early Musical Development of Louis Armstrong, 1901-1928*. Ph.D. dissertation, Columbia University, 1997.

______. "Louis Armstrong and the Clarinet," *American Music* 21/2 (Summer 2003), 137-58.

______. "'Telling A Story': Louis Armstrong and Coherence in Early Jazz," *Current Musicology* 63 (1999), 46-83.

Hodeir, André. *Jazz, Its Evolution and Essence*, trans. David Noakes. New York: Grove Press, 1956; reprinted New York: Da Capo Press, 1975.

Hüger, Florian H. "'Ory's Creole Trombone': Transkription und Analyse der ersten Schallplattenaufnahme einer schwarzen New Orleans Jazzband," *Jazzforschung* 23 (1991), 9-115.

Jackson, Robert. "Analysis of Selected Louis Armstrong Solos," *Jazz Research Papers,* Vol. 5. Manhattan, KS: NAJE, 1985. 74-81.

Lyttelton, Humphrey. *The Best of Jazz: Basin Street to Harlem, 1917-1930*. New York: Taplinger, 1978.

Magee, Jeffrey. *The Music of Fletcher Henderson and His Orchestra in the 1920s*. Ph.D. dissertation, Columbia University, 1992.

______. *The Uncrowned King of Swing: Fletcher Henderson and Big Band Jazz*. New York: Oxford University Press, 2005.

Poe, Gerald D. "An Examination of Four Selected Solos Recorded by Louis Armstrong between 1925-1928," *NACWPI Journal* (Fall 1975), 3-9.

Porter, Lewis, and Michael Ullman. *Jazz from Its Origins to the Present*. Englewood Cliffs, NJ: Prentice-Hall, 1993.

Reeves, Scott. "From Pops to Miles: The Evolution of the Jazz Vocabulary," *Jazz Research Papers*, Vol. 13. Manhattan, KS: NAJE, 1996. 113-22.

Russell, William. "Play That Thing, Mr. Johnny Dodds," *Jazz Information* (23 August 1940), 10-11.

Sargeant, Winthrop. *Jazz, Hot and Hybrid* (1938), 2nd ed. New York: E. P. Dutton, 1946; reprinted New York: Da Capo Press, 1975.

Schuller, Gunther. *Early Jazz: Its Roots and Musical Development*. New York: Oxford University Press, 1968.

Spencer, Peter. "Jazz and the Folk Process," *Sing Out* 32 (1986), 20-26.

Storb, Ilse. *Louis Armstrong: The Definitive Biography*, trans. Bertram Thompson. New York: Peter Lang, 1999.

Taylor, Jeffrey. "Louis Armstrong, Earl Hines, and 'Weather Bird,'" *The Musical Quarterly* 83 (Spring 1998), 1-40.

Tirro, Frank. *Jazz: A History*, 2nd ed. New York: W. W. Norton, 1993.

Winter, Keith. "Communication Analysis in Jazz," *Jazzforschung* 11 (1979), 93-133.

Other Titles

1920 Census—United States, City of Chicago.

Allen, Walter, and Brian Rust. *"King" Oliver*, rev. Laurie Wright. Chigwell, Essex: Storyville, 1987.

Anderson, Ernie. "Louis Armstrong, A Personal Memoir," *Storyville* 148 (1 December 1991), 125-48.

Anderson, Gene. "The Genesis of King Oliver's Creole Jazz Band," *American Music* 12/3 (Fall 1994), 283-303.

______. "Johnny Dodds in New Orleans," *American Music* 8/4 (Winter 1990), 405-40.

Anderson, Gillian. "Putting the Experience of the World at the Nation's Command: Music at the Library of Congress, 1800-1917," *Journal of the American Musicological Society* 42/1 (Spring 1989), 108-49.

Armstrong, Lillian. "Lil Armstrong Reminisces about Early Chicago Days," *Down Beat* 18/11 (1 June 1951), 12.

______. "Lil Tells of 1st Time She Met Louis," *Down Beat* 17/14 (14 July 1950), 18.

______. *Satchmo and Me: Lil Armstrong's Own Story* [recorded memoir]. Riverside RLP 12-120, ca. 1950-1959. Portions of this interview are reproduced in Berrett's *Louis Armstrong Companion*.

Armstrong, Louis. *Louis Armstrong: In His Own Words*, ed. Thomas Brothers. New York: Oxford University Press, 1999.

______. *Satchmo: A Musical Autobiography* [recorded commentary]. Verve Records 314-543-822-2, 1957; reissued 2001.

______. *Satchmo: My Life in New Orleans*. New York: Prentice-Hall, 1954; reprinted New York: Da Capo Press, 1986.

______. *Swing That Music*. New York: Longmans, Green, 1936; reprinted New York: Da Capo Press, 1993.

Avakian, George. "The Jazz Reissue Program," *JazzTimes* (October 2000), 43-45.

Banks, Ann, ed. *First Person America*. New York: Alfred A. Knopf, 1980.

Barker, Danny. *A Life in Jazz*, ed. Alyn Shipton. New York: Oxford University Press, 1986.

Bechet, Sidney. *Treat It Gentle*, 2nd ed. New York: Hill and Wang, 1960; reprinted New York: Da Capo Press, 2002.

Bergreen, Laurence. *Louis Armstrong: An Extravagant Life*. New York: Broadway Books, 1997.

Berlin, Edward. *Ragtime: A Musical and Cultural History*. Berkeley: University of California Press, 1980.

Berrett, Joshua. *Louis Armstrong & Paul Whiteman: Two Kings of Jazz*. New Haven: Yale University Press, 2004.

______, ed. *The Louis Armstrong Companion: Eight Decades of Commentary*. New York: Schirmer Books, 1999.

Billboard (1928).

Black, Charles L., Jr. "My World with Louis Armstrong," *Yale Review* 69/1 (Autumn 1979), 145-51.

Blesh, Rudi, and Harriet Janis. *They All Played Ragtime*. New York: Oak Publications, 1971.

Blumenthal, Ralph. "Digging for Satchmo's Roots in the City That Spawned Him," *New York Times* (15 August 2000), E: 1, col. 4.

Borgeson, Lillian. Interview with Ralph Peer (January-May 1958). Chapel Hill: Southern Folklife Collection, University of North Carolina.

Bradford, Perry. *Born with the Blues: Perry Bradford's Own Story*. New York: Oak Publications, 1965.

Bright, John. "Idle Musings on a Banjo Theme: Johnny St. Cyr," *New Orleans Music* 8/4 (December 1999), 6-9.

Brothers, Thomas. "Louis Armstrong: The 'Saints' and the 'Boys,'" *Musica Oggi*: *Louis Armstrong verso il ventunesimo secolo* 21 (2001), 5-21.

______. *Louis Armstrong's New Orleans*. New York: W. W. Norton, 2006.

Burkhardt, Werner. Liner notes to *The Louis Armstrong Connection: The Hot Five*, Vol. I Germany: Pastels, 20.1801-PA, 1989.

Charters, Samuel B., and Leonard Kunstadt. *Jazz: A History of the New York Scene*. Garden City, NY: Doubleday, 1962.

Chevan, David. *Written Music in Early Jazz*. Ph.D. dissertation, City University of New York, 1997.

Chicago Defender [city and national editions] (1923-1928).

Chicago Whip (1920).

Chilton, John. Liner Notes to *Armstrong's Hot Five and Hot Seven*. Vol. I, CBS Records CK44049, 1988. Vol. III, CBS Records CK44433, 1989.

______. *Who's Who of Jazz: Storyville to Swing Street* (1970), 4th ed. New York: Da Capo Press, 1985.

Cogswell, Michael. "Armstrong, Louis," *The New Grove Dictionary of Jazz*, 3 vols., ed. Barry Kernfeld. London: Macmillan, 2002. I, 67-73.

Collier, James Lincoln. *Jazz: The American Theme Song*. New York: Oxford University Press, 1993.

Crawford, Richard. "Notes on Jazz Standards by Black Authors and Composers, 1899-1942," *New Perspectives on Music: Essays in Honor of Eileen Southern*, ed. Josephine Wright. Warren, MI: Harmonie Park Press, 1992. 245-87.

Crow, Bill. *Jazz Anecdotes*. New York: Oxford University Press, 1990.

Dance, Stanley. *The World of Earl Hines*. New York: Scribner's, 1977; reprinted New York: Da Capo Press, 1983.

Dapogny, James. "Jelly Roll Morton and Ragtime," *Ragtime: Its History, Composers, and Music*, ed. John Hasse. New York: Schirmer Books, 1985. 257-67.

Davies, John R. T., and Laurie Wright. "The Other Take," *Storyville* 29 (1 June 1970), 172-73.

Dean, Demas. "Travellin' Man," *Storyville* 72 (August-September 1977), 207-25.

Dickerson, James L. *Just for a Thrill: Lil Hardin, First Lady of Jazz*. New York: Cooper Square Press, 2002.

Dodds, Warren "Baby," and Larry Gara. *The Baby Dodds Story, as Told to Larry Gara*, 2nd ed. Baton Rouge: Louisiana State University Press, 1992.

Driggs, Frank, and Harris Lewine. *Black Beauty, White Heat: A Pictorial History of Classic Jazz, 1920-1950*. New York: William Morrow, 1982; reprinted New York: Da Capo Press, 1995.

Edwards, Brent Hayes. "Louis Armstrong and the Syntax of Scat," *Critical Inquiry* 28/3 (Spring 2002), 618-49.

Ertegun, Marili. "Just Playing the Music I Love," *Down Beat* 18/16 (10 August 1951), 2, 16, 19.

Evans, David. Liner notes to *Female Blues Singers,* Vol. 1, 1924-32. Document Records DOCD-5505, 1997.

Foreman, Ronald. *Jazz and Race Records, 1920-32: Their Origins and Their Significance for the Record Industry and Society*. Ph.D. dissertation, University of Illinois, 1968.

Freeman, Bud. *Crazeology: The Autobiography of a Chicago Jazzman*. Urbana, IL: University of Illinois Press, 1989.

Friedwald, Will. *Jazz Singing: America's Great Voices from Bessie Smith to Bebop and Beyond*. New York: Charles Scribner's Sons, 1990.

Giddins, Gary. Liner notes to *The Complete Hot Five and Seven Recordings,* Vol. 1. Sony Music Entertainment, 2003.

______. *Satchmo*. New York: Doubleday, 1988.

Givan, Benjamin. "Duets for One: Louis Armstrong's Vocal Recordings," *The Musical Quarterly* 87 (Summer 2004), 188-218.

Godbolt, Jim. *The World of Jazz in Printed Ephemera and Collectibles*. Secaucus, NJ: Wellfleet Press, 1990.

Goffin, Robert. *Horn of Plenty: The Story of Louis Armstrong,* trans. James Bezou. New York: Allen, Towne and Heath, 1947; reprinted New York: Da Capo Press, 1977.

Green, Jeffrey P. "Spencer Williams: Composer," *Storyville* 123 (February-March 1986), 88-93.

Gushee, Lawrence. "How the Creole Band Came to Be," *Black Music Research Journal* 8/1 (1988), 83-100.

______. "Modes of Reception / Influence: The Influence of Louis Armstrong," *Musica Oggi*: *Louis Armstrong verso il ventunesimo secolo* 21 (2001), 22-27.

Hadlock, Richard. *Jazz Masters of the Twenties*. New York: Macmillan, 1965.

Hansen, Chadwick. "Social Influences on Jazz Style: Chicago, 1920-1930," *American Quarterly* 7/4 (Winter 1955), 491-507.

Harrison, Daphne Duval. *Black Pearls: Blues Queens of the 1920s*. New Brunswick, NJ: Rutgers University Press, 1988.

Henderson, Fletcher. "Henderson 'Had to Get Louis' for Roseland Ork," *Down Beat* 17/14 (14 July 1950), 4.

Hennessey, Thomas J. "The Black Chicago Establishment 1919-1930," *Journal of Jazz Studies* 2/1 (December 1974), 15-45.

Hillman, Christopher, and Roy Middleton. *Richard M. Jones: Forgotten Man of Jazz*. Tavistock, England: Cygnet Publications, 1997.

Hoefer, George. "Celebrated Mecca Flats to Go Way of Vendome," *Down Beat* 17/16 (11 August 1950), 11.

______. "Chicago Jazz Landmark Being Razed," *Down Beat* 17/2 (27 January 1950), 2.

______. "Will the Louis Sides on Cylinder Ever Turn Up?," *Down Beat* 17/14 (14 July 1950), 11.

Howatt, Roy. "Bartok, Lendvai and the Principles of Proportional Analysis," *Music Analysis* 2/1 (1983), 69-95.

Hubner, Alma. "Kid Ory," *Selections from the Gutter: Jazz Portraits from* The Jazz Record, ed. Art Hodes and Chadwick Hansen. Berkeley, CA: University of California Press, 1977. 112-15.

Jasen, David A., and Gene Jones. *Spreadin' Rhythm Around: Black Songwriters, 1880-1930*. New York: Schirmer, 1998.

Jones, Max, and John Chilton. *Louis: The Louis Armstrong Story, 1900-1971*. Boston: Little, Brown, 1971; reprinted New York: Da Capo Press, 1988.

Kenney, William Howland. *Chicago Jazz: A Cultural History, 1904-1930*. New York: Oxford University Press, 1993.

______. *Jazz on the River*. Chicago: University of Chicago Press, 2005.

______. "Negotiating the Color Line: Louis Armstrong's Autobiographies," *Jazzin' Mind: Essays on the History and Meaning of Jazz*, ed. Reginald T. Buckner and Steven Weiland. Detroit: Wayne State University Press, 1991. 38-59.

______. *Recorded Music in American Life: The Phonograph and Popular Memory, 1890-1945*. New York: Oxford University Press, 1999.

Kernfeld, Barry, ed. *The New Grove Dictionary of Jazz*. London: Macmillan, 2002.

Kirchner, Bill, ed. *The Oxford Companion to Jazz*. New York: Oxford University Press, 2000.

Klee, Joe. "George Avakian—In the Right Place at the Right Time," *Mississippi Rag* (September 1997), 1-3.

Laird, Ross, and Brian Rust. *Discography of OKeh Records, 1918-1934*. Westport, CT: Praeger, 2004.

Lambert, G. E. *Johnny Dodds*. London: Cassell, 1961. (*Kings of Jazz*, 10)

Lax, John. "Chicago's Black Jazz Musicians in the Twenties: Portrait of an Era," *Journal of Jazz Studies* 1/2 (June 1974), 107-27.

Levin, Floyd. "Kid Ory's Legendary Nordskog / Sunshine Recordings: A Seventy-Year-Old Controversy," *New Orleans Music* 2/4 (April 1991), 7-23.

Lichtenwanger, William. "Music and Copyright Law in the United States," *Music Publishing & Collecting: Essays in Honor of Donald W. Krummel*, ed. David Hunter. Urbana: University of Illinois Press, 1994. 69-94.

Lomax, Alan. *Mister Jelly Roll: The Fortunes of Jelly Roll Morton, New Orleans Creole and "Inventor of Jazz."* (1949), 2nd ed. Los Angeles: University of California Press, 1973; reprinted Los Angeles: University of California Press, 2001.

"Louis the First," *Time* LIII/8 (21 February 1949), 52-58.

Marquis, Don M. *In Search of Buddy Bolden: First Man of Jazz*. Baton Rouge: Louisiana State University Press, 1978.

McCusker, John. "Ory Baptismal Certificate," *The Jazz Archivist* (December 1994), 23-24.

Meckna, Michael. *Satchmo: The Louis Armstrong Encyclopedia*. Westport, CT: Greenwood Press, 2004.

Mezzrow, Mezz, and Bernard Wolfe. *Really the Blues*. New York: Random House, 1946; reprinted New York: Citadel Press, 1990.

Miller, Marc H. "Louis Armstrong: A Cultural Legacy," *Louis Armstrong: A Cultural Legacy*, ed. Marc H. Miller. Seattle: University of Washington, Press, 1994. 17-65.

Morgenstern, Dan. "Louis Armstrong," *The Oxford Companion to Jazz*, ed. Bill Kirchner. New York: Oxford University Press, 2000. 102-21.

______. "Louis Armstrong and the Development and Diffusion of Jazz," *Louis Armstrong: A Cultural Legacy*, ed. Marc H. Miller. Seattle: University of Washington Press, 1994. 95-145.

Morton, Ferdinand "Jelly Roll." *The Library of Congress Recordings*, 4 vols., ed. James Dapogny. Cambridge, MA: Rounder Records Corporation 1091-1094, 1993.

Neff, Wesley. "Little Mitch: A Biography of George Mitchell," *Jazz Information* 2/16 (November 1941), 32-36.

Norton, Richard C. *A Chronology of American Musical Theater*, 3 vols. New York: Oxford University Press, 2002.

O'Meally, Robert. "An Appreciation of Armstrong's Hot Five and Seven Recordings," in booklet for *Louis Armstrong: The Complete Hot Five and Hot Seven Recordings*. Sony Music Entertainment, 2000. 50-78.

Ory, Edward "Kid." "What Did Ory Say," *The Record Changer* (November 1947), 5-6, 12.

Ory, Edward "Kid," and Lester Koenig. "The Hot Five Sessions," *The Record Changer* (July-August 1950), 17, 45.

Ory, Edward "Kid," and Nesuhi Ertegun. "Louis Was Just a Little Kid in Knee Pants," *Down Beat* 17/14 (14 July 1950), 8.

Panassié, Hugues. *Louis Armstrong*. New York: Charles Scribner, 1972.

Pinfold, Mike. *Louis Armstrong: His Life and Times*. New York: Universe Books, 1987.

Ramsey, Frederic, Jr., and Charles Edward Smith. *Jazzmen*. New York: Harcourt Brace Jovanovich, 1939; reprinted New York: Limelight Editions, 1985.

Rand, Bill. Interview with Louis Armstrong for WERE Radio, Cleveland (ca. 1953). New York: Louis Armstrong Archives, Queens College, Cassette 26.

Russell, William. Interview with Lillian Armstrong (1 July 1959). New Orleans: Hogan Jazz Archive, Tulane University.

______. Interview with Louis Armstrong (5 May 1970). New Orleans: Hogan Jazz Archive, Tulane University.

______. Interview with Paul Barbarin (27 March 1957). New Orleans: Hogan Jazz Archive, Tulane University.

______. *New Orleans Style*, ed. Barry Martyn and Mike Hazeldine. New Orleans: Jazzology, 1994.

Rust, Brian. *The American Record Label Book*. New Rochelle, NY: Arlington House, 1978; reprinted New York: Da Capo Press, 1984.

______. *Jazz and Ragtime Records, 1897-1942*, 2 vols. Denver: Mainspring Press, 2002.

Rye, Howard. "Visiting Firemen 9: The Blackbirds and Their Orchestras," *Storyville* 112 (April-May 1984), 133-47, and *Storyville* 114 (August-September 1984), 211-17.

Sandke, Randy. Review of Edward Brooks, *The Young Louis Armstrong on Records: A Critical Survey of the Early Recordings, 1923-1928*, in *Annual Review of Jazz Studies* 12, ed. Edward Berger, David Cayer, Henry Martin, and Dan Morgenstern. Lanham, MD: Scarecrow Press, 2004. 205-12.

Sanjek, Russell, and David Sanjek. *American Popular Music Business in the 20th Century*. New York: Oxford University Press, 1991.

Schaap, Phil. "The Complete Hot Five and Hot Seven Recordings" in booklet for *Louis Armstrong: The Complete Hot Five and Hot Seven Recordings*. Sony Music Entertainment, 2000. 20-35.

Schenbeck, Lawrence. "Music, Gender, and 'Uplift' in the *Chicago Defender*, 1927-1937," *The Musical Quarterly* 81/3 (Fall 1997), 344-70.

Sengstock, Charles A. *That Toddlin' Town: Chicago's White Dance Bands and Orchestras, 1900-1950*. Urbana: University of Illinois Press, 2004.

Shapiro, Nat, and Nat Hentoff. *Hear Me Talkin' to Ya: The Story of Jazz as Told by the Men Who Made It*. New York: Rinehart, 1955; reprinted New York: Dover Publications, 1966.

Simeon, Omer. "Mostly about Morton," *Selections from the Gutter: Jazz Portraits from* The Jazz Record, ed. Art Hodes and Chadwick Hansen. Los Angeles: University of California Press, 1977. 92-93.

Smith, Charles Edward, Frederic Ramsey, Jr., Charles Payne Rogers, and William Russell. *The Jazz Record Book*. New York: Smith & Durrell, 1942; reprinted Westport, CT: Greenwood Press, 1978.

Spanier, Francis "Muggsy." "Louis, My Idol and Inspiration," *Down Beat* 17/14 (14 July 1950), 4.

St. Cyr, Johnny. "Jazz As I Remember It, Part Four: Chicago Days," *Jazz Journal* 20/1 (January 1967), 14-16.

______. "Jazz As I Remember It, Part Three: The Riverboats," *Jazz Journal* 19/11 (November 1966), 6-7, 9.

______. "The Original Hot Five," *Second Line* 5/9-10 (September-October 1954), 1-2.

Stearns, Marshall, and Jean Stearns. *Jazz Dance: The Story of American Vernacular Dance*. New York: Macmillan, 1968; reprinted New York: Da Capo Press, 1994.

Stuart, Dave. "Kid Ory," *Jazz* 1/1 (15 December 1944), 7.

Sudhalter, Richard M. *Lost Chords: White Musicians and Their Contributions to Jazz, 1915-1945*. New York: Oxford University Press, 1999.

______, and Philip R. Evans. *Bix: Man & Legend*. New Rochelle, NY: Arlington House, 1974.

Sutton, Allan, and Kurt Nauck. *American Record Labels and Companies: An Encyclopedia, 1891-1943*. Denver: Mainspring Press, 2000.

Swain, Virginia. "The Dance That Set America Wiggling," *McClure's* 58/4 (April 1927), 42-43, 120-21.

Talking Machine World (1918-1928).

Tichenor, Trebor Jay, ed. *Ragtime Rarities*. New York: Dover Publications, 1975.

Vaillant, Derek. *Sounds of Reform: Progressivism and Music in Chicago, 1873-1935*. Chapel Hill: University of North Carolina Press, 2003.

Variety (1927-1928).

Westerberg, Hans. *Boy from New Orleans*. Copenhagen: JazzMedia, 1981.

Whitburn, Joel. *Pop Memories 1890-1954*. Menomonee Falls, WI: Record Research, 1986.

Williams, Martin. *Jazz Masters of New Orleans*. New York: Macmillan, 1967; reprinted New York: Da Capo Press, 1979.

______. *The Jazz Tradition*. New York: Oxford University Press, 1970.

Wolff, D. Leon. "Bix Half-baked, Johnny Dodds Corny, Tesch Out of Tune," *Down Beat* 8/11 (1 June 1941), 8, 20.

______. "Bop Nowhere, Armstrong Just a Myth," *Down Beat* 16/11 (17 June 1949), 1, 19.

Wright, Laurie. *Mr. Jelly Lord*. Chigwell, Essex: Storyville Publications, 1980.

______. "Pieces of the Jigsaw Puzzle," *Storyville* (1998-99), 160-205.

Zenni, Stefano. *Louis Armstrong—Satchmo: Oltre il mito del jazz* [Beyond the Myth of Jazz]. Rome: Stampa Alternative / Nuova Equilibri, 1995.

Original Hot Five Copyright Deposits

Composers wishing to establish ownership of their work must submit at least one copy to the Copyright Office in Washington, D.C. Once assigned a registration number (always beginning with an "E"), the document is entrusted to the Music Division of the Library of Congress for cataloging and storage.[1] If the copyright was sold to a publisher, the published version (identified by a "cl" before the registration number) is submitted as well. The copyrights for slightly less than half of the Original Hot Fives were claimed by Consolidated Music Publishing House (CMP in Table A1.1). Because of the volume of materials, lack of archival space, and haphazard decisions for maintaining the collection, many items have been misplaced or lost. Such has been the fate of more than half of the Original Hot Five copyright deposits. Table A1.1 presents details for the thirty-three recordings under consideration.

Because only the melody and lyrics of musical works can be legally owned, the most common submission is a lead sheet—the form of most Hot Five deposits obtained for this study.[2] Four of these also designate harmonies, one provides lyrics, and one takes the form of a piano score. The most elaborate, "Savoy Blues," approaches the line-score status of a big-band arrangement.

By comparing the recording and copyright dates of extant deposits, marked with an asterisk (*) in Table A1.1, it will be noticed that a few were submitted before being recorded, but most were submitted afterwards—anytime from one month to over two years later.[3] The former might thus be designated "prescriptive," and the latter, "descriptive."[4] Prescriptive deposits—"Yes! I'm in the Barrel," "Cornet Chop Suey," and "Don't Forget to Mess Around"—show how works were conceived, and descriptive deposits—"Gut Bucket Blues," "Put 'Em Down Blues," and "Savoy Blues"

[1]The Music Division has served as the repository of music copyright deposits since its creation in 1896; see Gillian Anderson, "Putting the Experience of the World at the Nation's Command: Music at the Library of Congress, 1800-1917," *Journal of the American Musicological Society* 42/1 (Spring 1989), 119-20.

[2]See the informative chapter on Armstrong's copyright deposits in David Chevan, *Written Music in Early Jazz* (Ph.D. dissertation, City University of New York, 1997), 238-306.

[3]The fourteen and one-half-year delay in filing the copyright for "Ory's Creole Trombone" is related to its initial rejection by OKeh. Except for the lack of an introduction, the major structural differences between the deposit and the Hot Five performance are found in the number and order of repeats. The deposit contains no evidence of being transcribed from either the 1922 or the 1926 recording and may represent Ory's recollection of the tune.

[4]David Chevan, *Written Music in Early Jazz*, 226.

—indicate how they were realized. Differences between a prescriptive deposit and the recording represent the process of musical decision-making, and differences between a descriptive deposit and the recording represent the effect of inaccurate transcription or faulty memory.

Table A1.1. Original Hot Five Recording and Copyright Data

Title Composer	Copyright Date	Number	Release[5]
First Recording Session: 12 Nov. 1925			
"My Heart" Lillian Hardin	30 July 1920	E-483650	July 1926
"Yes! I'm in the Barrel"* Louis Armstrong	8 Dec. 1923	E-577785	Feb. 1926
"Gut Bucket Blues"* Louis Armstrong	19 Apr. 1926	E-640490	Feb. 1926
Second Recording Session: 22 Feb. 1926			
"Come Back Sweet Papa" Paul Barbarin and Luis Russell	1 May 1926	E-637450	July 1926
Third Recording Session: 26 Feb. 1926			
"Georgia Grind" Spencer Williams	19 Aug. 1926	E-643753	July 1926
"Heebie Jeebies" (CMP) Boyd Atkins	14 Apr. 1926	E-640106	May 1926
"Cornet Chop Suey"* Louis Armstrong	18 Jan. 1924	E-580818	July 1926

[5]Release dates are taken from *Talking Machine World* and label copy in the Sony Archives.

Table A1.1 Continued.

Title Composer	Copyright Date	Number	Release
"Oriental Strut" Johnny St. Cyr	1 Feb. 1926	E-634892	May 1926
"You're Next"* Lillian Armstrong	30 May 1926	E-640504	May 1926
"Muskrat Ramble"* Edward Ory	1 May 1926	E-637451	May 1926
Fourth Recording Session: 16 June 1926			
"Don't Forget to Mess Around"* Louis Armstrong and Paul Barbarin	10 Mar. 1926	E-635073	Sept. 1926
"I'm Gonna Gitcha"* Lillian Hardin	19 July 1926	E-643161	Sept. 1926
"Droppin' Shucks" Lillian Hardin	19 July 1926	E-643160	Sept. 1926
"Who'sit"* Beatrice Jones	19 July 1926	E-643164	Sept. 1926
Fifth Recording Session: 23 June 1926			
"King of the Zulus"* Lillian Hardin	19 July 1926	E-643162	Nov. 1926
"Big Fat Ma and Skinny Pa" Richard M. Jones	7 Sept. 1926	E-645932	Nov. 1926
"Lonesome Blues" Lillian Hardin	19 July 1926	E-643163	Nov. 1926

Table A1.1 Continued.

Title Composer	Copyright Date	Number	Release
"Sweet Little Papa" Edward Ory	30 Aug. 1926	E-645736	Nov. 1926
Sixth Recording Session: 16 Nov. 1926			
"Jazz Lips" Lillian Hardin	6 Dec. 1926	E-643162	15 Feb. 1927
"Skid-Dat-De-Dat" Lillian Hardin	6 Dec. 1926	E-654276	15 Feb. 1927
"Big Butter and Egg Man" Percy Venable	13 Oct. 1926	E-649013	3 Jan. 1927
"Sunset Café Stomp" Percy Venable	20 Dec. 1926	E-654632	3 Jan. 1927
Seventh Recording Session: 27 Nov. 1926			
"You Made Me Love You" Percy Venable	20 Dec. 1926	E-654633	25 Mar. 1927
"Irish Black Bottom" Percy Venable	20 Dec. 1926	E-654631	25 Mar. 1927
Eighth Recording Session: 2 Sept. 1927			
"Leave Mine Alone" Paul Barbarin	3 Dec. 1926	E-652281	rejected
"Put 'Em Down Blues"* Eloise H. Bennett	9 Jan. 1928	E-681076	15 Oct. 1927

Table A1.1 Continued.

Title Composer	Copyright Date	Number	Release
"Ory's Creole Trombone"* Edward Ory	28 Feb. 1941	E-250772	19 Nov. 1940
Ninth Recording Session: 6 Sept. 1927			
"The Last Time" Billy H. Ewing and Sara Martin	14 Oct. 1927	E-674699	19 Nov. 1940
Tenth Recording Session: 9 Dec. 1927			
"Struttin' with Some Barbecue" Lillian Armstrong	9 July 1928	E-695307	5 May 1928
"Got No Blues"* Lillian Hardin	10 May 1928	E-690493	15 Mar. 1928
Eleventh Recording Session: 10 Dec. 1927			
"Once in a While" William H. Butler	5 May 1928	E-690372	5 May 1928
"I'm Not Rough"* Lillian Armstrong	10 May 1928	E-690494	15 Mar. 1928
Twelfth Recording Session: 13 Dec. 1927			
"Hotter Than That"* Lillian Hardin	10 May 1928	E-690496	25 Jan. 1928
"Savoy Blues"* Edward Ory	9 Apr. 1928	E-687646	25 Jan. 1928

A late submission date, nevertheless, does not preclude prescription. Because the Hot Five used lead sheets in the studio,[6] there is no way of knowing that such materials were the ones submitted for copyright unless they indicated some vagary inimical to the recording. A goodly number of the Hot Fives fall into this indeterminate category. The following table of deposits and recordings itemizes their major differences, all of which could represent musical, aesthetic, or entertainment choices at work.

Table A1.2. Major Formal Differences between Original Hot Five Recordings and Copyright Deposits

Recording Title	Differences from Copyright Deposit
"You're Next"	Addition of piano introduction in F minor
"Muskrat Ramble"	A♭ major rather than F major No repeat of the first A chorus Additional repeat of the B chorus Repeat of the final A chorus Solo tag
"I'm Gonna Gitcha"	Reversal of chorus and verse first time through Breaks Vocal chorus
"Who'sit"	C major rather than D major Breaks No introduction
"King of the Zulus"	Spoken hokum Adjusted lengths of vamps and choruses Tag
"Got No Blues"	E♭ major at the beginning and end rather than F major throughout Different introduction Modulation from E♭ major to F major Breaks

[6]See Chapter 3, note 3.

Table A1.2 Continued.

Recording Title	Differences from Copyright Deposit
"I'm Not Rough"	B♭ major rather than A♭ major Different second ensemble chorus Double time Tag
"Hotter Than That"	Breaks Scat solo Ad libitum interlude Tempo transition Coda

Copyright submissions are not necessarily written in the owner's hand. David Chevan speculates that it is highly likely that Armstrong wrote out "I Am in the Barrel—Who Don't Like It?" and "Cornet Chop Suey" but holds that "Gut Bucket Blues" was transcribed by Lil and "Don't Forget to Mess Around" by Barbarin.[7] The deposits bearing Lil's name (given variously as "Lillian Armstrong" or "Lillian Hardin") are undoubtedly in her hand, including Beatrice Jones's "Whoosit," which was submitted the same day as Lil's "I'm Gonna Getcha" and "King of the Zulus." A different but presently unknown hand, possibly that of a professional copyist, seems responsible for three pieces claimed by Lil but not bearing her signature: "Got No Blues," "I'm Not Rough," and "Hotter Than That." If "Ory's Creole Trombone" were notated by its composer, then "Muskrat Ramble" probably was not, although the many years between their submission dates might account for some changes in manuscript detail. It is even more doubtful that Ory wrote out the complex "Savoy Blues" deposit, which, if he did, according to Lawrence Gushee, "would radically alter our notion of the kind of musician Ory was."[8] Finally, more examples of Eloise Bennett's musical manuscript style must be examined in order to validate her identity as the copyist of "Put 'Em Down Blues."

[7] David Chevan, *Written Music in Early Jazz*, 273-74.

[8] Lawrence Gushee, "The Improvisation of Louis Armstrong," *In the Course of Performance: Studies in the World of Musical Improvisation*, ed. Bruno Nettl (Chicago: University of Chicago Press, 1998), 307.

Why the keys of some copyright deposits differ from those of the recording can only be conjectured. The key disparity of "Who'sit," for example, could be resolved by assuming that Armstrong played from the lead sheet later submitted for copyright.[9] As transposing instruments, the cornet and clarinet, of course, sound a major second lower than read; hence, music notated in D would sound in C. But the differences of a minor third ("Muskrat Ramble" and "Put 'Em Down Blues"), of a perfect fifth ("I'm Not Rough"), or of a minor second ("Savoy Blues") between recorded and copyrighted keys cannot be explained by their use as parts. All these tunes were copyrighted six months or less after the recording, and most—if not all—were submitted after the release of the recordings. It would have been unusual for anyone in the Hot Five to have forgotten the correct key, particularly Lil and Ory, who both played and sounded in concert. The simplest explanation might be that these four deposits were copied by individuals who had no knowledge of or concern about the key of the recording—a further argument against "I'm Not Rough" being in Lil's hand or "Muskrat Ramble" and "Savoy Blues" being in Ory's.

Other than for purposes of analysis, perhaps the greatest value of the Hot Five's copyright deposits is their revelation that these gifted performers were complete musicians. Not only were they actively and collaboratively engaged in the creation of their own music, they possessed the requisite technical and theoretical skills to put it on paper and make informed judgments about changes and improvements. Armstrong, ever eager to improve his musicianship, credited David "Davey" Jones in Fate Marable's riverboat band for teaching him to read music.

> . . . it was Davey who really taught me to read music. He taught me the value of a note and how to divide and how to phrase and the rest. And because he liked me and I liked him and admired him so much . . . he was able to impress upon me the importance of knowing how to read and understand written music. He used to say to me, "Louis, you can blow, and you can swing because it's natural to you. But you'll never be able to swing any better than you already know how until you learn to read. Then you will swing in ways you never thought of before." And he was right. Davey Jones cared so much about my being trained better that he taught me for half an hour every afternoon through the six more

[9] David Chevan, *Written Music in Early Jazz*, 272.

> months we were on the river that summer. And I think he will say that I gave him my attention and learned fast.[10]

He never specifically acknowledged who showed him how to write music, but Jones, who later ran a music school in New Orleans, could have taught him the rudiments of music notation as well.

[10]Louis Armstrong, *Swing That Music* (New York: Longmans, Green, 1936; reprinted New York: Da Capo Press, 1993), 47-48.

Illustration A1.1.
Copyright Deposit for
"Yes! I'm in the Barrel"

Illustration A1.2.
Copyright Deposit for
"Gut Bucket Blues"

Illustration A1.3.
Copyright Deposit for
"Cornet Chop Suey"

Illustration A1.4.
Copyright Deposit
for "You're Next"

Illustration A1.5.
Copyright Deposit for
“Muskrat Ramble”

Illustration A1.6. Copyright Deposit for "Don't Forget to Mess Around"

Illustration A1.6
Continued.

Illustration A1.7. Copyright Deposit for "I'm Gonna Gitcha"

Illustration A1.8. Copyright Deposit for “Whos’it”

Illustration A1.9.
Copyright Deposit for
"King of the Zulus"

Illustration A1.10.
Copyright Deposit for
“Put ‘Em Down Blues”

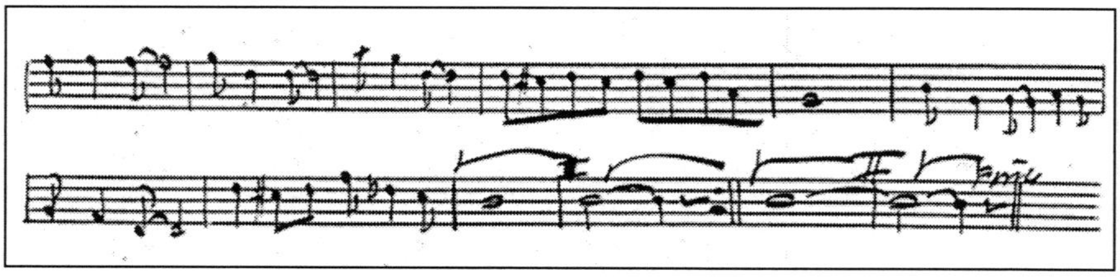

Illustration A1.11. Copyright Deposit for "Got No Blues"

Illustration A1.12. Copyright Deposit for "Ory's Creole Trombone"

Illustration A1.13. Copyright Deposit for "I'm Not Rough"

Illustration A1.14.
Copyright Deposit for
"Hotter Than That"

Illustration A1.15. Copyright Deposit for "Savoy Blues"

Two Memoirs

Johnny St. Cyr: The Original Hot Five

It happened in 1926 King Oliver completed his contract at the PLANTATION night club and decided to go to New York. Louis Armstrong, who was a member of his orchestra, decided to stay in Chicago and organize the Hot Five, which was only a recording combo as each man was with a different orchestra.

At the time I was working with Charley Cooke's orchestra. Johnny Dodds had his own combo at KELLY'S STABLES. Kid Ory was gigging with different bands. Lil Hardin, the pianist in King Oliver's orchestra, having married Louis, naturally remained in Chicago with him and became a member of the Hot Five.

Having recorded on numerous occasions with King Oliver for the Okeh label,[1] Louis became well known to Mr. Fern [*sic*] who was the recording engineer for that company at the time. Louis had no trouble getting a date for the Hot Five. Mr. Fern insisted that Louis record only his own compositions, and persuaded him to sign a five year contract, which Lil and I had advised Louis not to do. The first four numbers we recorded were: "I'm In The Barrel," "Potato Head,"[2] "Gut Bucket," and "Oriental Strut," which was my own composition. From this first recording date the Hot Five became staff artists for the Okeh company.

At that time we were only allowed two minutes and forty five seconds per record. Three minutes was the longest but that was only for special arrangements and that was a special privilege allowed staff artists. All bands that were not staff artists had to stick to the two minutes and forty five seconds limit. If the number ran over time the engineer would have to cut out a chorus or two to reduce the recording to the allotted time. We could not play at ease as the musicians do now as we had no microphones then, and we had to play into a horn which was attached to the recording machine. There were several of them, one to the piano, one to the reeds, and one to the brass, and one to the banjo. I would be sitting on a small ladder, or on several packing cases stacked on top of one another. Boy! We did it the hard way, but it was fun. Johnny Dodds could not play real hot without patting his foot so Mr. Fern got a pillow and put it under

[1]The spelling of the OKeh record label as "Okeh" has been kept as it originally appeared in this article.

[2]This is an error by St. Cyr. "Potato Head Blues" was recorded on 10 May 1927 by the Hot Seven.

Johnny's right foot which was the one he used when he got hot. They really got a kick out of that.

Boyd Adkins, who was not a member of the Hot Five, composed the "Heebie Jeebies" and he asked Louis to include it in our recordings, offering Louis an interest in the number, which was not necessary as Louis was always glad to do anything he could to help his fellow man, without compensation. It was while recording this number that the band got more kicks. The composition was only an instrumental and Mr. Fern insisted on a vocal chorus, so Louis wrote some words which he did not have time to rehearse or memorize, and he had to read them when it came time for him to sing. We were recording one way discs and we had to cut three test records and one master. On the "Heebie Jeebies" when we were recording the master and it was time for Louis to do the vocal he sang half of the words and the paper dropped from his hand. To avoid spoiling the record and having to do it all over again, he just gave out with some queer sounds such as Boo Boo Pa Doop, Boo Boo, Frinie, Nacki Sacki, and others that do not make sense, which was later known as the Scat theme. Nevertheless, we got a good laugh out of it.

On one of our recording sessions we had rehearsed only three numbers and after we had cut them Mr. Fern wanted a fourth and he asked Louis to do a blues, to complete the recording, and Louis said "Man, we have made so many blues and they all sound mostly alike!" So I suggested that I start the blues with a few bars on the bass strings of the banjo. So we made a short rehearsal and cut the number. When Mr. Fern asked "What shall we name it?," Louis thought for a while and then said "Call it The Gut Bucket." Louis could not explain the meaning of the name. He said it just came to him. But I will explain.

In the fish markets in New Orleans the fish cleaners keep a large bucket under the table where they clean the fish, and as they do this they rake the guts in this bucket. Thence The Gut Bucket, which makes it a low down blues.

Louis was a wonderful band leader. One felt so relaxed working with him, and he was very broad minded. He always did his best to feature each individual in his combo. It was not Louis Armstrong, it was the Hot Five, if you get what I mean. We got to the place where we would rehearse and time the numbers to be recorded, thus eliminating the tests, and making masters at the first recording. This was the original Hot Five. Later, when Louis become a member of Carroll Dickerson's Orchestra,

Carroll persuaded Louis to use members of his band to record the Hot Five—and so ended the Original.

I cherish the memories of my associations with Louis and the Hot Five. I have never worked with a nicer guy. He was very considerate of his men and always had something humorous to say, keeping his band in good cheer at all times. He was very modest and he had a comforting appreciation for whatever little the other fellow did. He was always open to suggestions and eager to try them out. He is a great guy and we did our best to make our recordings a success. We made money and we had lots of fun.

Johnny St. Cyr, "The Original Hot Five," *Second Line* 5/9-10 (September-October 1954), 1-2.

Edward "Kid" Ory: The Hot Five Sessions

I don't know who got the ideas for the Hot Five records. It may have been Richard M. Jones, who worked for the *Okeh* company[3] at that time. He worked for them in Chicago, as a pianist for different blues singers and writing and selecting tunes, and it may been through him that the *Okeh* company approached Louis.

Louis was in New York then, playing with Fletcher Henderson. I remember getting a letter from him. I was in California then, with my own band. Louis said he had the offer of a job for a band at the Dreamland in Chicago, and also the offer to record for *Okeh*. He said we'd both make some money, so I decided to give up my own band, go back East to Chicago. That was the end of 1925. I thought the world of Louis, so I was glad to go with him.

The idea was that we would have a regular band at Dreamland, and then that five of us from the band would make records together. I got to Chicago a few weeks before Louis, and played around at different clubs. Then Louis got there, and we rehearsed the band for a few days before we opened at the Dreamland. We had Johnny Dodds, Johnny St. Cyr and Lil with us.

We made our first records in Chicago at the *Okeh* studios, and of course when we made them we didn't have any expectation that they would be as successful as they became. The time was something like today, with people crazy about jazz and the Charleston, and our kind of music went over very well. Times were good, and people had money to

[3]In this article the name "OKeh" also lacks the capital K and is italicized as well.

buy records. One thing that helped the sales was the fact for a while the *Okeh* people gave away a picture of Louis to everyone that bought one of the records. When they did that, the sales went way up, because Louis was so popular.

Those days in Chicago were very happy. We had all played together before, and were friends from the old days. Louis, Lil, and Johnny Dodds played together in the Oliver band in 1923, so they had good experience together. And of course, I had played with Louis, Dodds and St. Cyr in New Orleans when they were in my band.

I remember the first night Louis sat in with my band in New Orleans, at National Park back before the first war. Louis was about 12 or 13 at that time. I remember Benny, the drummer, said how about letting my boy play the blues. Louis was quite a youngster so Benny picked him up and set him on the bandstand which was built quite high off the floor, and after I heard him play one number, I told him I thought he was going to be a great trumpet player, I wasn't mistaken in thinking so.

The only one of the Hot Five I hadn't played with was Lil, but that made no difference. She was a fine piano player, and from the first we all worked together very easily.

Everything was fine for a while, making the records for *Okeh*, and playing at Dreamland with the big band. It was a good sounding band, and very popular. People lined up in the snow to get in to hear us. But they didn't pay very well, and when Louis asked for more money for the band, they wouldn't come across, and so we left.

After that, Louis went with Erskine Tate, and I joined Oliver. Johnny Dodds had his own outfit at Kelly's Stables, and Johnny St. Cyr played in Cook's band. Lil was married to Louis then, and she didn't play with any band, as I remember, but just recorded.

Even though we were working in different clubs, we kept the Hot Five going. The records were very successful by this time, and *Heebie Jeebies* was what today would be called a hit record. That was the record where Louis forgot the lyrics and started scattin'. We had all we could do to keep from laughing. Of course, Louis said he forgot the words, but I don't know if he intended it that way or not. It made the records, though.

The Hot Five never played together as a band outside of a few benefits. We'd all take a short time off from the regular jobs we had and play for a half hour or so at some affair. We always would break it up, and then go back to our jobs.

Our recording sessions would start this way: the *Okeh* people would call up Louis and say they wanted so many sides. They never told him what numbers they wanted or how they wanted them. Then Louis would give us the date, and sometimes he'd call me and say I'm short of a number for this next session. Do you think you can get one together? I'd say all right, and that's the way *Savoy Blues* came to be composed, two days before we recorded.

We would get to the studio at nine or ten in the morning. We didn't have to make records at night, with the lights out, or get drunk like some musicians think they have to do before they can play. In the beginning we made records acoustically, and there was a separate horn for each man. The recording engineer would motion us if we were playing too loud or too soft, and then we'd know to move back or to move in closer. Then later, of course, we made records electrically.

When we'd get in the studio, if we were going to do a new number, we'd run over it a couple of times before we recorded it. We were a very fast recording band, in fact the records I made with the Hot Fives were the easiest I ever made. We spoiled very few records, only sometimes when one of us would forget the routine or the frame-up, and didn't come in when he was supposed to. Even then, we'd try to cover up. After we'd make a side, Louis would say: "Was that all right?" And if one of us thought we could do it over and do it better, why Louis would tell them we wanted to do it again, and so we would do it over.

I think one reason those records came out so well was that the *Okeh* people left us alone, and didn't try to expert us. Another reason was we all knew each other's musical styles so well from years of working together. And then, of course, there was Louis, himself. You couldn't go wrong with Louis. I always liked his style the best. That's not to take anything away from Oliver, but I always thought Louis was the greatest, and I still think so.

Edward "Kid" Ory and Lester Koenig, "The Hot Five Sessions," *The Record Changer* (July-August 1950), 17, 45.

Names, Titles, and Subjects

The following alphabetical list provides a guide to the names and titles cited in the body of the text, in the commentary of the footnotes, and in the legends to illustrations. The names of composers appear in parentheses after song titles, and an asterisk (*) identifies transcriptions. Subjects are listed generally under "Original Hot Five" and the individual names of its members.

Recorded Examples

All performances feature the members of the Original Hot Five except for the substitution of Hy Clark for "Kid" Ory on "You Made Me Love You" and the addition of guitarist Lonnie Johnson on "I'm Not Rough," "Hotter Than That," and "Savoy Blues." Details about the copyright deposits, the recordings, and the recording sessions are provided in Appendix 1.

1 My Heart (1925) [2:23]
2 Gut Bucket Blues (1925) [2:40]
3 Heebie Jeebies (1926) [2:52]
4 Cornet Chop Suey (1926) [2:55]
5 Oriental Strut (1926) [2:59]
6 Muskrat Ramble (1926) [2:30]
7 Who'sit (1926) [2:44]
8 King of the Zulus (1926) [3:03]
9 Sweet Little Papa (1926) [2:43]
10 Jazz Lips (1926) [3:00]
11 Skid-Dat-De-Dat (1926) [3:03]
12 Big Butter and Egg Man (1926) [2:57]
13 You Made Me Love You (1926) [2:51]
14 Put 'Em Down Blues (1927) [3:12]
15 Struttin' With Some Barbecue (1927) [3:04]
16 Got No Blues (1927) [3:24]
17 Once in a While (1927) [3:16]
18 I'm Not Rough (1927) [3:02]
19 Hotter Than That (1927) [3:03]
20 Savoy Blues (1927) [3:25]